A History of Mining in Latin America

D1736966

SERIES ADVISORY EDITOR:
Lyman L. Johnson,
University of North Carolina at Charlotte

A History of Mining
in Latin America

From the Colonial Era to the Present

KENDALL W. BROWN

University of New Mexico Press ✦ Albuquerque

© 2012 by the University of New Mexico Press
All rights reserved. Published 2012
Printed in the United States of America
17   16   15   14   13   12   1   2   3   4   5   6

LIBRARY OF CONGRESS CATALOGING-IN-PUBLICATION DATA

Brown, Kendall W., 1949–
A history of mining in Latin America : from the colonial era to the present /
Kendall W. Brown.
p. cm. — (Diálogos series)
Includes bibliographical references and index.
ISBN 978-0-8263-5106-7 (pbk. : alk. paper) — ISBN 978-0-8263-5107-4 (electronic)
1. Silver mines and mining—Bolivia—Potosí—History. 2. Mines and mineral
resources—Latin America—History. I. Title.
HD9537.B53B76 2012
333.8098—dc23
2011026644

BOOK DESIGN
Composed in 10.25/13.5 Minion Pro Regular
Display type is Minion Pro

To Margie, Matthew, Kimberly, and Mark

Contents

Graphs, Figures, and Maps

MAPS

Prologue

⚜ IN JUNE 1995 I TRAVELED TO POTOSÍ, BOLIVIA, TO DO RESEARCH in its archive. For a quarter century I had studied Potosí, Spanish America's greatest silver producer and perhaps the world's most famous mining district. I read with fascination about the flood of silver that flowed from its Cerro Rico (Rich Hill) and tried to visualize the toil and suffering of its miners, many of them indigenous conscripts dragged from their villages by the colonial state to serve in the *mita*, a system of rotating forced labor. Potosí symbolized fabulous wealth and unbelievable suffering. Its influence stretched around the globe as its silver traveled to Europe and then on to China to pay for silks and spices. As I arrived in La Paz, my trek to Potosí took on the character more of a historical pilgrimage than a mere research trip. I wanted to experience the awful grandeur of the (in)famous mines.

At the La Paz train station, I learned that the Ferrobus, a forty-passenger coach powered by a diesel engine, was the most comfortable, quick, and luxurious train to Potosí. It stopped en route only at Oruro, another colonial mining center, and had the additional advantage of being far more direct than the milk trains. I checked my suitcase and discovered that the luggage rode on top of the coach, wrapped in a canvas tarp. When a train worker brought out the tarp, a mouse hopped out and scurried away. We left at 5:00 p.m., on schedule. My seat was in the second row, and an old woman from Potosí was my seatmate. Her son had brought her to the station and provided her with two blankets. She folded one and sat on it (it made her three or four inches taller) and wrapped herself in the other. Her blankets made me worry about how cold the trip would be and how I would survive it. I had only a wool sweater and a light jacket, having relied on the assurance in the *South American Handbook* that the Ferrobus provided blankets.

For the first couple of hours of our journey, daylight held. The Ferrobus chugged its way up out of the La Paz basin along a narrow track strewn with garbage. We wound our way through urban sprawl, the houses made of mud bricks. The predominantly unpainted houses blended into the hillside when viewed from the valley floor. Arriving at the top of the ascent, we passed El Alto, a city near the airport that has grown due to an overflow of immigrants to La Paz. We were now on the altiplano, a bleak tableland about twelve thousand feet above sea level. Lack of moisture and cold temperatures make it unsuitable for most farming, but wild grasses offer fodder for livestock. I saw cattle, mules, and sheep but, to my disappointment, no llamas.

My pilgrimage alternated between boredom and surprise. Darkness descended on the altiplano, and a cook rustled up food for those who wanted to buy it. I chose fried chicken, fried potatoes, and rice, plus a Sprite, for two dollars. Not long afterward (around 9:30 p.m.), we reached Oruro, where another fifteen people boarded the coach. A little later, as we approached a small village, we saw what looked like a bundle of paper on the tracks. The driver slowed down, and one of the conductors got out to investigate. It turned out to be a drunk who had passed out on the tracks. The conductor dragged him to the side, with a few kicks for good measure, and we proceeded on our way, wrapped in the woolen blankets promised by the travel-guide writer. The night was already cold, and I was glad to bundle up.

After about 450 kilometers, we turned east off the main route (which continues on to Argentina) and headed toward Potosí. We also left the altiplano and began to move through broken, mountainous terrain. At Paso del Condor we reached the highest and coldest point of the journey, nearly five thousand meters, or sixteen thousand feet. The moisture from our breath froze on the windows, and the driver had a hard time keeping the windshield clear so he could see the track. My back ached and my legs were cold. I finally fell asleep, only to wake up about an hour before we reached Potosí. Knowing we would soon be there, I was too excited to sleep more. I hoped we would arrive after sunrise so that I might see the Cerro Rico. Across my mind flew the sobering thought of what it must have been like for the *mitayos*, Indian peasants conscripted by the Spaniards to toil in this isolated, harsh place. Some came from beyond La Paz, traveling for weeks to cross the more than six hundred miles to Potosí. And here I was complaining to myself about a twelve-hour Ferrobus ride.

Darkness still shrouded the city when we arrived at 5:30 a.m. I retrieved my bag and left the station. No taxis were in sight. Then one came around the corner, already carrying three passengers. It stopped for me, and after dropping off the others, took me to the Hostal Colonial, where I was to stay. A geographer friend, Alan Craig, had stayed there and recommended it to me. It offered two important attractions: its rooms had heaters, and it was only two blocks from the Casa de la Moneda (Royal Mint) where the archive was located. I did not want to face any strenuous walks right away at 13,250 feet. By the time I reached my room, I was cold and shivering. Inside the room, I turned on the electric space heater and got into bed. The cold sheets made me tremble.

I slept from 6:15 to 9:30 a.m. and then got up to go to the archive. The streets that had been deserted earlier were now filled with traffic. The Casa de la Moneda lay downhill from the Hostal Colonial about two blocks, just as Alan had told me. But he described it as a "head-splitting" walk because of the altitude. I didn't feel it; perhaps he meant the return uphill. The Casa de la Moneda, a wonderful example of colonial architecture that covered two city blocks, was built in the eighteenth century to house the royal mint. Making my way down the sidewalk, I looked off to the left, and there it was— the Cerro, a reddish hill scarred with tailings dumps and stripped of vegetation. I stopped to look for a minute, in tribute to the history of colonial Spanish America, and then walked on.

At the Casa de la Moneda, I went inside, found the archive, and made arrangements to conduct my research. The director and his staff were extremely friendly, as I had found Bolivians in general. I told him what I was looking for, and he made some suggestions that coincided with what I already intended to investigate. I spent the rest of the morning, until the archive closed for lunch, looking through the card catalogue produced by the Banco de San Carlos, the bank that the guild of silver producers formed during the second half of the eighteenth century. In its books I hoped to find data about the amount of mercury the bank had received each year to sell for silver refining, a process largely done through amalgamation. Although the first documents I read contained little useful information, other references looked promising. The afternoon's work proved very profitable, despite the cold that the archive's propane heater could not dispel. When the archive closed at 6:00 p.m. my fingers were numb, but my first twelve hours in Potosí had proved productive and enjoyable, as did subsequent days in the archive.

I also wanted to visit the Cerro Rico, to enter the mines and glimpse, even if faintly, what centuries of miners had experienced. Thus, I arranged to meet Raúl Braulio Israel, a former miner who now conducted mine tours, one morning at 8:45. He told me to eat a good breakfast and buy some chocolate for a snack. We were ready to go around 9:15, joined by his brother, a teenager who was their assistant, and a German tourist. Raúl's brother drove the jeep, and we headed toward the Cerro. Reaching the miner's market, we stopped for supplies. Raúl picked out a pair of boots, a hard hat, and a yellow raincoat for each of us. Then we bought some gifts for the miners and the Tío (the deity of the mine): a pound of coca leaves, three packs of L&M cigarettes, a bottle of 95 percent alcohol, a bag of ammonium nitrate, a stick of dynamite and an eight-minute fuse, plus fuel for the miner's lanterns that we would need for our underground venture. The dynamite was really for us: Raúl intended to let us set it off to see its force. My share of the supplies came to about three dollars.

Heading east of the Cerro, we stopped occasionally to take photographs. According to Raúl there were about six hundred mines honeycombing the hill. The first mine we visited was roughly 14,200 feet above sea level. Forty *socios* (partners), each of whom had his own team of workers, worked it as a cooperative. The partners shared the profits (or losses) of the operation, whereas the miners received a daily wage. Boys aged twelve to fourteen years earned about four dollars per day; older, experienced miners earned as much as twelve to fifteen dollars. This was a prosperous mine, yielding rich silver ores plus zinc and lead. Although Bolivia had been a great tin producer, that commodity's price now was so low that no one bothered with it. Industrialized countries had substituted aluminum and plastic for tin, making the mineral's future bleak. I picked up several ore samples to take home.

Work was in full swing. Miners pushed ore carts out and dumped them in areas assigned to their socios. Others shoveled the ore into dump trucks. We had already put our boots on, and Raúl took us along the track, which was three or four inches deep in water and ice, to the mouth of the mine. He pointed out a small shrine above the entrance that once housed a Catholic saint but was now empty. Apparently the miners wanted nothing to do with Catholic saints. Just below the shrine were timbers. They appeared to be coated with pitch. So much for appearances: The miners had smeared them with llama blood in ritual sacrifices. Over the weeks and months the blood had turned black. They had also daubed llama blood on sheds and other buildings, asking for luck and safety in their work. *Brujos* (shamans) carry out the most important rituals, making special offerings of llama parts or even human fetuses within the mine itself. I asked Raúl where they obtained the fetuses. He said it was a secret known only to the brujos.

Miners who had just finished their shift were sitting around, chewing coca leaves and drinking, as figure 1 shows. The coca increases their

Figure 1. Miners of Potosí's Rosario mine chewing
coca leaves after completing their shift.

endurance and suppresses hunger. Raúl offered us the chance to chew some,
but as the miners add a small bit of lye to the leaves in their mouths to acti-
vate the enzymes in the coca, I was not anxious to partake. The German
with us said he had tried it fifteen years earlier when in Bolivia, and his
gums burned from the lye for weeks afterward. The miners took turns with
a shot glass. Before downing the firewater, each miner spilled a few drops
on the ground for Pachamama (Earth Mother) and a few more for the Tío
before drinking the rest. We distributed cigarettes. American brands are a
welcome treat after the hand-rolled smokes of bitter tobacco that are all the
miners can typically afford. One told me he had been working in the mines
for thirty years. His skin was very dark, a sign of silicosis. Others kidded
him about how weak he had become, and he responded that he was even
too weak for sex now. The others were younger. All seemed content to chew
and drink.

Near the area where the carts dumped the ore, stood a shack inhabited
by an elderly Quechua widow. Her husband had worked in the mine until
his death, and her son was now a miner. She spent her time as a *palliri*,
one who picks through the dump to recover any bits of ore worth saving.
Ironically, her son had become extremely wealthy as a socio when his workers struck a large, rich vein of silver ore. He was now a millionaire with

investments and properties outside mining, but his mother preferred her traditional life at the mine head, working the ore her son provided and guarding the site.

Our next stop was the Rosario mine, which has been worked off and on since colonial times, to see the Tío. Tío means "uncle," and more colloquially "guy" or "fellow." The miners used the second meaning, referring to the "guy" with supernatural powers who rules the underground. Each mine had at least one, a god who controlled the workers' success or failure. Those who made gifts to the Tío might find rich ore; those who neglected their obligations to him might suffer accidents or death.

Decked out in rubber boots, raincoats, and hard hats, we went underground to visit the "guy." For the first fifty yards, colonial stonework lined the tunnel. Raúl said it had been constructed with mita labor. I thought the Tío would be just inside the entrance. I was wrong, and soon we were hiking deep inside the Cerro. To my dismay, the roof of the tunnel sometimes was too low to allow my six-foot three-inch frame to stand upright. Raúl pointed out veins of tin and deposits of arsenic oxide as we went along. The air was good, with a breeze blowing inward. I was all right when walking upright, but long stretches of trying to hike doubled over made breathing difficult. Of course, at that altitude there was not much oxygen to breathe anyway. Meanwhile, Raúl walked easily, usually remaining upright. I was very grateful for the hard hat because I probably hit my head twenty times, some of them good blows. With the hat none of them hurt me at all; without it, Raúl would have had to drag me out.

We still had not arrived at the Tío, but I noticed displays of flowers and colored ribbons left by miners on the walls at eye level. Those were also offerings for Pachamama and the Tío. Along the way we passed old colonial diggings. Rather than excavating systematically, colonial miners followed the veins wherever they led. At one point a step off to the left of the track meant a fall of a hundred feet or so into a colonial pit. Raúl said that occasionally a worker would get drunk and fall to his death.

As it turned out, the Tío was on the level below us. To get there we climbed down a rickety wooden ladder, which Raúl secured at the bottom. I was not happy to look down and see that if the ladder broke, I was going to fall forty or fifty feet. Then we set off to the right. Arsenic and antimony gases polluted the air. The upper level had been relatively cool. This level seemed hot: I had dressed for the cold outside and now had on a rubber coat besides. At times the ceiling was so low that I almost had to crawl.

And then we came to the Tío's gallery. He was an ugly, seated fellow, molded by a brujo out of black mud. This was Tío Jorge. Tíos were always named for one of the miners, Raúl said, someone very greedy, aggressive, and hard, just like the Tío. Other miners sometimes suspect a comrade has made a compact with the Tío to offer his own or other human lives in return for the Tío's riches. Someone had provided miner's boots for Tío Jorge. Colored ribbons draped around his shoulders and covered much of his chest. Reflecting Christian demonology, he had horns coming out of his head with a snake wrapped around one of them. In short, he was the devil. Another notable feature was his very large, erect penis. According to the miners, by copulating with Pachamama, the Tío produces the underground riches. Raúl lit an L&M and put it between the Tío's lips. He added more coca leaves to the little pouches on the idol's chest and poured alcohol on the ground for the Tío to drink. I also gave him some coca leaves and alcohol before we left.

Returning back down the same tunnel, we came to the ladder but passed by it. Raúl took us to a site where miners were working. Suddenly it seemed like things were falling out of the ceiling to the right. They turned out to be *kaipiris*, boys who haul forty- to fifty-kilo sacks of ore on their backs, who were sliding down the rock face from an upper level into our pit. Ahead stood a miner with a shovel, filling their sacks. All the workers were covered with sweat, as was I. The air was bad. We gave the crew chief, the fellow with the shovel, a pack of L&Ms, more coca leaves, and the remainder of our bottle of alcohol. Delighted, he immediately took a couple of swigs. The other gifts he would share later with his crew.

We then made our trek out of the mine. It was easier going up the ladder than down, but the low ceilings were even harder to navigate. By this time I was hot, tired, out of breath, and ecstatic to see daylight at the end of the tunnel. Emerging into the bright out-of-doors, our eyes took a while to adjust to the sun's brilliance. Our only light inside had been the carbide lanterns each of us carried. More thirsty than hungry, I gave my remaining chocolate bar to Raúl's *asistente* and he seemed delighted.

The visit to Potosí, to its archive, museums, churches, and especially to its mines was an unforgettable peek into a quintessential aspect of Latin American history, and thus, when I decided to write a general survey of Latin American mining, it was only natural that Potosí should assume its place as the main character in that story. This volume makes no pretense of being a complete, thorough study of the industry from the arrival of Columbus in the New World. It instead seeks to highlight major issues related to mining, the economic activity that has played such a prominent role in the region's history. New World bullion stimulated the formation of the first world economy. At the same time it had profound consequences for labor, as mine operators and refiners resorted to extreme forms of coercion to secure workers. Mining and metallurgical technologies flowed to and from the Americas. In many cases the American environment suffered devastating, long-term harm. All of this occurred in the name of wealth, for individual entrepreneurs, companies, and ruling states. Yet in the end, the question remains of how much economic development mining managed to produce in Latin America and what its social and ecological consequences were.

The following chapters address these and other topics. Chapter 1 examines the economic dimensions of gold and silver mining in colonial Latin America and how American bullion interacted with the emerging world economy. Chapter 2 analyzes the labor systems the Spaniards and Portuguese created and describes the mineral wealth they discovered in their American colonies. Chapter 3 considers social implications of colonial mining, especially the widespread resorting to forced labor, which often worked alongside more or less free-wage labor. Chapter 4 discusses the impact of Latin America's political independence for the mining industry and to what extent colonial structures survived in the new nations. Chapter 5 studies the transition toward mining nonprecious metals such as tin and copper in response to the demand for such materials in the industrialized world. Chapter 6 analyzes the introduction of new technologies, which changed transportation and refining for the mines, and the beginnings of labor organization in the industry. Chapter 7 looks at how their increasing proletarianization and changes in mining and metallurgical technology led workers to organize, sometimes by revolutionary actions, although not necessarily with long-term positive results. Chapter 8 concludes the survey with an examination of the ecological consequences of Latin America mining and how Andean cosmology enabled workers to find harmony despite the horror and misery of the mines. Each chapter will focus on the Cerro Rico of Potosí and its surrounding province as context for understanding mining elsewhere in Latin America.

I have incurred many debts over the years in preparing this study. The National Endowment for the Humanities and Brigham Young University provided funding for research trips. The late John TePaske started me on research related to colonial mining labor. George Addy continues to inspire a love of the Hispanic world. Lyman Johnson first suggested the project and offered invaluable suggestions along the way. I have benefitted from the scholarly support, critiques, and friendship of Alan Craig, Kenneth Andrien, Carlos Contreras, Richard Garner, Margarita Suárez, Rafael Varón, Inés Herrera, Julio Pinto Vallejos, Jeffrey Shumway, and Shawn Miller. My wife, Margie, and children Matthew, Kimberly, and Mark have lived for years with Potosí and have become fascinated with its history. All have contributed in important ways to my understanding of mining and its impact on the people and environment of Latin America, for which I am grateful.

CHAPTER 1

The Lure of Gold, the Wealth of Silver

From the first landing to the end of his days gold obsessed Columbus, directed his explorations and dominated his conduct.
—Carl Ortwin Sauer, *The Early Spanish Main*

⚶ WRITING IN THE SECOND QUARTER OF THE SIXTEENTH CENTURY, Gonzalo Fernández de Oviedo y Valdés, who had overseen gold smelting in the Caribbean and in New Spain for the Crown from 1514 to 1532, reported the story of three Spanish peasants who sailed to the Caribbean in search of their fortune. They had sold their scant possessions in Spain to finance the voyage, but a few weeks in the New World showed the futility of their ambitions. They searched and dug but found no gold to reward them. Exhausted, hungry, and destitute, they rested under a tree, cursing their luck. Finally, the one who had complained most loudly adopted a fatalistic tone. He recognized God's power to give them what they wanted and expressed confidence that in due time, He would reward them with the gold they sought. Just then one companion saw shining not twenty yards away a gold nugget. Looking around, they easily found other nuggets, enough to fill their boots. Delighted with their treasure and giving little thought to the future, the peasants took their gold and returned to Spain on the return voyage of the ship that had carried them to the Caribbean.[1] The people of Santo Domingo shook their heads in amazement.

1

Oviedo's story contains many of the themes found in the history of mining in Latin America. The newcomers from Europe considered the New World a treasure trove of precious metals. Many believed that in the Americas with a little work and God's blessing they could soon amass a fortune, which would permit them to return home to live in comfort. Their Christianity reassured them not only that God had placed gold and silver in the New World for their use, but also that He would intervene on their behalf. So firmly held was this belief that Spaniards and Portuguese were willing to confront great hardships and horrifying dangers as they searched for gold and silver. In so doing they brutalized the indigenous inhabitants, explored and settled the American continents, and changed the world economy. They established a culture that saw mining as a panacea for poverty and as a vehicle for economic prosperity. Those beliefs endured even when mining shifted from precious to industrial metals in the late nineteenth century. At the same time, however, mining brought misery and despair to many. Indians and African slaves toiled and died in the American mines. Many mine owners and refiners found temporary wealth and then lost everything when their lodes gave out. Unlike the three peasants in Oviedo's story, some Spaniards stayed on in the Indies, never able to satisfy their greed for gold no matter how much they found. Others despaired that they had found only a modest treasure when America's fantastic riches seemed so ready for the taking.

In the early years of discovery and exploration, gold obsessed the newcomers. This situation resulted in part from a remarkable conjuncture of Christian mythology and world monetary flows that provided the context through which Columbus understood his grand undertaking. Their Bible spoke to medieval Christians of the wealth of King Solomon, symbolized by the gold he obtained from the mines of Ophir. The Greek historian Herodotus had written of a desert land north of India where the sands were filled with gold. Giant ants, he claimed, guarded the treasure. Perhaps from reading Herodotus, Saint Jerome identified the land of Ophir with India. Other writers, including Saint Isidore, repeated and embellished the story, until they had situated Ophir far to the east. By the late Middle Ages, they had also substituted fantastic creatures like griffins and dragons for Herodotus's giant ants.[2]

Europeans consequently believed that somewhere in the East lay a great source of gold, where miners had only to shovel the sand from the beach and avoid the dangerous griffins. Venetian Marco Polo's account of his travels in China seemed to prove the existence of the land of Ophir. Polo also provided a new name for Ophir: Cipangu, the Land of the Rising Sun. As fate would have it, when Marco Polo visited China in the late thirteenth century, Japan was a major supplier of gold to the Asian mainland.[3] European cosmographers avidly read the Venetian's account and speculated on the relationship between Ophir and Cipangu (Japan). By the time Columbus sailed in 1492, he had convinced himself that the gold of the Orient lay in Cipangu, the biblical Ophir.

Thus, when Columbus and his men reached the West Indies, they immediately began searching for the gold of Ophir. His log for the days immediately after landfall shows him setting course "to seek the gold and precious stones" of "the island of Cipangu" rather than to find the Great Khan in China. Using signs and the Arabic-speaking interpreter he had taken with him on the assumption that the East Asians would have had contact with Muslims, Columbus repeatedly tried to question the natives about the source of any gold they possessed. On November 12 he imagined that the Arawaks had informed him that on the island of Babeque "the people collect gold on the beach by candlelight."[4] Perhaps such nocturnal labor was necessary to avoid the griffins and dragons. By December 24, he had decided that Cipangu, or "Cibao," as his Indian hosts called it, lay on the island of Hispaniola.[5] Arawak guides led the Spaniards to Cibao in the interior of the island, and then over the next decade the Indians showed the Spaniards the location of all their goldfields.[6] The Arawaks knew how to gather nuggets from the streambeds but apparently did not pan or mine for gold.[7]

Back in Spain, Columbus's exaggerated reports about his discoveries inflamed European imaginations. Gold seemed everywhere. All one needed to do was to dig along a riverbank to find the glittering grains washed clean by the flowing waters. "Gold constitutes treasure," wrote Columbus to Ferdinand and Isabella, "and he who possesses it may do what he will in the world, and may so attain as to bring souls to Paradise."[8] Enthused by his optimistic letters, the monarchs ordered in 1494 that four or five miners from the royal quicksilver mines of Almadén be sent to the Caribbean to raise the technical level of gold mining there.

Columbus and his comrades bartered with islanders for gold when possible, but indigenous trade could not satisfy the Spaniards. The next step was to demand tribute from the Arawaks and thereby force them to produce more gold. This seemed promising, given the sizable population of Hispaniola, which may have numbered a million or more.[9] In an infamous edict of 1495, the Admiral ordered all male Indians over the age of thirteen to produce a hawk's bell full of gold every three months.[10] Brutal punishment awaited anyone who failed to comply: his hand would be cut off. Columbus deemed such coercion necessary because the islanders lacked the discipline for heavy labor, but even this cruelty proved futile. The natives could not find enough gold to meet the Spaniards' tax, and many ran away rather than submit to the foreigners' mania. With the arrival of more and more adventurers from Europe, the demand for gold increased.

Some Spaniards turned to prospecting, as in the case of Oviedo's three peasants who discovered enough nuggets to fill their boots. Those fortunate enough to discover pay dirt resorted to forced Indian labor. Isabella had chastised Columbus for enslaving the islanders, but the Crown allowed Spaniards to make chattels out of Indians who rebelled or otherwise made war upon the invaders. Slaves were cheap. A horse cost the equivalent of one hundred Indian slaves.[11] Another solution to the labor shortage in the goldfields was the encomienda, a grant of Indian tribute to a Spaniard, the encomendero, who usually collected the obligations in labor. Although encomienda Indians were nominally free, conditions in the Caribbean provided little protection from extreme exploitation and abuse at the hands of the encomenderos. After Isabella's death, Ferdinand urged the Spanish to step up gold production, even if it meant forcing more Indians to work in the mines or taking Indians from other islands to those where gold was found.[12] Trying to protect the islanders, the missionary friar and humanitarian Bartolomé de las Casas condemned the encomienda "as the despotic slavery it actually is." The Indians, he noted, "died of the inhuman and bitter treatment they received in the mines and from other pestilential practices."[13]

Whether slaves or encomienda Indians, they worked the Spaniards' claims. In the goldfields, a work gang was generally a five-person team: two men to dig the gold-bearing dirt; two men to carry it to the river or other water source; and one person, often a woman who used a batea or pan, to wash away the gravel and dirt, leaving the grains, flakes, and nuggets of ore. The actual panning required dexterity rather than strength, and women excelled at the task. A Spaniard with a good claim might have ten such teams. The first problem was to reach gold-bearing alluvium. Sometimes that meant clearing forest and systematically processing layer after layer of dirt down to the bedrock to see if gold was present. Other Spaniards prospected along riverbanks. Because the water carried flakes of gold downstream, some Spaniards had their gangs divert streams so they could work the riverbeds.

Mining began its assault on the environment in the first decades. Verdant forests and grasslands became pockmarked by mining activity.

Areas of intensive gold panning left the rivers clouded with silt, harming aquatic plants, fish, and other organisms. Mercury the miners used to refine the gold contaminated the environment. Diverting the indigenous population to mining also changed the ecosphere. Hard labor and unhealthy conditions weakened the islanders and made them more susceptible to diseases such as smallpox that were unwittingly introduced by the Europeans. Early claim holders had little reason to protect their workers' health because they could obtain more labor by bringing in additional Indians from other islands and, later, from Mexico. Spaniards willing to trade a hundred Indians for a horse were not likely to worry much about the death of a few workers.

The Spaniards quickly exhausted the few Caribbean goldfields. Within a quarter century of Columbus's arrival, they had worked over the Cibao and San Cristobal fields on Hispaniola. As the Indians died out, labor became more expensive, forcing miners to abandon all but the richest claims. Production costs rose to levels that made gold mining unprofitable. Spaniards also found gold on Puerto Rico and Cuba, where mining began again. The demographic catastrophe provoked by Old World diseases soon raised Puerto Rican and Cuban labor costs in turn. By then Columbus was dead and the sands of Ophir had proved elusive. Yet new marvels promising rich golden treasures were on the horizon in Mexico and Peru and later in Brazil.

Metaphorically, the hunt for Ophir's riches continued throughout the centuries during which Spain and Portugal ruled their New World colonies. When Hernán Cortés and his men invaded Mexico, they received gold and other gifts from Aztec emissaries. The Aztecs later recalled that upon their receipt of the treasure, "the Spaniards burst into smiles; . . . They picked up the gold and fingered it like monkeys; . . . Their bodies swelled with greed, and their hunger was ravenous; they hungered like pigs for that gold."[14] The Aztecs were intrigued by a Spanish helmet and asked to take it to show Moctezuma, their ruler. Cortés agreed, on condition that they return it filled with gold, which they did, some three thousand pesos worth of small nuggets. More important, the gift showed the Spaniards "that there were good mines in the country."[15]

Spanish territory expanded as the Spaniards investigated rumors about gold. In 1532, Francisco Pizarro and a small company of Spaniards captured the Inca ruler Atahualpa, who then tried to ransom himself by filling a room once with gold and twice with silver. The Spaniards thus enriched must have been as enraptured as Columbus had been when he hurried back to Spain with the news that he had reached Cipangu. Later, Francisco Vásquez de Coronado roamed the area that is now the southwestern United States from 1540–1542 searching for the Seven Cities of Gold in the land of Cíbola. Expeditions penetrated the tropical heartland of South America seeking El Dorado. From the Brazilian coast, *bandeirantes* (frontiersmen) explored westward, hunting for gold and Indian slaves and staking Portugal's claim to the interior.

Although they never found the gold of El Dorado and Ophir, the Spaniards discovered great lodes of silver. By the mid-sixteenth century, they had found (or the Indians had revealed to them) the rich Mexican and Andean silver districts. Mining would undergird the social and economic structure of those two regions for the remainder of the colonial period. Mining came later to Brazil. Indians there had no metallurgical tradition, and they consequently could not reveal gold or silver deposits to the Portuguese. Aside from the Spaniards' working of alluvial deposits in the Caribbean, most of the gold they obtained during the first half-century in the Americas came from their plunder of Indian treasures, especially in Mexico and Peru. Eventually their expansion into Colombia offered them richer goldfields. The great gold boom in colonial Latin America began, however, in the 1690s, when bandeirantes from São Paulo discovered the golden riches of Minas Gerais.

Indigenous Mining and Metallurgy

In the Andes the Spaniards encountered the most highly developed indigenous metallurgy, which included work in gold, silver, copper, and bronze.[16] Metalworking and metallurgy in the New World developed in the Andes as early as 1500 BCE. Indians there worked native gold and copper and also smelted copper ore. Eventually they smelted silver and tin ores and also produced alloys, including bronze. Metallurgy spread to the region of Ecuador, Colombia, and Central America around 200 BCE. Indigenous metallurgists there chiefly worked gold. Only a few copper objects have been found, perhaps imported from the Andean region. In Mexico, metalworking emerged much later, around 650 CE in western Mexico. It yielded gold, silver, and copper objects. Some have conjectured that knowledge of metallurgy spread northward from the Andes. This would explain its relatively late development in Mexico. Most of the metal objects seem to have held religious significance in the indigenous cultures, rather than possessing merely utilitarian value.[17]

As use of metals expanded, especially of copper and silver, mining was necessary. The indigenous peoples obtained most of their gold through washing or panning gravels and sands in placer working of alluvial deposits. They also found some native copper and silver but in general obtained those metals through mining. The most famous pre-Hispanic Andean silver mine was at Porco, in modern Bolivia, where indigenous miners used deer horns to dig out silver ore and skin bags to carry it away. The largest cavity extended forty yards into the hillside, although the tunnel was so narrow that only one person could work at a time. Andeans smelted silver ores in small ovens. Lacking any form of bellows, a team of workers blew through long tubes to increase the heat of the fire. A variation of this technology was the *guayra*, a small ceramic oven placed on the hillside to use downdrafts of wind to raise the temperature.

Spaniards in Mexico found several important preconquest mining sites. The Tarascans were ancient Mexico's foremost metallurgists, working with gold from alluvial deposits, silver mined at Tamazula, and copper from La Huacana. Almost as soon as the conquest ended, Spaniards began exploiting Tarascan silver mines, including the famous Morcillo diggings (perhaps at Tamazula), which soon caved in and were abandoned.

Archaeological evidence of pre-Hispanic mining is difficult to obtain because later colonial exploitation of the sites destroyed almost all evidence of indigenous workings.[18] This happened in Peru at Huancavelica, where indigenous cinnabar diggings disappeared as early Spanish miners began to mine for mercury. Spanish excavations at Porco also obliterated preconquest diggings there. Nonetheless, some locales show considerable signs of indigenous mining. Anasazis in what is now the American Southwest extracted turquoise for trade with central Mexico, and sites such as Cerrillos, south of Santa Fe, New Mexico, are littered with the remains of their mining activity.[19] Found in a caved-in section of the mines at Huantajaya in northern Chile are the mummified remains of two Indian miners, along with a stone hammer and other aboriginal equipment, bearing witness to pre-Hispanic exploitation of that site.[20] Archaeological evidence, including hafted hammerstones and wooden wedges, has survived of pre-Columbian mining of copper, turquoise, and cinnabar in Mexico. Native miners also dislodged ore by fire-setting: building a fire in front of the ore face to heat it, then throwing cold water on the ore body to fracture it.

Throughout Mexico and the Andes, the indigenous population knew of great gold and silver deposits that by European standards had hardly been exploited. The conquistadors questioned their native allies and captives about the origin of gold and silver objects, hoping to learn where precious metals could be found. Spaniards probably learned about the earliest colonial mines from these sources. Spanish reports about new mining discoveries sometimes note that Indians had earlier worked the site. At times the Indians willingly provided information; at other times they were coerced. In the region of modern-day Taxco, Mexico, Spaniards found indigenous copper diggings, panned for gold, and eventually discovered veins that yielded millions of pesos of silver during the colonial era.[21] The same process occurred in Peru. After occupying Cuzco in November 1533, the Spanish invaders learned of Porco and soon worked it.

Self-interest and communitarian needs determined whether an individual Indian revealed an ore deposit to the Spaniards. Someone eager to curry favor with an encomendero or corregidor (governor) might show where Indians had mined. In 1563, for example, residents of the Peruvian village of Chacas showed encomendero Amador de Cabrera the location of cinnabar (mercuric sulfide) deposits that the Indians used for decorative and cosmetic purposes. Confusion and fantasy cloud the details of why the Indians told Cabrera about the cinnabar. According to one version, the wife of the *kuraka* (chieftain) told Cabrera's wife of the location. In another version of the story the kuraka's son had been holding Cabrera's hat while the encomendero participated in a Corpus Christi procession. The boy either lost the hat or through negligence allowed it to be damaged. His father, the kuraka Gonzalo Ñavincopa, compensated Cabrera by showing him the cinnabar. Visiting the site, Cabrera reported that the Indians had dug "great pits" and "very great adits, in such a way that almost all the said hill is countermined and hollow."[22] Indigenous miners crushed the ore on large stones and then washed it in a nearby stream to separate out the cinnabar. Those cinnabar deposits became the Huancavelica mercury mines, which supplied most of the mercury used to amalgamate and refine silver ores in colonial Peru.

The richest silver mines discovered in the mid-1500s lay within the western Sierra Madre mountain range of Mexico and in the Andes of South America. Mexico proved incredibly rich in silver: around the capital were discovered the districts of Sultepec (discovered 1530), Zumpango (1530), Tlalpujahua (1534), Taxco (1534), and Pachuca (1552); to the north were the great sites of Zacatecas (1546), Guanajuato (ca. 1550), Sombrerete (1558), San Luis Potosí (1592), and Bolaños (1740s); and still farther north lay Santa Bárbara (1567), Parral (1631), and Chihuahua (1703). The most famous silver mining district of all was Potosí (1545) in the mountains of modern Bolivia. Other Andean discoveries included Porco and Huantajaya (both Incaic),

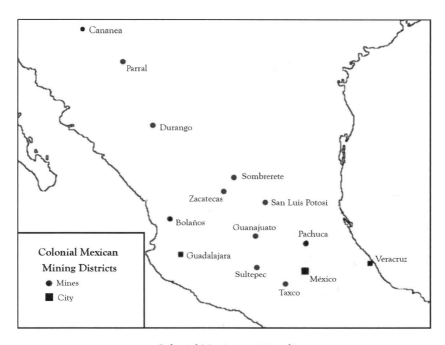

Map 1. Colonial Mexican mining districts

Castrovirreina (1555), Oruro (1606), Cailloma (1620), Cerro de Pasco (1630), San Antonio del Nuevo Mundo (ca. 1645), and Hualgayoc (1771).

Silver-bearing ores dated from Tertiary intrusions of argentiferous magma into faults and cavities during the upthrusting of the mountain ranges. In some places weathering, oxidation, and precipitation enriched the original ores. Most Andean mining districts were high enough to pose serious obstacles to human labor. Diggings at Potosí lay as high as 4,800 meters (15,600 feet). Mexican mines, however, were generally between 1,800 and 2,400 meters high (5,850–7,800 feet).

Colonial miners encountered both native silver (they extracted nearly pure and naturally occurring intertwined wires of silver at Huantajaya in northern Chile) and great quantities of enriched silver compounds. They found oxidized silver chloride (called *pacos* or *colorados*) above the water table and silver sulfide (*negrillos*) below it. The former proved far easier and more profitable to work: chlorides could be refined through smelting or amalgamation and since they lay above the water table, there was little

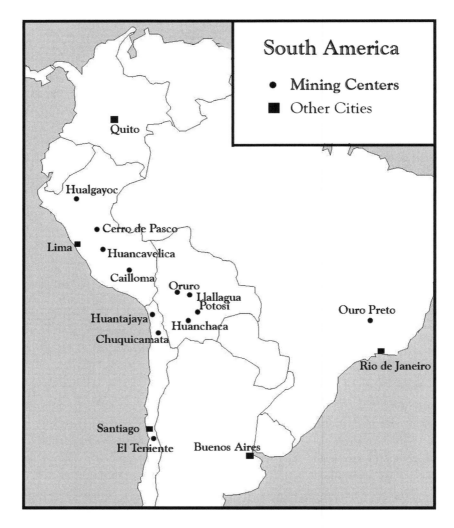

Map 2. Mining districts of South America

problem with flooded pits. Furthermore, because they lay near the surface, extraction costs were relatively low: mine owners did not have to dig expensive tunnels to reach them. The negrillos, on the other hand, were more complicated, although not impossible, to refine, and because they usually lay below the water table, drainage problems made their extraction costly.

Some Mexican and Andean districts also refined small quantities of gold found in the silver ore. The Spanish worked alluvial gold deposits in the Caribbean, Mexico, the Andes, and especially New Granada. Colonial mining concentrated almost exclusively upon precious metals. Some copper and iron were mined, but Spaniards could import base metals more cheaply from Europe than mine them in the New World. Aside from gold and silver, mercury was the only other commodity mined in significant quantities during the colonial period.

American Bullion and the World Monetary System

American bullion had a dramatic impact on European and global money supplies, and thus on the world economy. Precious metals either minted or in silver and gold bars acted as the medium of exchange for much national and international trade. Thus, the Crown, merchants, and bankers waited with anxious excitement for the return from the Americas of each treasure fleet. Once the ships neared Spain, the commander sent a fast-sailing sloop ahead to announce the fleet's arrival. Even then, however, there were still threats to the treasure, from English privateers lurking off the coast and from the dangerous bar at Sanlúcar that hindered entry into the Guadalquivir River. Escorted by the *capitana* and *almiranta* (armed naval vessels that generally carried the king's gold and silver, along with much of the privately owned bullion sent by colonists), dozens of merchant vessels made their way up the river. Those that were too heavy to cross the bar had to offload their cargoes. Using the flood tide to push them along, the other ships slowly sailed fifty miles inland to Seville. Galleys and small boats helped the ships dock along the river near the Golden Tower (Torre del Oro, built during the Muslim rule of Seville as a military fortress to control shipping on the river), while church bells pealed and guns fired a welcoming salute. Officials from the Board of Trade (Casa de la Contratación) boarded the ships to compare the cargoes with the bills of lading.

The crowds thronging the Arenal waited to catch a glimpse of the gold and silver hauled out of the ships' holds by a big two-wheeled crane. Workers loaded the king's share of the gold and silver bars onto ox carts that carried the treasure to the Board of Trade.[23] During the heyday of Potosí's production in the late sixteenth century, the treasure fleets amazed the spectators. For example, on 22 March 1595 the ships of the Indies silver fleet arrived at the docks of Seville, and began to unload and put in the Board of Trade 332 cartloads of silver, gold and pearls of great value. On 8 May 1595 103 cartloads of silver and gold were taken from the *capitana*, and on 23 May of said year they brought by land from Portugal 583 loads of silver, gold, and pearls, that were taken off the *almiranta* that had put in at Lisbon due to storms.[24]

Sometimes the treasure was so great that piles of silver and gold bars had to be left under guard on the docks. In the Seville mint, two hundred workers struggled to make coins out of the flood of bullion. Trying to give some idea of the amount of precious metal Seville received, a sixteenth-century observer, Alonso de Morgado, wrote that enough treasure had arrived by the 1580s to pave the city's streets with gold and silver.[25]

Even before Potosí's silver flooded into Seville, a Spanish writer, Pedro de Medina, opined in 1547 that "just as God provided Solomon with that gold and silver brought to built the material temple, so that it was the richest and most solemn in the world, he likewise wanted the Spaniards to bring from remote and distant places so much gold and silver and other riches to edify the spiritual temple, which is to bring the infidels to the society and council of the holy mother Church."[26] The deluge of American gold and silver seemed an answer to Columbus's dream of finding a westerly route to Cipangu's mythical gold in order to finance the Last Crusade.

Output from the American mines transformed Seville into one of the world's most dynamic commercial centers. The coins flowing out of the Seville mint were so abundant that gold and silver seemed to Sevillans "like they were any common merchandise."[27] Although they were precious metals, gold and silver were also commodities whose value fluctuated relative to each other. Scarcity of silver increased its value compared with gold, or vice versa. Heightened demand for bullion outside Spain and its colonies made gold and silver more precious within the empire. Gresham's law also held sway: namely, that bad money drives out good. This meant that when silver increased in value compared with gold, the silver tended to be drawn out of the economy. Once the silver strikes began in Mexico and Peru in the 1540s, silver dropped in value relative to gold.

Around 1500, silver's value relative to gold was comparatively high.[28] Europe had experienced a modest silver boom in the thirteenth century with the discovery and exploitation of important mines in Saxony and Bohemia.

In the early 1300s a mark of gold was worth about thirteen marks of silver. From 1350 to 1500 silver output lagged but demand for bullion grew because of heightened commercial activity. Trade with the Levant for goods from India and the Far East intensified, as did the import of fine furs from Russia through the Baltic. This drained bullion out of Europe, which was forced to use gold and especially silver to pay off its commercial deficit. Meanwhile, gold stocks increased because of imports of the yellow metal from sub-Saharan Africa over desert caravan routes.[29]

As a result, gold's worth declined against silver from 1350 to the time of Columbus but then rose once the Spanish American silver mines began producing. After 1600, silver's value declined rapidly until the eighteenth century, when the value of the two metals became relatively stable. The explanation for these changes in value is simple: Until the 1690s the Americas produced comparatively little gold in contrast to the quantity of silver that was refined. This meant that silver declined in value against gold. During the 1700s, the Brazilian gold boom offset the great contemporary surge in Mexican silver.[30]

Demand for precious metals in the Far East also influenced the value of gold and silver in Europe, an ironic situation given Columbus's search for the legendary Oriental Ophir's supply of gold. Europe's gold and especially its silver, much of it obtained from the New World, flowed to India, China, and the Spice Islands as payment for silks and spices. Around 1600 the value of silver to gold in Canton was 5.5–7:1, whereas in Spain, as indicated above, the ratio was 12–14:1. Thus, in terms of gold, silver was worth roughly twice as much in China as it was in Europe.[31] Indeed, one observer reported that to the Chinese, "silver is blood."[32] Although Europeans traded some woolen textiles, metal products, and other goods for the luxuries of the East, Asian demand for European goods was not nearly as strong as the European taste for Eastern luxuries. Given this negative balance of trade, European merchants often had to pay for 40 to 50 percent of their purchases in silver. East Asia used the bullion as a medium of exchange in its economies and thus was willing to trade luxury goods for the metals. The Indian subcontinent produced no precious metals, and its coinage was minted from bullion imported through trade. The collapse of Mongol power and extreme inflation in China brought an end to the use of paper money, which had circulated from the ninth to fourteenth centuries. The new Ming dynasty replaced paper with silver largely drawn from Spanish America via trade with Europe: "Silver—'white as snow' because it was mixed with antimony—was the basic instrument of large-scale exchanges in China, all the more so under the Mings (1368–1644) as a monetary and capitalist economy came to life."[33] Silver circulated both as coins and as ingots, with Chinese traders and merchants carrying scissors and scales to cut and weigh it.

All this made New World gold and especially silver alluring to the Spaniards. The bullion plundered by the conquistadors was just a foretaste of the New World's possibilities. Cortés, Pizarro, and their like were not thinking about balance-of-payments problems. They lusted after gold and silver for more personal reasons. In addition to the material comforts it could buy, bullion gave these men status and respect. Their dreams of gold and silver, coupled with the fantastic yet mysterious possibilities of the New World, promised freedom and adventure.[34] Back in Spain, Charles V was delighted to receive the royal fifth, the monarch's share of plunder seized from the Indians and the tax on mining production. The influx of precious metals promised to solve the Spanish monarchy's fiscal problems, along with Europe's commercial deficit with Asia.

CHAPTER 2

Potosí and Colonial Latin American Mining

~୧

The famous, always greatest, most rich and inexhaustible Hill of
Potosí; singular work of the power of God; unique miracle of nature;
perfect and permanent marvel of the world; joy of mortals, emperor
of mountains, king of hills, prince of all minerals; lord of 5,000
Indians (who extract its entrails); . . . lodestone of all wills; foundation of all treasures.

— Bartolomé Arzáns de Orsúa y Vela,
Anales de la Villa Imperial de Potosí

✢ OF ALL LATIN AMERICAN MINING DISTRICTS, POTOSÍ MOST FULLY
embodied the industry's grandeur and decadence, its dazzling wealth and
miserable poverty, the euphoria and the pain of mining. Indigenous artists
pictured the Hill as Pachamama, the Andean earth mother who created and
controlled mines and miners. Flemish engraver Theodor de Bry rendered a
famous sixteenth-century etching of the Cerro as a rocky cone with the interior hollowed out by naked Indian workers who toiled by candlelight. Potosí
was the most famous silver-mining district of colonial times, and Bolivians
today continue to work its Cerro Rico. The city that sprang up in colonial
times at the foot of the Hill lies at roughly four thousand meters (thirteen
thousand feet) above sea level. Less than twenty degrees south of the equa-
tor, Potosí falls within the tropics, but the elevation makes its climate cold.
Nighttime temperatures dip below freezing during half the year, and strong

winds often make days seem chillier than they really are. Situated on the eastern fringe of the Atacama desert, the Potosí region receives little precipitation from the Pacific but significant rain and snowfall from weather systems in the Amazon basin.

Legend clouds reports of Potosí's "discovery." According to some accounts, Indians considered the hill a *huaca* (sacred place). Andeans believed that deities and ancestors inhabited natural objects, including mountain peaks and crags. Thus, Indians from the vicinity of Potosí likely visited shrines on the Cerro and may have discovered outcroppings of silver ore. One oft-told story of the early colonial period claimed that the Inca ordered the Indians to mine silver at Potosí. When they attempted to comply, however, a thunderous voice ordered them to stop: "Take no silver from this hill, for it is for other owners."[1] Spaniards quickly saw in this story a prophecy of their own arrival, that God had prepared Potosí as their reward. Their desire to justify their conquest of the Incas and their seizure of Peru's wealth made it easy to believe such stories.

If Andeans knew of Potosí's silver prior to the conquistadores' arrival, they managed to conceal it until 1545. Even then, reports about the "discovery" conflict. In the most elaborate story, an Indian named Diego Gualpa made the find while searching for a huaca on the side of the Cerro Rico. Another version of the story has him searching the hillside for a llama that had strayed. While on the Cerro, a violent gust of wind threw him to the ground, and he found himself holding on to an outcropping of silver ore. According to a different account, he camped on the Cerro, built a fire to warm himself, and in the morning discovered his fire had smelted silver. Thereafter, Gualpa apparently tried to report his find to the Spaniards in Porco, but they paid him little attention. Another version of the story holds that Gualpa hid his find and secretly worked the lode. Eventually his good fortune attracted too much attention, and news of the strike spread rapidly.[2] Spaniards soon found several tremendously rich veins, and the celebrated history of Potosí began.

The word "Potosí" entered the Spanish language as "an object of incomparable value"; *vale un potosí* (it's worth a Potosí) came to mean "priceless." The royal government considered Potosí its most valuable American asset and supplied the mine operators there with forced labor, subsidies, and first claim on scarce resources. Spaniards almost inevitably compared new mining discoveries to Potosí. Its fame reached Mexico, where the silver district of San Luis Potosí was named for the great Andean site. When they found

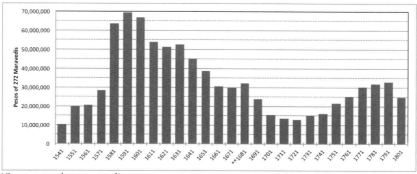

*One peso equals 272 maravedis
**The designation 1681 includes years between and including 1681 and 1690

Graph 1. Potosí silver output from 1545 to 1810, by decade. Data from John J. TePaske, *A New World of Gold and Silver*, ed. Kendall W. Brown (Leiden: Brill, 2010), 188–91.

silver at Cailloma in Peru around 1620, the enthusiastic prospectors and mine operators called those diggings the "new Potosí," hoping that fortune would bear out their prophecy. In Huarochirí province, east of Lima, still other mines were called Nuevo Potosí.

Of all the mining districts in Latin America, Potosí remains the archetype. It yielded a river of silver in colonial times, as graph 1 shows. Basing his calculations on mining tax data contained in colonial treasury records, John TePaske concludes that the Cerro of Potosí and mines in the surrounding countryside officially produced 22,695 metric tons of fine silver between 1545 and 1823.[3] To place this in context, Europe's silver stock in 1500 was 37,500 tons, plus 3,500 tons of gold.[4] Such figures are only informed estimates but nonetheless reveal the size of Potosí's official output, which by itself added to the European silver supply by 60 percent.

The history of colonial Potosí divides into three main periods. The first, from 1545 until the early 1570s, encompassed the discovery and first boom in silver production. Spaniards rushed to Potosí to take advantage of the strike, taking with them both Indians from their encomiendas and yanaconas (during colonial times, an Indian who lacked ayllu or clan affiliation and was tied permanently in a dependent relationship to a Spaniard). As news spread, even some Indians went there on their own to prospect. Andean natives provided nearly all the labor and most of the technology during the early phase, when work focused on the oxidized surface ores. These were very rich, sometimes even pure or native silver. Extraction costs were not high because only a modest amount of tunneling was necessary and drainage did not pose a problem.

Most of the Spaniards had no more than a rudimentary knowledge of mining techniques. To complicate matters, they soon discovered that their method of smelting did not work at Potosí. At Porco they had used Spanish-style furnaces equipped with bellows to heat the crushed ore and fuse the silver in a molten stream. Potosí's ore, however, seemed to lack flux, and the silver would not fuse. To solve the problem, they turned to indigenous techniques. In some cases it was sufficient to put the ore on top of wood, charcoal, or other fuel, light the fire, and raise the temperature by blowing on the fire through long cane or ceramic tubes. An ingenious alternative, the guayra, was a ceramic vessel that held the fuel and ore. Perforations in the vessel permitted air to circulate. Indians placed the guayras on hillsides and ridges where strong downdrafts of wind raised the fire's temperature and smelted the ore (see fig. 2). Of the guayras, chronicler Pedro Cieza de León wrote: "At night there are so many of them throughout the countryside and on the hills, that they appear to be luminaries."[5] Such techniques managed to produce more than 40,000 kilograms of silver per year, rising to nearly 64,000 in 1565. Then, however, production plunged to 21,000 kilograms in 1572.

Figure 2. *Estos Yndios están guayrando.* An early colonial depiction of Indians at Potosí smelting silver ore with *guayras.* Courtesy of the Hispanic Society of America (Atlas of Sea Charts, K3).

A shortage of ores suitable for smelting caused the crisis. In the twenty-five years following its discovery, Potosí gave up its rich surface ores. By the 1570s, miners had begun to tunnel into the hill. Moving earth and shoring up pits and adits cost more than surface mining. The ores extracted did not compensate for such expenditures, given the refining techniques the Spaniards used. Smelting also confronted environmental limitations: it required fuel, but Potosí's altitude limited the amount of wood and charcoal available for heating furnaces. Nonetheless, the Cerro offered an endless supply of lower-grade silver ore, great dumps of which had been discarded as too poor for smelting.

Desperation led to technological change. In 1555, Bartolomé de Medina had developed in Mexico a method of refining silver ores through amalgamation. Medina's process could refine lower-grade ores and required far less fuel than smelting. It involved mixing salt and mercury with crushed ore. Depending on the type of silver compound (oxides or sulfates, for example), the refiner then added a reagent (*magistral*), such as crushed copper or iron pyrites. The magistral started a chemical reaction in which the salt released the silver from the ore to form an amalgam with the mercury. Through flotation, the workers then washed away the dross, leaving the heavy amalgam, which they heated to volatilize or evaporate the mercury. This process resulted in silver. Medina called his discovery the "patio process." By 1572, Pedro Hernández de Velasco and others succeeded in adapting amalgamation to Potosí's ores.

Thus the stage was set for the great boom in Potosí production and the second period in the district's history. Ore suitable for amalgamation abounded. Refiners were called *azogueros* because they used *azogue* (mercury or quicksilver) to process their ores. Luckily for the colonial mining industry, cinnabar (mercuric sulfide) was plentiful southeast of Lima at Huancavelica and had been revealed to Amador de Cabrera in 1563. He and other Spaniards staked claims and began mining cinnabar and distilling mercury. Initially, they sold it to Mexican refiners, to whom the use of Medina's patio process had spread rapidly. Refiners also employed mercury imported from the Crown's mines at Almadén in Spain or quicksilver distilled from small Mexican deposits of cinnabar, such as at Cuernavaca. As amalgamation spread at Potosí, demand for Huancavelica mercury surged. After 1580, Potosí's refiners virtually abandoned smelting.

Peruvian viceroy Francisco de Toledo (1569–1581) clearly understood Potosí's importance to royal finances and the Peruvian economy. He also recognized that Huancavelica, the only major American source of mercury during colonial times, was critical to the prosperity of Potosí. Toledo aimed to ensure regular, abundant supplies of mercury for the silver refiners while at the same time give the government control over mercury distribution and thus over silver refining. According to Spanish law, subsoil rights belonged to the monarchy, which granted their use to miners upon payment of the appropriate taxes. Toledo insisted that the Huancavelica operators had no absolute right to their claims and expropriated their mines in the Crown's name. Despite Cabrera's protests and lawsuits, Toledo prevailed. He contracted with some of the former claimholders to continue operations and stipulated the amount of mercury they were to produce and the price the government would pay for it. Under his system, the Huancavelica treasury office bought the mercury and shipped it to Potosí and the other silver mines for sale.

The switch to amalgamation meant an increased demand for labor to extract and refine massive quantities of ore. Viceroy Toledo committed the colonial government to providing the mines and mills with workers. Prior to the Spaniards' arrival, the Incas had required adult males to take turns laboring on public projects. Toledo adapted this custom, called *mit'a* or "turn" by the Indians, and created the colonial mita, a system of forced Indian labor. He assigned an annual quota of thirteen thousand mitayos (mita workers) to Potosí, drawing them from a wide area stretching nearly to Cuzco, almost six hundred miles away. Adult male Indians in the mita provinces were to work every seventh year at Potosí. In 1571 at Huancavelica, Toledo had allocated the mercury refiners a mita of 900 workers, a number he raised to 3,280 in 1577 to meet the silver refiners' growing demand for mercury.[6] At both sites, mitayos received a wage, although it was lower than that paid to the free workers who were employed to supplement the mita contingents.

The new technology, Potosí's ores, and the Spanish government's coercion of indigenous labor caused an amazing surge in silver production. It outstripped anything seen during the earlier bonanza, when the outcroppings had yielded up their treasure. Potosí refiners had officially smelted 63,000 kilograms of silver in 1565. With amalgamation, they refined 194,000 kilograms in 1592. Only once from 1579 to 1610 did official output fall below 130,000 kilograms of silver, double the high point during the initial phase. Whereas many mining districts played out after a brief time, Potosí poured forth a river of silver year after year.[7]

Amalgamation was the critical element in Potosí's prosperity, although it was not the only factor. The new refining process allowed the mine operators to work medium- and low-grade ores. They built mills (*ingenios*) to pulverize and amalgamate the ores. An ingenio included storage rooms, living quarters, ore-grinding machinery, and facilities for amalgamation. Waterwheels powered the stamp mills, which raised and dropped heavy iron hammers to crush the ore. In the nearby mountains, refiners built a series of reservoirs to store runoff from rain and melting snow. This enabled them to grind ore year-round, except during infrequent severe droughts. Aqueducts brought the water into the ingenio to turn the wheel, then carried it on to other milling operations farther down the hill. Stout walls offered security to buildings, mill, and courtyard. See, for example, figures 3 and 4.

Processing took the ore through several steps before it yielded refined silver. At the mine on the Cerro, workers picked over the ore, discarding

Figure 3. Early colonial depiction of a refining mill at Potosí. Note the water-driven stamp mill (center left), the boxes containing a mixture of ground ore and mercury (bottom left), and the Cerro Rico. Courtesy of the Hispanic Society of America (Atlas of Sea Charts, K3).

Figure 4. Ruins of a colonial refining mill at Potosí. The water wheel was held in place by the upright masonry walls. The city of Potosí is located in the valley to the right.

any that appeared unprofitable. Indians transported the remainder to the ingenio on llamas, storing it in the deposit. Eventually, workers at the stamp mill pulverized the ore and sifted it through a screen. Then they shoveled it into a *cajón* (flagstone box), and the refiner added salt and crushed magistral. From a rough cloth bag he squeezed and sprinkled drops of mercury onto the ore, and workers mixed it in. Over the next three or four weeks workers occasionally stirred the mixture, until the refiner decided that no more amalgamation would occur. He could speed the process by heating the mixture, but this was more costly because of fuel scarcity. Washing the mixture with a flotation system, workers removed the amalgam from the dross. Next, they had to separate the mercury and silver. Compressing and hammering the amalgam removed some mercury. Workers then placed the lump of amalgam in a retort (a vessel fitted with a lid that had a long downward-sloping neck) and heated the amalgam to volatilize the mercury. The mercuric gases flowed out of the retort through the neck, where they cooled and condensed. Capturing and reusing the mercury was crucial, because mercury was an expensive element in the refining process. Azogueros called the porous spongelike silver that was left in the retort a piña (pineapple).

Royal law required the refiner to submit the piña immediately to the treasury office and pay taxes on it. Officials assayed the piña to determine its fineness or purity, charging a fee of 1.5 percent. On the remaining 98.5 percent of the silver they collected the royal fifth (*quinto real*), leaving the refiner with 78.8 percent of his original piña. The Crown forbade the circulation of silver in its untaxed piña form. At Potosí, which had a mint, a refiner could easily exchange his piña silver for coin. Sometimes officials simply smelted the silver into an ingot and stamped it with royal seals and identification numbers. However, most mining districts had no mint, and scarcity of coin was often a great hindrance, especially when the payment of small amounts, such as for workers' wages and the purchase of food and other necessities, was called for.

The government's financial stake in silver production at Potosí and other mining districts was substantial. Taxes on mineral production directly supplied a good part of the state's revenues. Of the surplus revenues remitted to the Peruvian capital by the provincial tax offices from 1607 to 1690, for example, Potosí supplied 110 million of the 180 million pesos received in the Lima treasury.[8] As silver and gold flowed through the economy, they stimulated other economic activities that generated tax monies. The state also monopolized the distribution and sale of mercury. It collected the royal fifth on the Huancavelica distillers' mercury, but sold the quicksilver at cost plus the expense of transporting it to the silver mines. To make quicksilver more accessible to refiners, the treasury sold it on credit. Some azogueros never paid for the mercury advanced to them, creating huge fiscal deficits. In the late seventeenth century, the Potosí refiners owed the treasury more than a million pesos in mercury debts, most of which the Crown never collected. Lending money to the guild of mercury distillers at Huancavelica also resulted in huge losses for the government, but these deficits were small when compared with the revenues obtained from mining. The mercury monopoly gave the government some control over silver refiners. Early on, officials recognized a rough relationship (*correspondencia*) between the amount of mercury used and the quantity of silver refined. They judged that an azoguero ought to produce at least one hundred marks of silver for every one hundred pounds of mercury he purchased. Officials suspected someone whose correspondencia fell much below that ratio of avoiding taxes. It was easier, however, to suspect than to prove contraband production.

The second period of Potosí's colonial history, which began with the introduction of amalgamation in the early 1570s, ran until approximately 1720. From its height, when yearly output reached nearly 200,000 kilograms in 1593, Potosí began a long, gradual decline. By 1700 its official annual production had fallen to 30,000–40,000 kilograms. The Cerro still yielded silver, but a quarter to a third of production came from other mining camps in the province. Although the tax burden, a shortage of mitayos, and the lack of mercury contributed to Potosí's decadence, foremost was the poor quality of the remaining ore available in the Cerro. Whereas Potosí azogueros had, in general, refined 130–140 marks of silver for every hundred pounds of mercury over the middle half of the 1600s, the average correspondencia for the first decade of the eighteenth century was only 100 marks. This seems clear evidence of the poorer quality ore and the inability of the operators to significantly improve their refining techniques to extract a higher percentage of silver from their ores. Part of the lower correspondencia probably stemmed from increasing contraband production as well. The assay fee and the quinto tax took 21.2 percent of the silver, and mine operators and refiners looked for ways, both licit and illegal, to cut their costs. During the late seventeenth and early eighteenth century, French, English, and Dutch smugglers infested the Pacific coast, anxious to exchange their wares for Potosí's silver. It mattered little to them, of course, whether the silver had been taxed or not, although they did worry about the fineness of piñas as compared with official stamped ingots. Clandestine trade with the Portuguese in Brazil also offered untaxed silver another outlet.

It is hard to determine the extent of such illegal silver refining. Let us assume, however, that Peter Bakewell's estimate of 12 percent contraband is correct for 1635. That would mean that azogueros were producing about 150 marks of silver for each hundred pounds of mercury they purchased, even though the official correspondencia was only 130 or so marks. In the early 1700s, officials at the Huancavelica mercury mines apparently believed the correspondencia was still around 150 marks.[9] This would have meant, however, that ore quality had not declined during the intervening years, and this was unlikely. From 1710 to 1714, for example, treasury officials in Potosí distributed 7,348 hundredweight of mercury and registered about 850,000 marks of silver. This yielded a correspondencia of 116 marks per hundredweight, down significantly from the 1635 figure and reflecting poorer ore, greater smuggling, or a combination of both.

Even during Potosí's gradual decline, the district continued to yield great wealth. Its riches attracted tens of thousands of fortune seekers to the arid site. By the early seventeenth century, the city had a population of over one hundred thousand. (Even today, it remains the highest city in the world, with seventy thousand inhabitants). Visitors admired its richly decorated churches. Public celebrations ostentatiously emphasized Potosí's stature in the Hispanic world. The procession marking Philip III's marriage in 1600 included a large float pulled by a dozen white horses that depicted in worked silver the Cerro Rico, with a girl clad in silver, diamonds, and other precious jewels representing the city below. Extending her hand toward a picture of the monarch, she offered him silver ingots.[10] For another procession, refiners literally paved the thoroughfare with silver ingots.

Its population and wealth made Potosí a predominant market for regional and international commerce. Declared chronicler Pedro de Cieza de León, "In Potosí there was the richest market in the world, in the time that these mines were in their prosperity."[11] Potosí yielded vast fortunes for some, as exemplified by Antonio López de Quiroga. Born in Galicia, Spain, López immigrated to Peru as a merchant and within a few years moved to Potosí. By 1653 he was a silver merchant, making loans to mine and ingenio owners and receiving from them piñas at a discounted price. Through his commercial contacts he also sold merchandise to them. As his capital grew, López bought property in Potosí and agricultural estates nearby. He also saw opportunities in the mines and began to renovate old flooded workings. López was apparently the first to apply blasting on a broad scale in Spanish American mining. To earlier generations of miners, in fact, detonating charges of gun powder seemed more likely to collapse the mine than increase productivity. Nonetheless, López perceived the benefits that blasting offered, especially when coupled with careful planning to minimize risks to the mine itself. His crews blasted slightly rising tunnels or adits to reach the deep, flooded pits of abandoned mines. Doing so drained the pits and gave access to their ores. Such endeavors required massive capital outlays, which were beyond the capacity of many operators, but López had the foresight to understand how his commercial assets could be invested to produce even greater wealth in mining. Before his death in 1699, López's business endeavors extended throughout Upper Peru. "The master maker of silver in the New World," he was clearly one of Spanish America's greatest entrepreneurs, whose fortune was made ironically at the same time Potosí's glory was fading.[12]

By the mid-1600s Potosí's profits had begun to wane, a fact symbolized by civil strife among Spaniards and a scandal at the local mint. With mercury and mita labor in short supply and rising production costs cutting into the refiners' profits, two factions arose among the azogueros: the Basques, who controlled most of the refining mills; and the *vicuñas*, the non-Basque

Spaniards and Creoles. Between 1622 and 1624 the two factions engaged in a murderous feud that killed sixty-four and wounded many others. On the surface the strife was ethnic, but more critical was its economic dimension. With fewer profits to go around, the vicuñas wanted for themselves more control of Potosí's silver output.

Factional hatred lasted long after the murderous rampage ended, but it faded into the background once the scandal at the mint seized public and government attention. Although colonial mints stamped royal coins, during the sixteenth and seventeenth centuries the mints were operated by private entrepreneurs who paid the Crown handsomely for the position of treasurer, which oversaw the mint. In Potosí, for example, the office of treasurer sold for 260,000 pesos in 1612.[13] To recover his investment in the office and make a profit, a treasurer earned a small amount for each coin the mint produced. Refiners and silver merchants took much of their silver, once it had been registered and taxed, to the mint for coinage. The latter were investors who advanced operating funds to refiners and received silver at a discounted rate in return. They then took the silver to the treasury office, paid taxes on it, and carried it to the mint, where it was converted into coins. By the 1630s, Potosí's heyday had passed, and there was less silver to mint, which meant less income for the treasurer and fewer profits for silver merchants. In connivance with some of the mint officials, some silver merchants solved the problem of less silver by going to the mint after hours and making debased coins that contained less than the legal amount of silver. As officials became aware of the problem, they assumed that inattention, incompetence, or technical problems had led mint operators to produce coins of substandard quality. Despite royal warnings, the Potosí mint continued to stamp coins that contained less than the required amount of silver. The Council of the Indies, which oversaw colonial affairs for the king, had to proceed cautiously. On the one hand, it could not jeopardize confidence in Spanish coinage by allowing the adulteration to continue. But on the other hand, if it removed and arrested everyone suspected of the crime, it might upset Potosí's delicate credit market. Potosí's mine operators and azogueros depended on working capital they obtained from several of the silver merchants who were accused of involvement in the mint scandal.

Finally, the council sent Francisco de Nestares Marín to investigate and clean up the mess. A priest of austere and unforgiving character who had served in the Inquisition in Spain, Nestares Marín arrived in Potosí in late 1648. He soon concluded that some of the city's principal silver traders had paid off mint officials to produce defective coins from the silver they submitted. Some of the accused sought sanctuary in the city's main church; two others tried to flee Peru. Among the accused was Captain Francisco Gómez de la Rocha, one of Potosí's wealthiest, most generous citizens. Nestares Marín negotiated with Gómez de la Rocha a fine of five hundred thousand pesos (the fines levied against all the culprits amounted to 1.5 million pesos). Gómez de la Rocha agreed to pay the fine over five years and left his sanctuary in the church.

Things did not end happily for the silver merchant. Pressed by Nestares Marín to begin paying the fine, Gómez de la Rocha allegedly conspired to have the priest's cook poison his food. Persuaded that the silver merchant was trying to kill him, Nestares Marín ordered Gómez de la Rocha's arrest and then his execution. In January 1650, Gómez de la Rocha was garroted in Potosí, after which his head was cut off and displayed as a warning to others who might debase the royal coinage or attack the king's emissaries.[14]

The third and final long-term cycle in Potosí's colonial history began around 1720 and lasted until independence in the early 1820s. From 1720 to 1726 the treasury registered less than thirty thousand kilograms of silver per year. Slow improvement began in 1736, when the Crown halved the principal mining tax from a fifth to a tenth (*diezmo*), hoping the lower tariff would stimulate silver output by increasing the industry's profitability. Despite the poor quality of ore, silver production increased gradually, reaching seventy thousand to eighty thousand kilograms per year from 1770 to 1800.

A number of factors enabled the modest recovery. The Crown supplied more mercury and by the 1770s had dropped its price to the refiners. This was possible because output at the royal quicksilver mines at Almadén increased dramatically. The government also purchased mercury from the Idria mines in Slovenia, which were owned by the Austrian Habsburgs. In 1779 the refiners joined together to establish the Bank of San Carlos (Banco de San Carlos), which provided capital and credit and took over the sale of mercury from the treasury office. A technological mission of central European mining and metallurgical experts headed by the Baron of Nordenflicht arrived at Potosí in 1789. Sent by the Crown, the group worked to improve refining techniques by demonstrating a new method of amalgamation developed by Baron Ignaz von Born. Using rotating barrels to mix the ore, mercury, salt, and magistral, it completed amalgamation in three or four days rather than weeks. The "barrel" method also required heating of the ores to speed amalgamation. Initially optimistic about its potential, the azogueros eventually rejected the method, put off by both the cost of building the new machinery and the method's disappointing results in experiments.

Another important factor in Potosí's late colonial resurgence was more intense exploitation of mita labor to offset production costs. Mine operators and refiners increased the amount of work they demanded of mitayos while they held wages down. So crucial was the mita's labor subsidy, writes historian Enrique Tandeter, "that the survival of mining in the *Cerro Rico* depended on the annual *mita* migration."[15] By severely underpaying the mitayos relative to what their labor would have cost on the free market, the azogueros continued profitable operations. But the azogueros' profits came at great cost to the mitayos, who were required by the colonial government to labor in horrible conditions for below-subsistence wages in a forced transfer of wealth from the indigenous population to the Spaniards.

After 1800, the final years of colonial rule brought new crises to Potosí, occasioned first by its dependence on Almadén in Spain for mercury and later by the outbreak of the war for independence. Almost immediately a mercury shortage occurred. Because of war with Great Britain, Spanish shipping could not reach the Americas with quicksilver from Almadén. In 1800, Potosí received only 1,479 hundredweight of mercury, about half of its normal consumption, and by the end of the year all the mercury had been distributed. No quicksilver arrived during the next two years. Most ingenios stopped grinding ore because the refiners had no way of amalgamating it. In 1801, Potosí registered fewer than forty thousand kilograms of silver, whereas it had been producing nearly eighty thousand kilograms per year in the 1790s. Another shortage occurred when Napoleon invaded Spain in 1808 and the French seized Almadén. The Bank of San Carlos did not run out of mercury completely, but supplies were very short. Spanish liberals, who managed to form an interim government in Cádiz, abolished the mita in 1812 and outlawed all types of forced indigenous service, ending the profitable exploitation of indigenous laborers by the mine operators and silver refiners.[16] Meanwhile, the fight for independence began, with patriot and royalist armies ravaging the region. The Bank of San Carlos no longer had funds to make credit available to refiners, only a handful of mills continued to grind ore, and mercury, when available, was much more expensive. In 1820 Potosí registered only twenty-seven thousand kilograms of silver, and its mining industry was nearly moribund.

Silver Production Elsewhere in Colonial Spanish America

In the late 1500s, Potosí's flood of silver was so great that it obscured the output of other mining districts. Many imperial officials echoed the sentiments of a Peruvian viceroy, Pedro de Toledo y Leiva, the marquis of Mancera, when he wrote that Huancavelica and the great silver mines of Potosí "are like two poles which support this kingdom and that of Spain."[17] During the great amalgamation-fueled boom of around 1600, the Potosí district produced more than half the silver registered in Spanish America. Treasure fleets sailing back to Spain carried the Crown's share along with huge amounts of private silver to pay for the textiles and other merchandise the colonists imported. When the king lived beyond his means, waging hugely expensive wars to protect Catholicism from Protestantism or to hold the Spanish Netherlands, he could borrow from European bankers, who knew that the next American convoy would bring New World bullion. Upon receiving reports that disaster had befallen the Invincible Armada in 1588, Philip II reportedly remarked: "I give thanks to God by whose hand I have been so endowed that I can put to sea another fleet as great as this we have lost whenever I choose. It does not matter if a stream is sometimes choked, as long as the source flows freely."[18] The silver of Potosí seemed an inexhaustible resource. As one of the king's biographers noted, "His revenues from the New World permitted Philip, who was no absolutist in theory, to practice in effect royal absolutism. In his dominions he was freed from too much dependence on representative assemblies, which constrained other European monarchs, and could push ahead when he wished with unpopular policies, intimidating or buying off those who opposed him."[19]

In two ways, however, these perceptions of Potosí were wrong. As already noted, Potosí was not inexhaustible. Its ores and output of refined silver experienced a gradual decline. The Crown's other American revenues also had limits, as Philip II's successors learned in the 1600s, when their domestic and international commitments outstripped Spain's economic resources. Neither did Potosí continue to dominate New World silver production. Its portion of total silver output subsided as mining expanded in other parts of Spanish America, particularly in Mexico. By 1700, Potosí registered only 15 percent of American silver production, and that slipped to 10 percent by 1801–1810, reflecting both Potosí's decadence and higher levels of output elsewhere.

Colonial silver mining in Mexico first centered around the capital, especially to the southwest at Zumpango, Amatepec, Sultepec, and Taxco. Little more than a decade after the conquest ended, Spaniards were trumpeting the discovery of rich mines.[20] Hernán Cortés himself owned several of the first Spanish mines at Taxco.[21] The conquerors had little mining or metallurgical experience, and Indian servants and slaves probably found most of the early sites. They worked the surface ores, using primitive smelters to refine the silver. In the mid-1530s, several German experts arrived at Sultepec and helped improve smelting techniques; their improvements included adding lead-based compounds (litharge) to the ore as a flux for the smelting process. By 1540, however, the Spaniards had exhausted most of the rich outcroppings, and the profitability of smelting had declined.

Two developments changed the fortunes of Mexican mining. The first was the discovery of new mines such as Zacatecas, Guanajuato, and Pachuca to the north of Mexico City. The second was Medina's development of the patio process in 1555, which allowed the refiners to amalgamate rather than smelt medium- and low-grade ore. Unfortunately for the refiners, Mexico had no Huancavelica to supply mercury, as Potosí did. They had to depend on sometimes irregular and meager shipments of mercury from Almadén.

Whereas the mines south of Mexico City lay in densely populated areas, most of those in the north had no nearby sedentary indigenous population.

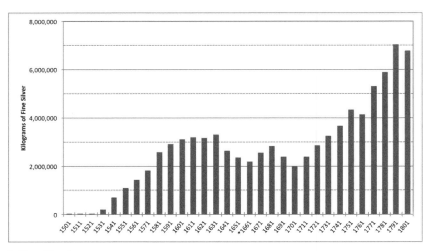

* 1661=1661–1670

Graph 2. Spanish American silver production from 1501 to 1810, by decade. Data from John J. TePaske, *A New World of Gold and Silver*, ed. Kendall W. Brown (Leiden: Brill, 2010), 113.

This situation affected the nature of the labor pool. At Sultepec and Taxco the Spaniards made encomienda and enslaved Indians work in the mines. As the native population declined due to epidemic diseases, the Spanish forced the neighboring towns and villages to provide rotating labor drafts (the repartimiento) around midcentury. Forced labor was less common in the north, although the miners and refiners occasionally used slaves, both indigenous and African. Generally, however, they relied upon wage labor. Some employers advanced wages to the workers, then held them at the mines in debt peonage. But many worked voluntarily, attracted by the wages and, perhaps even more important, by the custom that allowed them to take a share of the ore (*pepena* or *partido*) for their own profit.

Mexican silver production rose rapidly from the establishment of the mining camps through the depletion of the surface ores and during the decades following the introduction of the patio process (for total Spanish American output, see graph 2). This followed the pattern seen at Potosí. Despite some setbacks during the seventeenth century, however, Mexican output did not experience a prolonged decline, as was true of Andean mining, especially at Potosí. Exploitation of Fresnillo and Sombrerete, for example, compensated to some extent for Zacateca's setback between 1635 and 1660.

Historian Woodrow Borah advanced the theory that Mexico suffered a prolonged economic depression during the seventeenth century.[22] The cause of the economic crisis was, according to Borah, the demographic catastrophe that befell New Spain's indigenous population after the conquest: mistreatment, war, and especially the introduction of Old World diseases against which the Indians had no biological immunity triggered a tremendous population plunge, from 11 million in 1519 to 1.5 million around 1650.[23] Dependent on indigenous labor, the colonial economy, including the mining industry, lacked sufficient workers to maintain former levels of production. Meanwhile, the Spanish population, which parasitized indigenous economic output, grew. This, concluded Borah, caused the long depression, which ended only when the indigenous population began to recover around 1700. Data indicate, however, that Mexican mining suffered no century-long depression. The downturn lasted only from the 1640s to approximately 1670, and it probably had more to do with depletion of the surface ores and the scarcity of capital and mercury than with the demographic crisis. In terms of total population, mining employed a much smaller percentage of workers than agriculture did. Borah's century-long crisis seems, in fact, to fit the mining data for the Andes better than it does for Mexico. Silver output at Potosí experienced a prolonged depression from 1630 until it began to increase again in the early eighteenth century.

During the final third of the seventeenth century, Mexican silver mines surpassed Andean mine production. From 1700 to 1750 the margin widened to the point where Mexico refined twice as much as the southern viceroyalty. At century's end, the amount was nearly three times greater. Although New Spain (as the Mexican viceroyalty was called) had no Potosí within its territory, several conditions favored its long-term supremacy. First was simply the greater abundance of rich lodes of silver-bearing ores throughout its jurisdiction. Second, whereas most Andean mines lay above 3,500 meters, Mexican diggings were lower, at 2,000–2,500 meters. Workers at Potosí confronted the oxygen-poor atmosphere of 4,500 meters, 2,000 meters higher than Zacatecas and 2,500 meters above Guanajuato, two of the chief Mexican mining districts. Labor for both humans and draft animals was much easier at the lower Mexican altitude. Altitude also affected the availability of fuel for smelting. The scarcity of wood made its use impractical throughout the Andes, but smelting remained a common refining technique in some Mexican districts throughout the colonial period.

A third factor was the availability and cost of mercury. During the sixteenth and seventeenth centuries, Huancavelica in Peru typically supplied Andean refiners with mercury, while refiners in New Spain received quicksilver from the Crown's mines at Almadén in Spain. Worked since Roman times, Almadén's old mines were nearly exhausted and hardly sufficed to meet the needs of Mexican refiners. Royal officials earmarked Huancavelica's output for Potosí because of the region's fame. The result was more abundant mercury for the Andes than New Spain. Nonetheless, around 1700 the tables turned. Rich newly discovered mines came on line at Almadén that eventually yielded four or five times more mercury than Huancavelica, and at a cost of five or ten pesos per hundredweight, compared to fifty-eight to seventy-three pesos at Huancavelica. Transoceanic shipping costs added only ten pesos or so to the cost of each hundredweight. Meanwhile, Huancavelica's production began declining with the depletion of its ore, making it "an old woman whose fangs and molars are falling out," according to one of its governors.[24] Almadén's prosperity made mercury relatively plentiful in Mexico and allowed the Crown to cut the price it charged Mexicans for quicksilver. A hundred pounds of mercury fell from eighty-two to sixty-two pesos in 1767 to forty-one pesos in 1778. For Andean refiners the government briefly reduced the price to fifty-five pesos in 1779 but then had to raise it again because of problems at Huancavelica. Thus, Mexico derived far more benefit than did Peru from abundant and cheap mercury during the eighteenth century.

Royal tax policy also made for lower operating costs in Mexico than the Andes. Whereas Potosí and other Andean silver producers paid the royal fifth on their silver until 1736, when the Crown reduced the tax to a tenth (diezmo), the Mexican refiners had enjoyed the lower rate since the early 1600s. Some of them had paid the diezmo as early as 1548. Its legendary reputation probably worked against such concessions at Potosí: the Crown believed Potosí was a limitless treasure that could support heavier taxation.

These advantages helped make the Mexican industry more profitable, and consequently mining in New Spain attracted more investment from other economic sectors than was true in the Andes. The need to rehabilitate old mines, flooded in their deepest levels where discoveries of new ores were most likely, required large infusions of capital. Mexican mining entrepreneurs staked their own money on the risky but potentially lucrative task of renovating flooded mines, and their successes attracted capital from merchants as well as financial concessions from the government.

Guanajuato glistened as the greatest Spanish American silver district after 1750, far surpassing decadent Potosí and any other Mexican mining area. Discovered in the mid-1500s, Guanajuato symbolized Mexico's Age of Silver. Its eighteenth-century bonanza resulted in part from the opening by 1768 of the Valenciana mine, whose output between 1780 and 1810 constituted 60–70 percent of the district's total.[25] Antonio Obregón y Alcocer's workings at the great mine so impressed the Crown that it ennobled him as the Count of La Valenciana.[26] Mine owners such as Obregón prospered due to lower mercury prices and managed to reduce labor costs by paying workers only a wage rather than permitting them to also take a share (partido) of the ore. Heavy investment in pumps and drainage equipment and more efficiently designed shafts and other workings allowed access to an abundance of good ore. Mine owners had traditionally depended on the *aviadores* (financial backers) and "silver banks" of Mexico City to provide capital for such infrastructure. Thus a significant portion of the mines' profits ended up almost immediately in the pockets of Mexico City's merchants. After 1750, however, Guanajuato output was so great that much of the capital improvement came from local investors, as silver was recirculated back into the mines.

Mexico's most famous eighteenth-century mining entrepreneur was José de la Borda, who initially worked mines at Taxco and Tlalpujahua. When lavish spending and mining reversals left him nearly broke, Borda moved to Zacatecas in 1767. There he laid plans to drain the flooded depths of the Quebradilla mine, rumored to hold rich ore. Several merchants had tried but failed to drain it, losing three hundred thousand pesos in the bargain. Borda's project required massive investment, and he persuaded the government to exempt him from the diezmo tax and sell him mercury at a discounted thirty pesos per hundredweight until the renovations were completed. Waiting to line up private investors for the Quebradilla, Borda worked several successful mines at Vetagrande, built refining mills, and purchased a nearby estate to grow food for his workers and mules. In 1775 he finally began work at the Quebradilla. His well-designed whims (animal-powered hoists) drained it, establishing Borda's reputation as the viceroyalty's greatest miner. Of him Viceroy Carlos Francisco de Croix remarked: "José de la Borda is without doubt the person in this kingdom who knows most about mines and the machinery for their excavation and drainage."[27] Over a long career Borda made and lost several fortunes before he died in 1779. His son reported in 1790 an estate largely inherited from his father that was worth a million pesos.[28]

During the late eighteenth century, the Spanish Crown made a conscious effort to improve the technological level of mining in its American colonies. Prior to 1700, miners in the Andes and Mexico sometimes developed new technologies. Medina's patio process was a chief example. Another was the *horno busconil*, an oven for distilling mercury that was invented around 1629 by Lope de Saavedra Barba, a doctor living in Huancavelica. His oven had exterior tubes in which the mercury vapors condensed, thus doubling the productivity of the distillation process. A few years later, in 1646, Juan Alonso Bustamante, who had seen Saavedra's ovens in Huancavelica, introduced them in Almadén as his own invention, which gave him such renown that the king ennobled him and made him superintendent of Almadén.[29] After 1700, however, colonial innovation slowed, and technology flowed from Europe to the colonies. At Almadén, experts and technology obtained by the Spanish government from central Europe modernized the mines. The king then sent personnel from Almadén to the New World. In 1778, officials at Almadén also began formally instructing future engineers, metallurgists, and technicians, some of whom were assigned to the colonies. A royal academy of mining and metallurgy soon evolved out of those efforts.

Meanwhile, the Spanish government also sent scientists and technicians to the mines of central Europe for training and to learn new technologies. Antonio de Ulloa, a leading figure of the Spanish Enlightenment, participated in such a mission. Upon Ulloa's return to Spain, the minister of the Indies appointed Ulloa governor of Huancavelica (1758–1764). The Crown also dispatched the Elhuyar brothers (Juan José de and Fausto de) to study at the Mining Academy of Freiberg. The former was then appointed director of mines in New Granada (1783–1796), and Fausto became director general of the Mexican Mining Tribunal (1788–1821). In that capacity he played a critical role in the dissemination of mining and metallurgical technology in New Spain. The Elhuyars championed the Born method of amalgamation, which Baron de Nordenflicht attempted to introduce at Potosí around 1790.

The Crown promoted the organization of colonial mine owners and refiners in new guilds, hoping to make the industry more efficient and profitable. In 1783, Charles III authorized the Mexican operators to form an official guild, the *Real Cuerpo de Minería*. The guild oversaw the Mining Tribunal, which drew up mining ordinances for the industry and adjudicated legal disputes and also supported the mining school established in 1792 in Mexico City. A tax of one real for each mark of registered silver provided revenue for the tribunal and school. The Crown approved a similar guild for Peru in 1787, with regulations and ordinances based on the Mexican model, and another for Upper Peru in 1794 that was headquartered in Potosí. The guilds acted as a lobby for miners' interests.

Besides the great Mexican silver boom of the 1700s and Potosí's modest recovery, other areas of Spanish America produced substantial amounts of the metal as well. Several sites in Chile, Central America, and especially Peru added to the bonanza. Around 1800, in fact, azogueros at Cerro de Pasco in Peru surpassed the output of Potosí. Sites such as Hualgayoc, Cailloma, and Huantajaya also added to the Andean total. Most of these strikes, however, were small compared with the discoveries at Potosí, Zacatecas, or Guanajuato, and within a couple of decades their ores were in general exhausted.

Gold in the New World

Gold had drawn Columbus, Cortés, and Pizarro to the New World. Rich mines existed, but colonial gold production did not rival the total value of the silver output, except in the first half of the eighteenth century. The chief gold-mining zones were New Granada and Brazil, with Chile, Mexico, and Peru yielding lesser amounts. For the Spanish colonies, the northern Andes, especially the territory of modern Colombia, held the richest goldfields, and the Spaniards exploited them from the sixteenth century. Brazil was ultimately

the greatest gold producer of colonial Latin America, but its riches were discovered only in the late 1600s. Analysis of production levels is problematic
due to tax evasion and contraband. Because gold was worth ten to sixteen
times more than silver, miners were more likely to mine it secretly and smuggle it to avoid paying taxes than was the case with silver. Thus, calculating
production according to tax records and other data is even less reliable for
gold than for silver.

Drawn by rumors of El Dorado, Spaniards eagerly explored the mountains of New Granada, searching for "The Gilded One." They never found the
legendary king who ritually powdered his body with gold dust before bath-
ing in a mountain lake. Nonetheless, this region proved the richest in gold of
all Spanish America. Indigenous peoples had worked alluvial deposits prior
to the invaders' arrival, and the region possessed "the foremost goldsmiths
of aboriginal America, whose golden artifacts were traded over a wide
area."[30] Spaniards eventually exploited deposits in the Chocó region along
the Pacific coast; the Cauca drainage system, especially around Popayán and
Antioquia; and the Magdalena valley. A form of macabre pseudo-mining,
the robbing of pre-Hispanic graves, also yielded considerable gold.

Colonial miners used both placer and vein mining. The most simple
placer method was panning the gravel and sand from stream and river bottoms. Sluicing was the most common technique to wash gold in colonial
New Granada. Below a mineralized terrace or hillside, workers cut a sluice
or channel and paved its bottom. Using bars and other tools, the workers
then dislodged earth from the terrace into the sluice. Sometimes they also
directed water against the terrace, using its force to excavate the hillside and
deposit it gradually into the sluice. In these mines, networks of bamboo tub-
ing constructed as small aqueducts carried water from higher locations to
the face of the terrace for sluicing. As water flowed through the sluice, it carried off the dirt, leaving heavy minerals, including gold, on the bottom of the
sluice. After picking out any gold nuggets, workers took the residue out of
the sluice to work it with bateas, or pans. By adding water and swirling the
mixture in the batea, they little by little spilled lighter material over the edge
of the bowl. This left the heavier metals concentrated in the batea.

Miners used several techniques to separate gold from the concentrate.
When dealing with black sands (*jagua*) containing gold flakes and iron
oxide, the colonial miners used indigenous inventions. They mixed the concentrate with sap from any of several tropical plants, and "the iron oxide
flakes adhered to the foamy, glutinous material, leaving pure gold dust at

the bottom of the batea."[31] The European technique of using magnets could also sometimes separate out the iron oxide. Gold miners apparently did not use mercury to amalgamate the black sands because quicksilver was expensive and the indigenous method worked efficiently. In the Chocó region of northwestern Colombia, gold sometimes occurred with platinum, and refiners there had to use mercury to separate the two metals. Until the mid-eighteenth century, platinum (platino), as it was called for its resemblance to silver, had no value, and miners either discarded it or mixed it with gold to fleece the unwary.

Graph 3 shows gold output. New Granada dominated official Spanish American gold production for most of the colonial period. Prior to 1700, the yield was comparatively meager, although it had important economic ramifications for the region. During the eighteenth century, however, gold mining and washing boomed in New Granada and also expanded in Mexico and Peru. The increases in yield reflected more mining activity and perhaps a decline in contraband gold due to more rigorous fiscal oversight of mining after 1700. More striking was the sudden bonanza in Brazilian gold mining in the 1690s, which peaked in the mid-1700s. From the sixteenth century, the Portuguese, encouraged by the Spanish discoveries in Mexico and Peru, had roamed Brazil in search of precious metals. Many of these explorers were the famous frontiersmen (bandeirantes) from São Paulo. Descended from Portuguese and the native Indians, these men were slavers and prospectors.

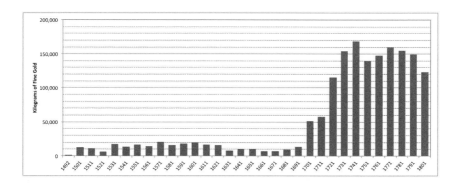

Graph 3. New World gold output from 1492 to 1810.
Data from John J. TePaske, *A New World of Gold and Silver,*
ed. Kendall W. Brown (Leiden: Brill, 2010), 56.

Despite finding a few small goldfields, they failed to make great strikes such as the Spaniards had uncovered in their colonies. The Brazilian economy consequently developed around agriculture, producing sugar, tobacco, and dyewoods for export. Around 1692 the bandeirantes finally hit pay dirt: rich alluvial deposits in the region that became known as Minas Gerais. Would-be miners hurried across the mountains from Rio de Janeiro and São Paulo to the mining district. Thousands more pushed southwest from the coast of Bahia, where the colonial capital of Salvador was located, through the São Francisco River valley into Minas Gerais. The gold rush was on. On the arduous trek to the goldfields, the miners took with them great numbers of African slaves. Migrants from Portugal, Madeira, and the Azores also joined the throng searching for gold.[32]

The sudden, massive migration quickly pushed tens of thousands into the Brazilian frontier. Although the *paulistas* (natives of São Paulo) understood the backcountry, many who entered Minas Gerais were unprepared for the primitive conditions. Few brought sufficient provisions, and the initial wave did not worry about growing enough food in the backlands to feed the burgeoning population. Although food could be brought in from Bahia along the São Francisco River, the journey took two months. The distance to São Paulo and Rio de Janeiro was shorter, but the trails were much more difficult. As a result, many prospectors starved and malnutrition sapped gold's allure.

Back in the sugar-growing regions of the northeastern coast, the gold rush provoked labor shortages. Sugar planters in Bahia and Pernambuco complained that the gold rush was draining away labor they needed to plant and harvest sugarcane and tobacco. With their gold, miners could easily outbid planters for the best slaves, and the gold bonanza also touched off inflation along the coast as mine operators bought up foodstuffs and other merchandise at much higher prices than the planters could afford to pay. The inflation in turn stimulated more migration to the goldfields by individuals who could not earn enough to survive in the coastal agricultural economy.[33]

Early on, the Portuguese government paid little attention to these gold discoveries, because previous finds had quickly petered out. Eventually, however, it became obvious that the discoveries in Minas Gerais, Mato Grosso, and Goiás were large and enduring. Yet the Crown saw the long-established sugar plantations as more stable and, over the long run, more profitable. The plantations were a renewable resource, whereas mines typically provided a brief bonanza, then their ores were exhausted. The wave of migration worried the Crown that coastal Brazil would become depopulated and unable to defend itself and that tobacco and sugar production would falter. Thus, in 1701 Portugal issued decrees to stop further migration to Minas Gerais, but they had little impact. Some Portuguese saw the gold mines as divine retribution inflicted on Brazil. Jesuit André João Antonil wrote that "the worst is that the greatest part of the gold taken from the mines passes in dust and in coins to foreign kingdoms," adding, "God permitted the discovery of mines with so much gold to punish Brazil."[34] He did not clarify exactly why God was angry with the Portuguese colony.

By the middle of the first decade of the eighteenth century, Portugal attempted to impose order in the gold districts and collect the royal fifth on output. This was no easy task, for near-anarchy reigned in the mining camps and the miners resisted the obligation to pay the fifths. Open conflict broke out in October 1708 between the paulistas and the *emboabas*, as the frontiersmen derisively called new settlers from Bahia and Portugal. The War of the Emboabas lasted over a year, with the more numerous outsiders driving most of the paulistas out of their diggings. By December 1709, the Crown's representatives had engineered a settlement, which also tenuously established royal power in the mining districts.

Gold production continued to increase. By 1720, prospectors had discovered the principal goldfields in Minas Gerais, Mato Grosso, and Goiás, and production continued to expand rapidly until midcentury. Meanwhile, the government organized the migrants into townships and established the rudiments of state bureaucracy. It opened assay and smelting houses at Taubaté and Parati, but their distance from the goldfields hindered tax collection. Around 1720, diamonds were discovered in the goldfields around Villa do Príncipe. According to the story, miners had often found crystal-like stones while searching for gold and occasionally collected them to use as chips while playing cards. Eventually, someone who had been to India recognized that the worthless crystals were in reality diamonds. He and his friends tried to gather as many of the stones as possible.[35] But just as Gualpa could not keep secret forever his discovery of silver at Potosí, word about the diamonds became public, adding to the mining fever in Minas Gerais. It is impossible to know the value of Brazilian diamonds mined during the eighteenth century because of widespread smuggling at the time. British mineralogist John Mawe, who visited the diamond fields in the first decade of the nineteenth century, claimed that smugglers had taken two million pounds sterling in diamonds out of Brazil, but his estimate was little more than an informed guess. Even the legal output is impossible to calculate because contemporaneous government accounts have not survived. Nonetheless, it was not unusual for Brazil to produce several hundred thousand carats of diamonds during a single year.[36]

Brazilian gold miners worked some veins but primarily used washing or placer techniques. In this regard, Brazil resembled the conditions in Spanish New Granada, although the indigenous population of the Portuguese colony had no metallurgical skills on which the gold rush could depend. Sluices and *bateias* (wooden or metal pans similar to the batea) were the chief equipment for separating gold from the gangue. As in New Granada, the miners sometimes diverted riverbeds to get at gold-bearing gravels. Given the general backwardness of Portuguese mining and metallurgy, claimholders often tried to purchase slaves from the gold-producing regions of West Africa, especially from the Costa da Mina (Bight of Benin), because of their mining expertise.

As with diamonds, the precise dimensions of Brazilian gold production during the eighteenth century are nearly impossible to ascertain. Most historians agree that the goldfields reached their apogee between 1730 and 1755, when Brazil's output probably reached eighteen to twenty tons annually. During the eighteenth century, mines and placers yielded nearly one thousand tons. This was a sizable treasure in light of the fact that Europe's total gold stock in 1500 was probably 3,500 tons. Yet all these figures are little more than educated guesses, given Portugal's lax control over the mining districts and immense amount of contraband. Rumors abounded about priests, whose ecclesiastical privileges exempted them from search, who carried saintly statuettes hollowed out to smuggle gold. Throughout the era, huge, untaxed diamonds appeared in Lisbon. Without doubt, however, the volume of gold in Brazil outstripped that mined in Spanish America by a wide margin.

The Economic Ramifications of Colonial Mining

The economic impact of colonial mining reached far beyond the frontiers of the New World. Spain and the rest of Europe felt its power, and the rest of the world responded to the lure of American gold and silver. No mining district wielded greater influence than Potosí. Around 1600 it was Europe's main source of silver. Andean and Mexican silver and Brazilian gold production stimulated the economy of Western Europe, helped capitalism triumph over feudalism, enabled Europeans to trade for the goods of the Spice Islands and China, and touched off inflationary pressures in Spain that spread across the continent. Little concerned about the effect of mining upon life in the New World, Spanish and Portuguese statesmen and political economists focused instead on the advantages and difficulties American bullion created for the Iberian economies.

More so than their Portuguese cousins, Spanish monarchs saw American gold and silver as a windfall they could use to achieve political goals. Spanish monarchs undertook geopolitical campaigns such as crusades against Protestantism and preserving the Habsburg empire, encouraged in the quest by the scale of American treasure. Such extraordinary revenues made them less dependent on feudal assemblies such as the *cortes* and thus allowed them to pursue more absolutist policies than otherwise would have been possible. It is hard to imagine the Spanish empire without its American silver.[37] Brazilian gold created similar conditions in Portugal. It was not coincidental that the Portuguese Cortes (representative assembly or parliament) of 1698 was the last to convene until 1808: with Brazilian gold the Portuguese monarchy no longer needed the Cortes to approve new tax revenues.[38]

Meanwhile, American bullion helped form the European economy that developed with the rise of capitalism. Its effect on prices in Europe in particular struck sixteenth-century observers. By the mid-1500s, Spain began suffering from inflation (although the level was low compared to twentieth-century hyperinflation), and contemporary writers, including Tomás de Mercado, Jean Bodin, and Martín de Azpilcueta, blamed the rise in prices on the imports of American gold and silver. The abundance of precious metals reduced their value relative to other commodities, more so in regions where gold and silver were most plentiful. Within Europe, Spain felt the effects of the "Price Revolution" most strongly, although other nations also experienced inflation. Precious metals from the New World enabled Spaniards to consume imported manufactured goods rather than establish their own industries. Compared to the Low Countries or Italy, Spain had lots of bullion and a backward manufacturing sector. Competing regions possessed comparatively strong and efficient industries but lacked bullion. Given such market conditions, bullion flowed out of Spain in exchange for manufactured goods produced elsewhere. This happened despite royal decrees forbidding the export of gold and silver from Spain.

American bullion helped foster the economic transformation of Europe during the sixteenth to eighteenth centuries, when the population rose, manufacturing expanded, capitalism replaced feudalism, European commerce intensified, and the Industrial Revolution began. A larger monetary supply was crucial to these interrelated economic trends. Europe's commercial expansion of the eighteenth century depended on the increased monetary stock provided by the Latin American mines and would have been impossible without it.[39] Europeans solved the monetary shortage through bills of exchange, national banks, paper money, and especially American gold and silver.

Also important was the role of American gold and silver in increasing world monetary flows. "China and India," writes economist Charles P. Kindleberger, "were sponges that soaked up the streams of silver flowing through Europe (and the Philippines) from Spanish America."[40] The exact volume of American silver arriving in the Orient defies calculation, in part because private shipments and contraband constituted a sizable portion of the flow. Nonetheless, for the late 1500s and most of the seventeenth century, the Far East ultimately received 90 percent or more of the American output. Nearly as much Andean and Mexican silver made its way to China across the Pacific as through Europe.[41] Little ultimately remained in the New World colonies or Spain itself.

Equally important, however, were the consequences for manufacturing and other economic activities in response to the demand for New World specie. Demand for silver stimulated mining activity in Spanish America. German mines could not compete with the lower cost of American silver and stagnated in the sixteenth century. With the Brazilian gold rush, demand for labor increased, stimulating the Atlantic slave trade. This in turn provoked ethnic warfare as African tribes fought to take captives to sell to the European traders on the coast. Asians expanded spice and silk production to exchange those commodities for bullion. Facilitated by the Methuen Treaty, commerce between Britain and Portugal grew, and a good part of Brazilian gold found its way to London. There it proved vital among conditions leading to the onset of the Industrial Revolution. Yet the Portuguese ministers quickly learned that the flood of gold arriving from Brazil did not really enrich the mother country. It flowed instead via Portugal to the nations that manufactured the goods consumed in Portugal and Brazil. Like Spain before it, Portugal discovered that mineral wealth did not necessarily promote national economic well-being or stimulate production.

The impact of mining was even more pronounced in the Ibero-American colonies. It dominated economic life in the Spanish Andes, and its influence was nearly as strong in Mexico. Potosí, for example, constituted the foremost market in South America. Its population of over one hundred thousand made it the largest city in the hemisphere at the time, and its silver enabled its residents to consume goods from the surrounding hinterland, from Europe, and from the Far East. Foodstuffs arrived from Cochabamba, coca leaves from the eastern slopes of the Andes, wine and brandy from southern Peru, woolens from Quito, fine cloth from Europe, and silk and spices from the Orient. The Portuguese and Brazilians expanded south to the northern bank of the Río de la Plata estuary, from whence they sold contraband goods for Potosí's silver. Lima, the viceregal capital, depended on Potosí. As an administrative center, Lima drew much of its revenue from mining taxes paid on silver at Potosí. A commercial entrepôt, its merchants imported merchandise to sell at the mines. From Cuzco southward, the mita propelled Indians to Potosí to work. In central Peru mitayos labored at the Huancavelica mercury mines, which produced the quicksilver for Potosí's refiners. There were, in short, few places in the Peruvian viceroyalty that were unaffected by Potosí's economic pull.[42]

For better or worse, mining colored the exploration and settlement of vast portions of Latin America. Mineral-rich districts attracted people, and towns sprang into being. This occurred even in territories that previously were sparsely populated, such as the lands of Zacatecas and the *reales de minas* in northern Mexico. Aside from its silver, Potosí offered little to hold human inhabitants, except for the occasional llama herder. In Brazil, the colonial population remained clustered along the Atlantic coast until gold and diamonds enticed heavy migration to the interior. Forays by the bandeirantes through the Brazilian interior left few permanent traces until they discovered gold.

Mining's effect on the economic structure of the colonies also merits consideration. The mines obviously produced great amounts of wealth for the colonial empires and capital for the colonial economy. Precious metals also created economic opportunities for agriculture and manufacturing. Prosperous mines reached out to those who grew or made the goods consumed in mining towns and cities. Like magnets, Potosí, Guanajuato, and Ouro Prêto were markets that attracted and consumed large volumes of industrial and consumer goods.

For the colonies, however, little of the capital obtained from mining seems to have been reinvested in activities that might have made these economies more dynamic and self-sustaining. Instead, the colonial system tended to drain bullion and capital out of the Americas. Merchants and state bureaucracies shipped vast quantities of gold and silver from the mining centers to colonial entrepôts and from the New World to Europe and beyond. In part this was coercive, through imperial taxation. But market forces also facilitated the outflow of specie. Its abundance made bullion cheap in Spanish and Portuguese America. Silver's value in Potosí or Mexico City was low compared to its worth in Madrid or the Spice Islands. Even mitayos at Huancavelica received higher wages than did mercury miners at Almadén. This resulted in part from the relative availability of labor and the cost of living at the two mercury mining districts, but it also reflected the abundance of silver in the Andes compared with Spain. Trade consequently carried gold and silver to where they were more highly valued.[43]

In exchange, the Portuguese and Spanish colonies received consumer goods. The Latin American colonies might have produced these items. An early observer in Peru, fray Martín de Murua, remarked on the self-sufficiency of the Andes: "All Peru lacks is silk and linens, for they have a surplus of everything else, and do not have the need to beg nor wait for any other kingdom or province in the world."[44] This was the "'Dutch Disease,' in which brilliant success in one activity (silver) raises wages to the point where they stifle the rest of the economy."[45] The export of natural resources (in this case bullion) adversely affected production in other economic sectors that had to compete with imports. Because rising gold and silver output increased the colonies' foreign purchasing power, European and Oriental manufactured goods flooded in, undercutting demand for their locally produced counterparts (i.e., tradable goods). With the mining boom and the liberalization and expansion of transatlantic commerce in the eighteenth century, for example, foreign textiles flooded into the Andes, depressing the demand for woolens from Quito. At the same time, it tended to cost more (in terms of the declining value of silver) in the colonies to produce consumer goods for which there was no import competition (i.e., nontradable goods). Market agriculture, for example, had to compete with mining for capital, whereas Brazilian agriculture had great difficulty in competing with the gold mines for labor. The inflated price of slaves due to the gold boom substantially cut the profitability of sugar production.[46]

What then were the economic consequences of silver and gold mining for colonial Latin America? Although the mines yielded great treasures, they did not produce conditions leading to self-sustaining growth in other parts of the economy. Although Brazilian gold may have helped lay the foundation for the Industrial Revolution in Great Britain, it had no such result in South America. Gold and silver rippled through the colonial economy stimulating commerce and agriculture, but such stimulus perpetuated economic dependence on mining. From his study of Mexico in the eighteenth century, historian Richard L. Garner concludes that despite the great silver boom, mining did not make structural changes in the economy: "They did not lead to many other fundamental economic changes. Mining and mining camps largely became more highly specialized in the business of extracting and processing metal and did not broaden in any significant way the colonial economy."[47] Mining absorbed much of the capital investment in Mexico and the Andes, capital that thus was unavailable for use elsewhere. By the late colonial period, it should also be remembered, the profitability of mining had declined in many districts with exhaustion of ores and higher operating costs. As to the social impact of mining, its effects were profound, as we will see in the next chapter.

CHAPTER 3

Spanish and Portuguese Colonialism and Mining Labor

∼ℓ

The greedy pit had swallowed its daily ration of men; nearly seven
hundred of them were now toiling in this immense ant-hill, bur-
rowing in the earth, riddling it with holes like old, worm-eaten
wood.

—Emile Zola,
Germinal

✦ POPULATION AT POTOSÍ WAXED AND WANED WITH THE PROSPERITY
of the mines. In 1545, shortly after the Spaniards learned of the Cerro Rico's
riches, less than two hundred Spaniards and three hundred Indians resided
at the site. Within two years the lure of silver had increased the population to
fourteen thousand, enough that Emperor Charles V gave the city the title of
villa imperial. In the words of economic historian Dennis Flynn, "the population of Potosi surged to equal or exceed that of London or Paris by the
early seventeenth century. It may have been world history's most spectacular
boom town. Profits were gigantic because the cost of producing silver had
fallen suddenly, while its world price declined only gradually."[1] Because of
the region's large transient population of laborers, merchants, and bureaucrats, census figures are ambiguous, but Potosí probably hosted more than
100,000 inhabitants for decades, and perhaps as many as 150,000 during

its years of peak silver production around 1620. Of these, perhaps half were Indians, some of whom lived permanently at the mining site and others of whom were there to fulfill mita obligations. Another quarter of the population would have been Creoles and mestizos. Europeans, especially Spaniards and Portuguese, comprised most of the remainder, along with a few thousand African slaves and freedmen.

This vast enterprise depended on the labor of thousands of Indians, who like miners everywhere toiled in unhealthy, perilous conditions. What distinguished much of colonial mining, however, was the coercion employed to obtain workers and the state's role in this coercion. This was particularly true of Potosí. The colonial government allowed almost nothing to stand in the way of silver production. It gave silver producers cheap mita labor and supported other forms of economic and legal incentives to force Andeans into the mines as wage laborers. Potosí played a central role in dislocating indigenous peoples, acculturating them into the colonial world and defining the type of society that developed and endures in the Andes.

Most laborers came from agricultural villages and were either forcibly taken to the mines or were attracted there by the wages they could earn. Such migration, whether temporary or permanent, had important consequences for the villagers' ability to preserve traditional ethnic practices. Andeans forced to work periodically in Potosí's silver mines had to leave their homes and extended families for a year, after which some returned to their villages and others remained at the mines to work as free laborers. Africans taken as slaves to the Brazilian goldfields also faced an alien culture and a new language, but they had no possibility of returning home. They were forced to construct a new culture and society. Even in Mexico, where workers were freer to come and go, mining weakened their ties to the villages they left behind.

The introduction of capitalist mining also initiated the process of proletarianization in the mines and refining mills. The proletariat is the lowest class of industrial workers, those who have no capital or any other means of production except their own labor, which they consequently must sell for wages to support themselves. A mining proletariat would thus be workers who are totally dependent on the wages they earn at the mine for their survival. They have no farmlands on which they can grow food for their own consumption. They are mining specialists, workers dedicated to the process of ore extraction and refining, or some phase of it. Mine and refinery operators benefit from employing proletarians because the latter become experienced in mining and metallurgy and because they are completely dependent upon the industry for their livelihood. Owners and operators, the capitalists, try to increase their profits by reducing the wages paid to the proletariat. In the early colonial period, few mine workers were proletarians, and in fact, proletarianization was very slow in coming to the Latin American mining industry. It nonetheless was a measure of the industry's capitalist progress and modernization: the greater the proletarianization, the more advanced the capitalist mining industry.

In colonial mining, technology had great impact on social change, including the first halting steps toward proletarianization. A new technology might improve conditions for mine workers if, for example, it substituted animal or machine power for human energy. By the eighteenth century, some Mexican mines expanded outward from a central vertical shaft, out of which workers could use a winch to haul equipment and ore, rather than carry it out on their backs up long flights of stairs. But technological change did not always benefit the workers. Such was certainly the case at Potosí in the 1570s.

From Potosí's discovery in 1545 until the 1560s, Spaniards relied heavily on indigenous technical skills as well as labor. In early years, yanaconas, Andeans who had been state servants of the Inca empire and who had no clan affiliation, produced much of the silver. No longer tied to the Inca state after it was toppled by Pizarro and his men, yanaconas often sought the protection of a Spaniard and worked for him. At Potosí, a yanacona had to give his Spaniard two marks of refined silver per week but could keep everything above that amount. As a result, a few became relatively wealthy and Hispanicized. At one point indigenous miners reportedly had fifteen thousand guayras (indigenous smelting ovens) in operation at Potosí.[2] Spaniards also sent encomienda Indians to the Cerro to mine silver as a way to pay their tribute obligations to the encomenderos. Unlike the yanacona, the *hatunruna* (indigenous peasant) worked temporarily at Potosí to pay tribute to his encomendero but then returned to his agricultural lands and home village.

By the 1560s, however, the encomienda workers and yanaconas had exhausted Potosí's rich surface ores, and new technology and labor arrangements were necessary. The yanaconas' guayras could smelt rich ores but not the growing volume of lower-grade ore. Profits declined and crisis engulfed Potosí. The Spaniards needed new refining techniques to satisfy their lust for silver. The technological solution to the crisis arrived in 1572, when

Pedro Fernández de Velasco adapted to Andean conditions the amalgamation techniques he had learned in New Spain. This new refining method required mercury plus milling equipment to grind great quantities of ore. Indigenous miners had neither access to quicksilver nor capital to build water mills, and thus Spaniards came to monopolize the new refining process. Amalgamation even marginalized the yanaconas, whose technical expertise with the guayras had given them a relatively high status and considerable independence at Potosí.[3] Instead, the new technologies created a demand for a large pool of less-skilled workers to mine and handle the ore. The crisis of the 1560s, however, had stripped Potosí of most of its labor force, and Spaniards doubted the Indians would return.

Rather than admitting that the crisis and the new refining technique had removed most of the Indians' economic incentive for going to Potosí, Spaniards mounted a propaganda campaign to justify a greater coercion of labor. State intervention was necessary, according to Spanish legalist Juan de Matienzo in 1567, to overcome the opposition of the kurakas (ethnic lords). The hatunrunas would not go voluntarily to work at Potosí, either because the kurakas would not permit it, opting to exploit the laborers themselves, or because the hatunrunas knew that the kurakas would confiscate any wages they earned at the mines.[4] Viceroy Toledo recognized that Andeans had little appetite for the prolonged underground physical labor and the dangers associated with production of precious metals. He considered them lazy and unwilling to work, preferring instead to spend their time "in eating and drinking and sleeping."[5] Indeed, Spanish authorities and economic interests echoed similar sentiments for generations. In the late colonial period, one of Potosí's intendants, Pedro Vicente Cañete y Domínguez, wrote:

> [B]eing slow and stupid of mind, but robust and strong of body, it seems that nature subordinated them economically and politically to other more enlightened men, so that they live under their protection. . . . Their decline into idleness, their repugnance for all service, by the custom in which they were born and raised to wander aimlessly, without property, and to live from the scarce harvest of their wild homes; their lack of self-discipline and worse education, dragged them perceptibly to the innate vices of drunkenness, idolatry, and adultery, separating themselves from all lucrative and honest work.[6]

Such apologists of Spanish colonialism contended that to let the Indians remain idle would hamper the economic development of Andean natural resources, particularly the mineral wealth. Furthermore, they insisted, Indians owed Spain an infinite debt for bringing them Christianity, a debt they could partially repay through their toil in the mines and refining mills.

With this sort of rationalization, Spaniards devised several forms of coercion to mobilize labor for their mines, but none led to proletarianization. Of these the mita was the most infamous. But the state's intervention to supply labor did not end there. It also used indirect means to provide workers for the mines. The two most important were tribute and the *reparto de mercancías*. Most adult male Andeans had to pay tribute to an encomendero or to the Crown.[7] Villages originally paid in commodities that they produced, such as cloth and grain. Eventually, however, the state demanded tribute payment in coin, thereby forcing Andeans to earn cash wages to pay the tax. They found they could make tribute money at the mines, working there temporarily, then returning to their village.

The reparto, or commercial distribution, worked in the following manner. To fill their own pockets, local governors made Andeans buy merchandise at exorbitant prices, thereby forcing them into debt. In partnership with a merchant who supplied goods and credit, a governor might force a villager from his district to purchase a mule for fifty pesos, for example, when the market value was only fifteen pesos. The villager had no access to credit to buy a mule for the lower price, however, but neither could he resist the governor's insistence that he take the animal for fifty pesos. As the chief magistrate and judge in the province, an abusive governor could arrest, jail, and flog peasants who refused to take reparto goods or pay for those they received. To meet reparto obligations, villagers often worked temporarily in the mines.[8] Many of Potosí's wage laborers ended up at the mines because of the colonial system's indirect but still coercive push. They needed the wages to pay tribute and reparto debts. Thus, mita, tribute, and repartos all sent Andeans temporarily to the mines, but only a minority remained there permanently. The government intended that the mine labor be temporary so as to avoid disrupting agriculture and village life any more than necessary. This, of course, worked against proletarianization.

The mita came to characterize Andean mining labor because of its importance at Potosí. But such an image is misleading: the mita was not representative of all labor in Peruvian mines. Only three Andean mining districts (Potosí, Huancavelica, and Cailloma) had a mita for a significant length of time. Silver producers at Oruro clamored for the government to assign them a mita also, without success. They consequently had to utilize wage labor, which also occurred at other important Andean sites such as Hualgayoc, Huantajaya, Castrovirreina, and Cerro de Pasco. Indirect state coercion helped push workers to those mines, but those districts did not receive the degree of government support that Potosí enjoyed.

Mining elsewhere in colonial Latin America likewise combined forced labor with wage earners. African slaves did most of the work in the gold and diamond fields of Brazil, and the gold and emeralds of New Granada were mined by the toil and sweat of slaves as well. Yet in both cases considerable itinerant prospecting took place. Searching for their own El Dorado, roving prospectors remained independent, beyond the control of large-scale producers and even the fiscal constraints of the colonial governments. Mexico was less dependent on forced labor, but even there mine owners used slavery, impressment, and debt peonage to supplement wage laborers. Spaniards initially forced indigenous peoples to work in the mines either by enslaving them or by instituting repartimiento labor (which was similar to the mita). This worked in the densely populated areas of New Spain but proved less efficient in the more sparsely inhabited north, the site of important mining centers such as Zacatecas and Guanajuato. Wage labor predominated there, although not to the exclusion of more coercive forms. Of course, colonial taxation gave wage laborers, whether Mexican or Andean, a strong push into the mines.

Even so, the Potosí mita epitomized the coercive nature of the colonial mining industry. In no other mining district was the full power of the state brought so forcefully to bear over such a long period.[9] Slavery in the goldfields of Brazil's Minas Gerais was, of course, horribly oppressive, perhaps more so than what mitayos typically experienced at Potosí. But the Portuguese government had no direct hand in that labor system. Meanwhile, the Potosí mita survived with government support from the 1570s to the end of the colonial period. Silver refiners at Potosí clung to their mita quotas with a tenacity inversely proportional to the declining quality of their ores. The imperial government itself was psychologically dependent upon Potosí's silver output, which remained higher than for any district in the Andes until the late 1700s. Despite rare discussions about abolishing the mita out of humanitarian concern for the workers, the Crown feared to endanger Potosí's silver output. Viceregal officials who tried to tamper with the mita met overt resistance, threats, and real danger. Consequently, the Potosí mita provides a useful starting point for an examination of colonial mining labor.

The Potosí Mita

Amalgamation heightened Potosí's appetite for labor, but desolate and inhospitable Potosí lacked a resident population to man its mines and refining mills. By 1570 most of the miners who had migrated there during the early bonanza had left. Amalgamators had to persuade thousands of new workers to migrate to the Cerro Rico. Labor, like everything else from food and mercury to merchants and clergy, had to be imported. Fortunately for the azogueros, Viceroy Toledo supported their interests. Searching for ways to revive Potosí, Toledo recognized that its vast dumps of low-grade ore, when refined with mercury from recently discovered Huancavelica, could yield great quantities of silver. Toledo promised the amalgamators that if they built the refining mills at their own cost, the government would provide them enough workers. The refiners agreed.

Philip II had prohibited Spaniards from forcing Indians to work in the mines, but Toledo could see no other solution to the labor shortage except coercion. The viceroy inquired of Peruvian mining, ecclesiastical, and legal experts whether the common good dictated that the state use force to supply Potosí with workers. Their response was no surprise: it was almost as though he had asked foxes whether for the common good they ought to be permitted to enter the hen house. With their predictable backing, Toledo instituted the Potosí mita in 1573, dressing the Incan practice of mit'a in more exploitative colonial garb. The Inca empire had required villagers to take turns working on public projects as a labor tribute to the state, but these demands were less onerous than the mita. Back in Spain, Philip II fretted about the arrangement but went along with Toledo's plan as there seemed no other way to resurrect the mines.[10]

The azogueros built their refining mills, and Viceroy Toledo conscripted mitayos. Potosí drew from an area stretching over hundreds of miles from Chichas south of the mines to Lampa, Asángaro, and Paucarcolla, which lay between Cuzco and Lake Titicaca far to the north, as map 3 shows. Mitayos from the distant northern provinces faced a trek of many weeks just to reach Potosí before they even began their year of labor. Toledo's plan compelled the mita provinces to send approximately one-seventh of their tributary population (males of the ages of eighteen to fifty) to Potosí each year. Around 1580 this

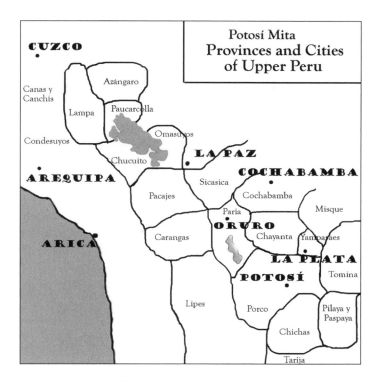

Map 3. Provinces serving in the Potosí mita

amounted to over thirteen thousand mitayos. A third of the contingent worked in the mita each week, while the other two-thirds rested or hired themselves out. Toledo apparently believed the mita only a temporary necessity: once mitayos worked at the mines, a sufficient number would be enticed by wages to stay on as free laborers. The government would then eliminate the mita.

A detailed firsthand account of a mitayo's experiences would make fascinating reading and offer compelling insights into indigenous perceptions of Spanish colonialism. Such a narrative does not exist, however, and the historian is left to piece together evidence from other, primarily Spanish, sources. In the mita provinces something similar to what follows was played out each year. A few weeks before the mitayos departed their villages for the mines, the local Spanish corregidor (governor) prepared a list for the governor of Potosí indicating the number of mitayos being sent, along with their individual names and villages. The contingent then assembled and readied itself for the journey. The entire village gathered in front of its church, where the mitayos received the priest's blessing. Many sought the protection of local huacas and participated in shamanistic rituals. Despite the cleric's benediction, sorrow hung over the square as the mitayos and their families bid farewell to family and friends.

They would be gone for a long time: a year at Potosí plus the weeks needed to travel there and return. In the back of their mind lingered the knowledge that some would never return from Potosí. Accidents and disease took their share of the workers, some decided to stay on at the mines, and others fled to regions where they would no longer be subject to the mita. Some mitayos took their families with them. In part they did so for companionship but also so that wives could cook food and wash clothes for their husbands and perhaps find ways to supplement the men's meager mita wages. Children worked in the ore dumps and at other menial jobs. All mitayos suffered the sorrows of separation from their extended family and village. Elderly parents might die while sons and daughters were at Potosí. Babies would be born at the mines, far from grandparents and the huacas that protected the ayllu. Aside from all this, the disconcerting knowledge of what work was like at the mines troubled the minds of the mitayos. They faced months of brutal physical labor and meager rations in working conditions that were at best unhealthy and often perilous.

After the Mass ended, the church bell began to toll, adding to the doleful mood. The caravan of mitayos, wives, and children set out for Potosí, jewel of the Spanish empire and bane of its Indian inhabitants. Tears dried as the church bell sounded in the distance. The people moved slowly, taking with them herds of llamas and as many provisions as their village could spare. Each year the village leaders earmarked part of the harvest to sustain the mitayos. With Potosí's high cost of living, mita wages could not feed a family at the mines.

After several weeks' trekking across the windswept high plains of the Andes, the mitayos reached Potosí, where the indigenous mita captain who accompanied them reported their arrival. According to law, the mine owners and refiners were supposed to pay each mitayo a half wage, or *leguaje* (calculated at one-half real per league traveled) for each day the journey took. The azogueros usually cheated the mitayos out of the leguaje for the journey to Potosí on the pretext that the subject towns had not supplied the full quota of workers. Nor did the azogueros usually pay the costs of the mitayos' trek home, and this forced some workers to remain in Potosí because they were unable to afford the travel back to their villages. Those who tried to return home often were forced to beg along the way.

In the early years, when the city and the mita were newly established, Potosí offered only the barest accommodations for the workers. Straw huts around the plaza sheltered them temporarily. Lack of space forced many to live in the streets. Eventually more permanent housing grew up on the city's outskirts. This evolved into thirteen indigenous parishes that divided along ethnic lines. Every Monday morning, workers gathered at the base of the Cerro Rico so that Spanish officials and mita captains could organize the work gangs. Mitayos received a variety of work assignments, particularly tasks requiring little skill or training. Some were *apiris*, who carried heavy bags of ore out of the mine; some worked in the mills, crushing ore and performing the heavy labor associated with amalgamation; others used their own llamas to carry ore from the mouth of the mine down to the refining plants. Officials checked the number of mitayos presented by the ayllus against the assigned quota. Each ayllu had to make up any shortages by providing *indios de plata* (silver Indians), paying the mine owner or azoguero so that wage laborers could be hired to take the place of the missing mitayos. A wage laborer (*mingado*) earned eight to ten reals per day, two or three times what the forced laborers received, and paying for missing mitayos drained a village of its resources. The Spaniards fined, beat, and imprisoned mita captains and kurakas who failed to provide workers or money. An indigenous observer reported:

> They hang one noble *cacique* by his feet, and they seat another one on a llama and whip him. Others are bound, stark naked, to the whipping post, where they are punished and their hair is roughly shorn. Still others are kept in the public jail in stocks and fetters, without being given any food or water or being allowed to provide their own. All of this abuse and shaming is done to them under the excuse that a few Indians are missing from the *mita*.[11]

Such intimidation of indigenous leaders helped ensure compliance with the demands of the mita.

Not all workers at Potosí and other mines were mitayos. More or less voluntarily some chose to live as miners, their motivation varying from individual to individual. Perhaps they had lost their ethnic affiliation and had no right to ayllu lands and thus had to perform nonagricultural labor to earn a living. Furthermore, during the colonial period, many peasants, including mitayos, worked part-time as *mingados* (free laborers) at Potosí. Viceroy Toledo's coercive system did mobilize indigenous workers to provide some free labor for the mines. By the early 1600s mingados made up over half the miners and mill workers, and that ratio seems to have endured to the end of the colonial period.[12]

Conditions for the mingados were marginally better than those for the mitayos. In terms of wages, mingados usually earned two or three times more in cash and other benefits, such as foodstuffs and coca leaves. Mingados were also entitled each day to take the *corpa*, a piece of ore that they could then sell to their own profit.[13] Often a mine owner or refiner had to advance wages to the mingado to secure his services. Because the mingado was relatively free to leave if he wanted, employers could not impose quota labor, as they did with the mitayo apiris. To control labor at Potosí, Spaniards generally did not use debt peonage, whereby workers received money or goods as an advance on their wages but could not leave until they had paid off their debts. Although common in Mexico, such bondage was rare in Potosí, perhaps because the mita mobilized sufficient workers for the mining operations.

At Potosí there was a substantial secondary industry of silver production that competed with the main Spanish operations and that the great mine owners and azogueros tried but never managed to eradicate. This subsidiary production centered on *trapiches*, small mills operated by human or animal power. These dated back to the earliest years of mining at Potosí, when mining and refining lay chiefly in the hands of the yanaconas. Trapiches processed rich ores either smuggled out of the mines by mitayos and mingados, obtained through the *pallayta* (high-grading, or selecting small bits of profitable ore from ore dumps and abandoned mines) or the *kajcheo* (workers mining for themselves as a supplement to their wages during the weekend, which custom allowed), or discovered by prospectors in the district. Even though crews of mitayos and mingados usually stayed underground in the mines the entire work week, it was a relatively easy matter for the workers to slip rich pieces of ore they had discovered to their wives, who brought them food on Wednesdays. On the weekends, anyone could enter the mines. When owners worked their mines only during the day, *kajchas* invaded the workings at night. Owners responded by mining round the clock, but they had no solution to the kajcheo on the weekend, however much they hated it and wanted to eradicate the practice. Mingados jealously guarded their right to the kajcheo, and many earned more from weekend prospecting in the mines than they did from their wages.

The kajcheo had evolved from Potosí's early ore trade.[14] Yanacona refiners bought ore from prospectors, miners, and high-graders to smelt in their guayras. The shift to amalgamation did not completely eliminate such production. Indians with ore to sell gathered each morning near the city's main plaza.[15] To obtain enough for processing, Indian refiners had to buy a small amount from many sellers, including the bits and pieces brought in by miners' wives and larger quantities from the kajchas. Because this ore had been carefully selected, it was richer than what the apiris carried out to fill their work quotas for Spanish refiners. In the second half of the eighteenth century, trapiches processed far less ore than the water mills yet sometimes produced nearly 40 percent of all silver registered at Potosí.[16] Although trapiche output varied over the colonial era and mill owners often tried to eliminate indigenous competition, the guayras and trapiches largely remained beyond Spanish control. They provided an important income to at least some elements of the indigenous mining community.

The kajchas resisted any attempts to eliminate their activities, sometimes with violence. In early 1751, for example, some mine owners hired guards and ordered them to keep kajchas from entering the diggings on the weekend. The owners believed the kajchas harmed the mines with their disorderly work and, more important, that they were stealing ore that should have been mined during regular shifts. A mine owner, Francisco Velarde, ordered his guards to shoot any kajcha who tried to invade the mine. On January 31, 1751, his guards killed a young kajcha and wounded three others. Rumors soon circulated that other kajchas had been arrested and that kajchas planned to demonstrate against and even attack the guards. Recently arrived in Potosí, Governor Ventura de Santelices feared a general uprising, despite assurances from local leaders that such disputes and tensions had occurred frequently over the previous thirty years with more bark than bite. Nonetheless, Santelices mobilized the provincial militia and ordered the arrest of a half dozen kajcha leaders, even though it soon became apparent that the mine owners themselves had fomented rumors in order to entice the governor into cracking down on the kajchas. Santelices eventually ordered the execution of Asencio Patapata, a kajcha accused of murdering a mine guard.[17] Despite such occasional outbursts, however, the trapiches and the kajchas remained crucial to the overall output of silver at Potosí and a means whereby indigenous miners and refiners enjoyed some autonomy in the mining industry.

Although men shouldered most of the direct burden of mine and mill work, women and children found niches in Potosí's labor market also. Due to the long turn they served in the mines, many mitayos took their families with them to Potosí. The high cost of living there forced all to contribute to the family income to survive. Women and children hired themselves out in the city, adding to the floating labor pool. Some worked in the mining industry itself. Custom did not permit females to work underground, but women

worked as high-graders, or palliris, who searched through ore dumps, selecting out any rocks containing small pieces of ore. Using hammers, they then
broke off the mineralized parts and saved them for refining. This was a primitive form of ore concentration. High-graders earned whatever refiners were
willing to pay for the ore, but few earned more than a pittance.[18] Nonetheless,
such earnings by a woman or child added to the mitayo's meager wage and
helped offset the extremely high cost of living at Potosí.

Women were crucial to the mita in other ways. Unmarried men, whether
bachelors or widowers, needed access to feminine domestic skills. For food
preparation, single mitayos probably depended on female relatives who had
accompanied their husbands to Potosí. Back in the villages, women wove
cloth to sell so that the ayllu could pay for any workers missing from its
assigned quota. Single women also had to farm and graze livestock, replacing labor that might have been performed by the mitayos.[19]

In the Mines

Colonial miners faced terrible conditions, as was true in nearly all early
modern mining districts. In Mexico and the Andes most colonial mining
was underground work, whereas Brazilian gold and diamond mines operated at the surface. In the Andes, mine owners imposed little organization
on the diggings. Tunnels followed the silver veins, climbing and descending
according to the vagaries of the ore bodies. Rarely did a central shaft connect the various levels of the mine and permit the use of whims or pulleys
to haul ore and workers up from the depths. Lack of planning hindered the
application of such labor-saving techniques. The availability of cheap mita
labor made owners reluctant to invest capital in systematic excavation and
machinery. Instead, workers descended hundreds of feet into the Rich Hill
on ladders made of rope or twisted leather thongs and wooden steps. They
were crude but sturdy enough to support the weight of workers and ore.
Many were wide enough to hold three men abreast. Wooden platforms provided a place to rest when workers had to negotiate a series of ladders, which
sometimes extended three hundred to four hundred feet to the next level or
to the surface. Although miners undoubtedly grew accustomed to them, just
as sailors do to a ship's rigging, the ladders frightened new mitayos. They
climbed down into the dark, the first in line with a candle tied to his thumb
to light the way, and eventually they reached their assigned pits.

Crews consisted of both mingados and mitayos. The former, experienced miners, worked as *barreteros*. They used a steel-tipped thirty-pound pry bar, hammers, and chisels to chip away at the ore face. With the introduction of blasting in the second half of the seventeenth century, barreteros also drilled holes and set off explosive charges to dislodge the ore. Two barreteros generally labored together, one working while the other rested. Many mitayos served as apiris, carrying ore rather than performing more skilled tasks in the mines.

All too often, mine owners preferred to exploit workers rather than install labor-saving machinery. Until the eighteenth century, technology aside from amalgamation remained primitive. This was especially true in the Andes, as compared with Mexico. At Potosí the silver producers neglected to construct central shafts and install simple winches to haul ore to the surface, for example. Mita labor made it cheaper to have human beasts of burden carry the ore up rope ladders to the surface. In the seventeenth century, after population decline made it more difficult to fill the mita quotas and deeper tunneling made ore extraction more costly, mine owners began to cut *socavones*, horizontal passageways that gave access to the lower pits of a mine.[20] This permitted the miners to use llamas to carry ore out in some cases, although the llamas were usually restricted to transporting ore from the mouth of the mine to the mills. Antonio López de Quiroga, the great seventeenth-century entrepreneur of Potosí, initiated the use of blasting to cut such tunnels and thereby amassed a vast fortune.[21]

Neither mingados nor mitayos worked without sucking on a chaw of coca leaves (*acullicar*). Coca's use long predated the conquest. Before the Spaniards arrived, indigenous rulers restricted consumption of coca to the elite. The Spaniards swept away such prohibitions and organized production as demand skyrocketed. Europeans took over many of the preconquest *cocales* (coca plantations) and expanded production. Pack trains laden with leaves arrived each year in Potosí and other markets where profits could be made. Workers at the mines had complicated motives for turning to coca. Coca leaves were attractive as a formerly restricted elite good that commoners suddenly could buy. The leaves also held religious significance for Andeans, and miners ritually offered them to Pachamama and the *supay*, deities who guarded the underground riches and who, if properly placated, might be induced to protect and reward the miners.[22]

Perhaps Spaniards ignored the cultural inducements to coca consumption, but they were aware of indigenous claims that chewing the leaves made arduous, high-altitude labor more tolerable. Indians refused to work without coca leaves. In fact, "the custom of not entering the mines without placing this herb in the mouth is so well established that there is a superstition that the richness of the metal will be lost if they do not do so."[23] Workers did not chew the coca leaves but sucked on a wad placed between the cheek and gum. To the wad in the mouth, they added *llijta*, made from the ashes of corn cobs and potatoes. Llijta contained lye, which released the ecognine, an alkaloid with narcotic effects, in the coca leaves. Workers claimed that coca preserved teeth and more importantly inhibited thirst, hunger, and fatigue. When using coca, some miners regularly worked double shifts. Spaniards who experimented with coca, however, generally rejected such claims.[24] Ecognine also helped workers absorb carbohydrates. This, to the thinking of ethnohistorian Thierry Saignes, was the chief physiological benefit of coca: because their diet was heavy in potatoes and other carbohydrate-dense food, mine workers needed coca to obtain more nutrition from their sustenance. Spanish diets contained fewer carbohydrates, and thus Spaniards noted less benefit from coca.[25] Even so, coca consumption dropped in the seventeenth century, probably due to the decline in indigenous population and the increasing preference among workers for alcohol and other drugs.

Teams usually stayed in the mine for the entire work week. Laboring by candlelight, their strength sapped by the humidity, subterranean heat, and oxygen-poor high-altitude air, the miners gouged at the entrails of the Hill. Jesuit José de Acosta visited Potosí in the late sixteenth century and recorded his impressions of work in the mines:

They labor in these mines in continual darkness and obscurity, without knowledge of day or night. And forasmuch as those places are never visited with the Sun, there is not only a continual darkness, but also an extreme cold, with so gross an air contrary to the disposition of man, . . . Those that labor therein use candles to light them, dividing their work in such sort, as they that work in the day rest by the night, and so they change. The metal is commonly hard, and therefore they break it with hammers, splitting and hewing it by force as if they were flints. After, they carry up this metal upon their shoulders, by ladders of three branches made of neat leather twisted like pieces of wood, which are crossed with staves of wood, so as by every one of these ladders they mount and descend together. . . . A man carries ordinarily the weight of two *arrobas* [fifty pounds] of metal upon his shoulders, tied together in a cloth in manner of a skip, and so mount they three and three. . . . to mount so great a height which commonly is above a hundred and fifty *estados* [an estado was the height of a man], [is] a fearful thing and . . . breeds an amazement to think upon it, so great is the desire of silver, that for the gain thereof men endure any pains.[26]

Or, one might add, in their greed, they force other men to endure any pains.

Viceroy Toledo had issued regulations to protect the mitayos from Spanish abuse, but it was one thing for the government to issue decrees and quite another to enforce them. He set the wage for mitayos working as apiris at 3.5 reals per day. Other mitayos who performed unskilled labor in the refining mills, usually grinding ore, received 2.75 reals per day. Nonetheless, azogueros commonly found pretexts to cheat mitayos of their wages. Toledo also decreed that mill and mine operators could not require mitayos to meet a quota of piece work: for example, hauling a certain amount of ore from the mine. Yet during nearly the entire colonial period, apiris routinely had to meet such quotas. Spaniards justified their demands on the grounds that without quotas mitayos would produce nothing. Sometimes operators used violence in an attempt to increase output. Luis Capoche, who described Potosí in the early 1580s, reported that physical abuse was common. Overseers and owners commonly called mitayos "dogs" and beat them for having transported too little ore. Capoche recounted that one terrified leader of a gang of mitayos tried to run from a beating inside the mine but fell into a deep pit and "broke into a thousand pieces."[27]

The work week began on Monday morning, when the workers gathered near the Cerro Rico for distribution among the miners and mill operators, and continued until Saturday afternoon. Laborers originally received their wages on Sunday, although the practice shifted to Monday, probably because of the kajcheo: on weekends many men were in the mines working as kajchas to supplement their regular wages. On payday, indigenous magistrates representing the sixteen mita provinces paraded through Potosí's Indian parishes to the sound of a bugle, instructing the mita captains to assemble the previous week's workers at Guayna, the small hill in front of the Cerro Rico, to receive their wages.

Mine work was dangerous and unhealthy. Potosí's altitude made labor especially arduous. Although some Andeans lived temporarily above four thousand meters to graze llamas and other livestock, no sizable pre-Hispanic villages or cities lay at that height. Cuzco, for example, was 3,500 meters above sea level, and highland urban centers typically fell in the range of 2,500 to 3,500 meters. Inhabitants of these high-altitude cities had undergone some biological adaptation over the generations. Their blood contained more red corpuscles than that of people living at lower elevations, which enabled them to absorb more oxygen. Even so, these high-altitude residents had trouble at Potosí (and nearly all of the other principal Andean silver districts, which lay at similarly high elevations). Many workers who migrated, whether voluntarily or through coercion, to the mines suffered from altitude sickness (*soroche*), their bodies at least temporarily unable to adapt to the new environment. Production of additional red corpuscles made their blood too viscous to circulate easily. The result in many cases was some combination of these symptoms: headaches, nausea, insomnia, fatigue, depression, and tingling in the extremities.[28] Father Acosta alluded to a personal experience with the pernicious effects of life at high altitude when he visited the Potosí mines: "Such as newly enter are sick as they at sea. The which happened to me in one of these mines, where I felt a pain at the heart, and beating of the stomach."[29]

Altitude was not the only thing that made work onerous and dangerous in Potosí's mines. For mingados who worked permanently in the mines or the stamp mills, the risk of silicosis was even greater than for the mitayos. Years of inhaling metallic dust almost guaranteed lung disease, as the purplish faces and lips of older mingados bore witness. Writing in the early 1800s, a British military officer serving in the patriot army that liberated Upper Peru from Spanish rule claimed that mine labor at Potosí was fatal to 20 percent of the workers. He added: "So dreadful was the labour of the mines considered, that each individual on whom the lot fell regarded it as a virtual sentence of death."[30]

Prolonged breathing of dust within the mine left lungs impregnated with silica and miners suffering from silicosis, which developed gradually. An afflicted worker first suffered repeated, long-lasting colds. Later, as lungs suffered more damage from the dust, the worker experienced severe fits of coughing, vomiting, and chest pains. In such a weakened state, miners became more likely to contract infectious diseases. Some survived and tried to work. Damaged lungs cut the oxygen carried by the blood, forcing the heart to work much harder. Those in the advanced stages of silicosis were spectral from loss of weight and too weak for almost any physical activity.[31] It also made them susceptible to pneumonia and tuberculosis. Consumptive workers suffered lingering coughs, fevers, weight loss, and chronic fatigue, coughing up bloody sputum as the disease devastated their lungs. Tuberculosis was "the coffin in which life lies dead or in which death lives."[32] Extremes in temperature confronted by the miners, especially the apiris, made illness more likely. Those working underground sweated profusely from the heat and the labor. Yet outside the air was frigid, with temperatures often falling below freezing at night. Ore carriers reached the surface covered with sweat, only to plunge into the icy air outside. Ore compounds in the mines sometimes contained arsenic, making the ubiquitous dust even more poisonous. Smoke from candles and torches contributed to pollution within the mines. By decreasing the miner's lung capacity, silicosis accentuated the symptoms of altitude sickness. Whereas a miner could cure soroche by migrating to lower elevations, he had no way to reverse the ravages of silicosis.

Mine cave-ins threatened both free and forced workers. One of the worst occurred at the royal quicksilver mines of Huancavelica, which supplied mercury to Potosí's amalgamators. In 1786 the top half of the Huancavelica mine collapsed and crushed more than two hundred workers.[33] Timber to shore up dangerous pits and tunnels was expensive. At Potosí mine owners and their foremen often lacked knowledge of engineering, and few knew how best to shore up tunnels or secure their diggings. Workers and overseers routinely postponed needed maintenance, thinking repairs could wait a little longer. The owners' illegal demand that mitayos produce a quota of ore each day forced barreteros and apiris to put off construction of timber or masonry buttresses and other protective fortifications, only to suffer the disastrous consequences. Attempting to make the work safer, the state provided for an *alcalde mayor de minas* (mining magistrate) and *veedores* (inspectors) to supervise conditions in the mines. Regulations required the veedores to remain on the Cerro during the work week and periodically to inspect the galleries and tunnels. All too often, however, the veedores were inexperienced and willing to accept bribes, permitting mine owners to put their workers in danger.[34] When officials tried to curb such abuses, owners sometimes protested and brought suit, delaying enforcement of orders. This occurred around 1580 in the Muñiza mine at Potosí, operated by two Spaniards with two twenty-eight–man work crews. Veedor Francisco de Oruño ordered work stopped until the owners repaired the mine. The operator sued on the ground that Oruño had acted out of personal malice and that the mine was safe. As charges and countercharges flew, work began again, and two days later a cave-in killed all twenty-eight miners of the night crew.[35]

Although it was less perilous than underground mining, work in the refining mills was as unhealthy. Laborers inhaled noxious dust as the stamp mills ground the ore. The falling hammers not only pulverized ore but also the arms, legs, and heads of careless and exhausted workers. Mercury poisoning was another health risk. Refining silver by amalgamation required that the pulverized ore be mixed with mercury. Workers poured mercury on a mound of ground ore and then, rather than using shovels, trod the mixture with their feet. In so doing they inevitably absorbed the poisonous mercury. Once amalgamation had occurred and the mercury had combined with the silver, the workers washed away the dross, leaving the lump of amalgam. They then heated the amalgam to separate the silver and mercury. This was a very dangerous step in the refining process: workers had to be careful to avoid breathing the extremely poisonous fumes that could escape if the lid was not securely fixed to the retort. Between industrial injuries and illnesses, the city hospital generally held around a hundred patients.[36] Each year a few hundred workers probably died from mining accidents at Potosí, and many others suffered the ravages of respiratory diseases until finally succumbing to them.[37]

Compared to the Andes or to Brazil, colonial Mexican mining was less overtly coercive. True, the Spaniards exploited both African and indigenous slaves to work early discoveries, such as those around Taxco, and used the repartimiento (coatéquitl in Mexico) and encomienda to provide additional labor drafts. This changed with the discovery in the mid-1500s of great silver deposits in the sparsely populated north, such as at Zacatecas and Guanajuato. To obtain workers for these mines, Spaniards tried to subdue the seminomadic Chichimecas. A favorite strategy was to capture them in real or fake wars and then sentence them to a term in the mines as punishment, although this offered no permanent solution to the labor problem. Neither the encomienda nor the repartimiento proved useful in mobilizing workers in the north. Instead, mine operators and refiners relied primarily on wage labor, supplemented occasionally with the labor of slaves. Nevertheless, most of the estimated forty-five thousand Mexicans working in the mining industry did so voluntarily.[38]

Similar to those in the Andes, Mexican miners performed tasks requiring brute strength but also considerable skill. Barreteros used picks and pry bars to dislodge ore. If the rock proved especially hard, they set fire to the

Figure 5. Tenateros (ore carriers) at Guanajuato. From T. A. Rickard,
Journeys of Observation (San Francisco: Dewey Publishing, 1907).

ore face to heat it, then threw cold water on it to fracture the stone. Drillers
(*coheteadores* or *barrenadores*) using blasting powder became widespread in
the eighteenth century. Mexican *tenateros*, as figure 5 shows, lugged heavy
ore-filled bags (*tenates*) to the surface, where other workers used hammers to
break off bits of ore from worthless rock. When this primitive form of concentration was completed, the mine owner transported the ore by mule to
his refining mill (*hacienda de minas*). Carpenters and masons shored up the
mines to make them safer.[39]

At times, the colonial state tolerated and even supported coercive measures to supply the Mexican mines and mills with workers. The mining industry used debt peonage as a tool for retaining workers much more commonly
than was true in the Andes.[40] Such peonage involved enticing or forcing workers to go to the mines, lending them money or advancing them wages to make
them indebted to the mine owner or the refiner, then making them stay until

the debts had been paid off. Workers often found it very difficult to discharge such debts, and employers sometimes manipulated accounts to make sure that peons remained in debt. Mexican mine owners also used *lazadores* or (labor recruiters) to scour the countryside, impressing idlers into the work gangs. The government generally exempted Indians from such impressments, but press gangs were not always careful about whom they conscripted. Peasants found themselves kidnapped from farms and villages and hauled off to the mines.

If Mexican silver producers usually had to be satisfied with wage labor, this placed them at a disadvantage compared with refiners at Potosí, who enjoyed the mita subsidy. It is difficult to determine the labor costs of these mining operations and even more difficult to establish the wage level of Mexican miners. At Zacatecas in the late sixteenth century, for example, workers and their families lived in quarters supplied by the mine owner and received free provisions. Living and working together fostered solidarity, and strife sometimes festered between rival owners' work gangs. How long workers typically remained at a given mine is unclear. News of rich strikes elsewhere was sufficient inducement for many to migrate. Nor is it clear how many worked only occasionally in the mines and were employed otherwise as peons on Spanish estates or as day labors in the city. Mining paid better, although it was harder and more dangerous work.

At first glance, Mexican wages appear lower than those paid to free laborers at Potosí. An eighteenth-century pickman at Potosí, for example, earned a wage of eight to ten reals per day, compared with the four reals paid in many Mexican mines. Yet Mexicans miners probably realized more from selling a share of the ore they were allowed to take from the mine than they did from the cash, housing, and food the owner supplied. Each day, a mine worker had to fill his *tequío* (ore quota), after which custom permitted him to gather a bag of ore for himself (the pepena or partido). For obvious reasons, rather than giving the best ore to the mine owners, workers tried to reserve it for their own pepena. The pepena was therefore a form of profit-sharing. Owners did not like it because they lost part of the ore, but they recognized that desire for better pepenas motivated workers to explore and expand the diggings.[41]

Ore sharing potentially gave a Mexican worker as much as twenty reals per day over and above his wage. This probably exceeded what a Potosí miner typically earned even if he worked on the weekend as a kajcha. Mexican mine owners tried to limit worker predations by stationing an overseer, or *quitapepena*, at the mine entrance to make sure that workers did not take more than the customary share of ore. Workers tenaciously defended this traditional form of profit sharing, and mine owners usually considered it an essential cost of production. At Bolaños, in fact, workers received no wage at all but were allowed a third of the ore they produced.[42] In lean times the partido enabled Mexican mine owners to shift part of their costs to the workers, who earned less because their share of the ore was worth less. During prosperous times, however, owners occasionally tried to cut the amount of pepena or to eliminate it altogether.

Whereas Potosí's mitayos were theoretically free, Brazil's slaves did most of the work in the colony's gold and diamond fields. Word of the Brazilian strikes in the 1690s touched off a massive migration, which included slaves taken by prospectors from the Brazilian littoral and from Portugal who rushed to the goldfields:

> The insatiable thirst for gold incited so many to leave their lands and set out by roads so rough as are those of the mines, that it would be difficult to count the number of persons that presently are there. . . . The mixture is of every condition of people: men and women, young and old, poor and rich, noble and plebeian, lay and clerical, and religious of diverse institutions, many of which have in Brazil no convent or house.[43]

With them went thousands of African slaves. As the demand for mine labor grew, slave traders imported more and more captives from the Bight of Benin, where Africans had long mined and refined gold. Portuguese mining technology was so primitive that the Portuguese needed the slaves' expertise, which was also backward and showed little improvement well into the nineteenth century. When British adventurer Sir Richard Francis Burton visited Minas Gerais in 1867, he compared methods used in the goldfields to those of the ancient Romans.[44] The great profits earned in the gold and diamond fields meant that owners could easily outbid sugar planters for slaves arriving from Africa. Even after gold production dropped and the economy became more diversified in the nineteenth century, the traffic in slaves for the mines reached such heights that Minas Gerais had the nation's largest population of bondsmen.[45] Brazil's mining boom stimulated a massive inter- and intracontinental migration, playing a decisive role in opening the Brazilian interior to settlement and economic development.

In the goldfields, working conditions for the slaves depended on the type of mining. In some rich mining areas, gangs of slaves used sluices to wash gold-bearing hillsides and river banks. These workings (*lavras*) required capital investment to move large amounts of earth, to rechannel water, and to build the sluicing apparatus. A gang of slaves generally worked a lavra under the close supervision of the master or his overseer. Except for what the slave might steal from the lavra, he received little or no benefit from the gold produced. Although owners searched slaves as they left the diggings, in an attempt to prevent theft, these measures were ineffective. In the lavras the size of a claim depended upon the number of chattels an owner could assign to the operation. Portuguese mining codes generally allocated 2.5 square *braças* (a braça was roughly a fathom, or six feet) per slave.[46] Because the wealthy could afford more slaves, they could obtain larger claims.[47]

By the mid-1700s, slavery in the goldfields began to change, with important social and cultural ramifications for the province. On the one hand, imports of African slaves dropped as the profits from gold mining declined. Some mine owners moved their slaves to new strikes in Mato Grosso or sent them back to the coastal areas. But many remained in Minas Gerais, which had become a largely Afro-Brazilian province. A 1776 census showed that its population was three-fourths African or Afro-Brazilian. In 1738, less than 2 percent of slaves in Ouro Preto were Creole, but by the end of the century more than half were Brazilian-born. Furthermore, many slaves in Minas Gerais gained their freedom. In 1786 roughly 40 percent of Afro-Brazilians in the province were free.[48]

Owners who had offspring by female slaves sometimes freed the children. In Ouro Preto during the peak mining years, baptismal records show that about a quarter of slave infants were manumitted by their owners. Female infants were a little more likely to be freed than were males, perhaps because neither children nor women provided the labor necessary to mining.[49] The gender ratio meant that male slaves had limited opportunity to establish families. Furthermore, because slave children offered the mine operators no immediate economic benefit, the owners apparently discouraged slave marriages and family formation.[50] As the proportion of Brazilian- to African-born slaves rose, acculturation proceeded more rapidly.

Adult slaves gained freedom through purchase or as a gift from the master. It was no easy matter for a slave to save enough to buy manumission, although some miners blessed by rich strikes accomplished it. Some female slaves managed to accumulate their purchase price by working in petty commerce, which often included part-time prostitution. It was difficult, however, to meet the master's labor demands and also save money. Many resorted to *coartação*, a conditional manumission. In these cases the owner granted the slave autonomy, subject to the fulfillment of certain labor requirements. Once those requirements were met, the slave received full liberty. The slave might agree to pay the master over several years a sum equivalent to the cost of another slave. The *coartado* then worked as he was able and bought his freedom. Sometimes masters required good conduct or limited amounts of additional service for several years before granting the slave outright freedom. The possibility of manumission probably affected slave behavior, making a slave temporarily more willing to tolerate his enslavement.

These changes sped up cultural assimilation. Children learned Portuguese more easily than their parents and grandparents had done, especially if the latter had arrived in Brazil as adults. The Afro-Brazilians, whether slave or free, began to identify more closely with Brazil, weakening the ties that early generations of slaves had with their African ethnic groups of origin. Mining towns sprang up almost immediately, with slaves, freedmen, and Europeans living and working in close proximity. Chief among the towns was the Vila Rica de Ouro Preto. One observer called it a "golden Potosí," linking it to the archetype of colonial Latin American mining. Like Potosí, Ouro Preto soon attracted merchants, bureaucrats, gamblers, priests, and others hoping to claim their share of the miners' profits, but much of its population descended from Africans brought to Brazil as slaves.

Colonial Latin America's mines spewed forth a great stream of silver and gold. Spain and Portugal's European rivals envied the Iberian powers' good fortune and plotted ways to also enrich themselves from the lands of El Dorado. That Spain and Portugal were able to organize the political, commercial, and technical resources to exploit their colonies' vast mineral riches is a testament to their imperial prowess. Yet the great flood of American bullion had far-reaching human costs. It involved massive migration, whether the horrendous enslavement and shipping of Africans across the Atlantic to Brazil's gold and diamond fields, the coerced movement of mita workers to Potosí's silver and Huancavelica's mercury mines, or the flights of peasants to avoid mita service. The great northern mining districts of Mexico such as Zacatecas and Durango could not have flourished without the migration of workers to those districts. Of course, wage labor also existed in the Mexican and Andean mines and refineries, but tribute and reparto demands by the colonial system helped drive free workers into the mining industry. An early Spanish observer, Domingo de Santo Tomás, avowed that "what is being sent to Spain is not silver, but the blood and sweat of the Indians."[51]

CHAPTER 4

Workers' Response to Colonial Mining

By the beginning of the seventeenth century about half the Indian labor force directly engaged in producing silver in Potosí was voluntary.

—Peter Bakewell,
Miners of the Red Mountain

ALTHOUGH DIRECT AND INDIRECT COERCION PLAYED A CRUCIAL ROLE IN THE supply of labor for the colonial mines, it did not explain completely why workers went to work at Potosí, Guanajuato, or the Brazilian gold and diamond fields. Nor did it explain why some coerced workers stayed on at the mines at the end of their required terms. The mita and slavery provided large numbers of laborers, but so did daily wages and ore-sharing arrangements such as the kajcheo and the pepena. Nor did the coercion so thoroughly repress mine workers that they became completely compliant to the mine owners' wishes. Many miners found ways to resist the operators' demands or to garner greater personal benefit from the labor they were forced to do in the mines.

One such individual was the kajcha and trapiche operator Agustín Quispe. On a September day in 1725, Bartolomé Arzáns de Orsúa y Vela, a chronicler of Potosí, was on the Rich Hill with four Frenchmen when they passed near the chapel of the kajchas. There they happened upon Quispe, famed throughout Potosí for his bravery and brawling. Quispe owned a trapiche in which he ground and smelted the ores he and other kajchas extracted from the mines at night or on feast days and weekends. The chronicler obviously admired

71

Quispe and reported that when they met that day on the Hill, Quispe offered him a jar of chicha, the indigenous maize beer. He also offered chicha to the four Frenchmen, who were Arzáns's friends. They haughtily rejected the indigenous brew. The offended Indian grabbed a flagstaff and launched himself at the Frenchmen. He broke one's head with the stick. The drawn swords of the other three provided them no protection from Quispe's onslaught, and they fled, hastened onward by fifty kajchas who began to stone them. With difficulty Arzáns stopped the kajchas from killing the Frenchmen.

On another occasion the kajcha Quispe was visiting the Bethlehem sanctuary some distance from Potosí and encountered a militia unit drawn up in formation. When the soldiers refused to let him pass through their lines, Quispe took his harquebus and fired it through the lined-up soldiers, sending men running in all directions. The captain took two swipes at Quispe with his pike. The kajcha parried the first blow with the harquebus but suffered a chest wound by the second. Quispe fell to the ground, where he was wounded two more times. Just as the soldiers gathered to finish him off, six of Quispe's companions arrived and threw themselves into the brawl to save the fierce kajcha. Despite his injuries, Quispe wounded the captain, his sergeant, and four soldiers before the village priest intervened to restore peace.

Quispe's boisterous and assertive example shows that mining at Potosí was more than gangs of oppressed Indians toiling mournfully under the pitiless control of Spanish azogueros and their overseers. In his brawls with European visitors and even with militia troops, the kajcha leader Quispe often received help from other kajchas and mitayos, as well as from some local clergy who protected him. To many he was a hero, an Indian who defied authority and yet also enriched himself as an "ore thief." To the chronicler Arzáns, Quispe was not dangerous or threatening: although he worked abandoned diggings or snuck into operating mines, "he took out ore without knocking down buttresses or causing substantial damage." Some kajchas were not so careful, stripping ore out of the mine's natural buttresses and causing cave-ins. It was probably inevitable that mines owners detested Quispe as a leader of the kajchas and wanted "to drink his blood." Indeed, his most serious fights were with the owners and their guards, and as a result Quispe took to carrying a pair of pistols with him into the mines.

Not long after his brawl with the Frenchmen, Quispe had a serious run-in with Magistrate Antonio Rodríguez and twelve Spaniards. They had tracked him down because of complaints made by the son of a mine guard, who had tried to keep Quispe and his kajchas from entering the mine. Quispe and his companions managed to enter anyway, and out of spite for having been denied entry extracted all the good ore in the mine. Rodríguez and his henchmen located the kajcha while he celebrated his saint's day. Members of his ayllu who were present tried to protect Quispe but finally had to give way in the face of twenty-six firearms. Tied hand and foot, Quispe was taken to a house in the country, where he was held prisoner. Loaded down with chains and kept in stocks, Quispe was "cruelly mistreated" until his clerical friends finally intervened on his behalf. As Quispe's case shows, Andean mining labor was clearly a more complex subject than might be expected.[1]

In the 1570s, the Indians initially cooperated with Toledo's reforms. Many had, after all, worked at Potosí during the first decades when wages and profits were high. Kurakas consequently supplied the assigned quota of mitayos from their ayllus. They found the ore dumps easy to work, and azogueros earned heady profits for a few years until the tailings were exhausted.

Furthermore, underground labor was not foreign to native understandings of nature. For pre-Hispanic Andeans the *ukhupacha*, or underground, was a mysterious, sacred realm inhabited by the supay, or shadows of the dead. A supay was "that aspect of the soul that is its personal identity, . . . the shadow that, before Christian evangelization, would be liberated forever from the sufferings of this world (*kay pacha* 'the present time-space') to rest beside the other shadows of its ethnicity, in the *(s)upaymarca* 'the land of shadows.'"[2] Surviving relatives took great care to provide offerings of food and drink so that the supay did not suffer from hunger or thirst. Although the living did not seem to fear the spirits, the deceased's relatives knew that the supay could behave generously if given the appropriate offerings but could also cause injuries or inflict other punishment if offerings were neglected. Miners "perturbed subterranean life and the spirits that ruled it; they yielded to a sacredness that did not belong to the familiar universe, a deeper and riskier sacredness."[3] Such ancestor worship was an integral part of Andean ritual life prior to the Spanish conquest, and reciprocity established harmony between the beings of the ukhupacha and *kaypacha*.

The arrival of Christianity modified Andean beliefs concerning the underworld and the supay, and mining itself caused other changes. Catholic missionaries interpreted Pachamama, the Andean earth mother, as the Virgin Mary, mother of God, in their attempts to convert the indigenous population. But the clerics saw indigenous ancestor worship as a threat to Christian orthodoxy. The Indians' ancestors had died without baptism and thus were the damned (*condenados*), consigned eternally to hell. The spirits of the ukhu-pacha were therefore devils. Catholic clerics emphasized the evil nature of the supay, although native Andeans continued to believe in the supay's dualistic nature, capable of both good and evil. With the Catholic hierarchy trying to prevent traditional ancestor worship, Indians found it difficult to openly pro-vide offerings to satisfy the supay. The Taki Onqoy movement, which began in 1565–1566 around Huamanga (Ayacucho) in the central Andes, was one of several attempts to resist the Spanish and restore traditional Andean religious practices. Adherents of Taki Onqoy reported that the huacas, which included the supay, "went about in the air dried out and dead from hunger because the Indians no longer sacrificed to them, nor poured *chicha* [maize beer]."[4] The huacas were angry with those who had become Christians and threatened to kill all who refused to forsake their baptisms and make the old offerings.

For the colonial Indian laborers, the underground was a living entity rather than a mere geological formation, and it was inhabited by the spirits of ancestors. The ukhupacha was the manifestation of Pachamama and its rich ores the fruits of her reproduction. Just as Pachamama generated corn and potatoes on the surface (kaypacha), underground she created gold, silver, tin, and other metals: "Like the agricultural products, the metals were considered fruits of nature, with whom relations of reciprocity had to be undertaken to assure an abundant 'harvest.'"[5] The cosmic serpent (*amaru*) slithered from the underworld through the kaypacha to the overworld (*janajpacha*), medi-ating life between the three levels and giving them harmony. Miners saw the serpent's presence in subterranean water flows carrying riches and power to the surface.[6] To get at the rich ore, miners poured alcohol on the ground for Pachamama before entering the mines. Meanwhile, Catholic priests encour-aged the workers to build subterranean chapels to the Virgin Mary. By the end of the sixteenth century, clerics and Spanish officials had prevailed on the min-ers to construct chapels and shrines to the Virgin/Pachamama in many mines within Potosí's Cerro Rico. Worship at Christian mining shrines included contributing gifts of alcohol, food, incense, and other offerings to create *ayni* (harmony).[7] Those chapels always lay near the mine entrances.

The realm of the supay was deeper inside the Rich Hill. Influenced by Christianity, miners endowed the shadows with demonic characteristics yet retained beliefs about the supay's ambiguous nature. Peasants arriving as mitayos understood the supay's power and mystery because the ukhupacha was part of their cosmos: to them, "agrarian and mining activities appear[ed] related. . . . [T]he vein was conceive[d] of as a plant."[8] Thus, Indians were familiar with the underground, and their cosmology helped them as they entered the mines.

Even so, they did not respond passively to the mita's growing oppression. By the 1620s, after the great silver boom associated with the introduction of amalgamation began to wane, azogueros' costs rose and they sought to maintain profit levels by squeezing the mitayos even harder. They withheld travel allowances mandated by law; required mitayos to meet excessive production quotas that were banished by law, which cut the already below-subsistence-level wages even further; and physically punished recalcitrant or sluggish conscripts. Discontent festered but did not flare into open rebellion. Instead, many Indians tried to escape the mita's compulsory and disruptive intrusions. As population dropped in provinces subject to the mita, some potential conscripts fled to other regions. By abandoning their village ayllu, they became *forasteros* (strangers or outsiders) who were not subject to the mita in their new location.[9] Priests, kurakas, corregidores, and hacendados (landowners) sometimes hid workers from census takers, hoping thereby to reduce the amount of labor exported to the mines and retain it for their own exploitation. With so much indigenous movement, the colonial government struggled to muster sufficient manpower to keep the refining mills stocked with ore to grind, and azogueros complained constantly about the shortage of mita laborers. Nevertheless, the mita remained a state subsidy at the indigenous population's expense, which for centuries permitted refiners to produce silver that in free-market conditions would have been unprofitable.

Despite the attractions of migration, many chose to stay in their home villages even though it meant serving in the mita. Indigenous response to the mita was framed by the economic and social interests of individual villages and ethnic groups. Communities and individuals manipulated the mita system to their own benefit as much as possible, although in ways that were not always clear to the external observer.[10] Toledo's ordinances required the Indians to appear in Potosí in person (*efectivos*) to perform the assigned mita labors, but mine and mill owners frequently allowed them to buy their way out. Thus, villagers had to decide whether to provide mita workers in person or pay in silver. These "silver Indians" (indios de plata) and their ayllus paid the mine owners enough to hire substitutes from the free labor pool.[11] In the early seventeenth century, the closer Indians lived to Potosí, the more likely they were to pay rather than serve personally in the mita. This reflected an indigenous response to economic opportunities at Potosí. Workers who lived close enough to Potosí to go there during slack periods in the agricultural calendar, for instance, might earn enough as mingados and from the kajcheo to pay their mita obligation and still have money left over. This was not feasible, however, for those living far away. Villages that produced commercial goods for Potosí also found it more profitable to concentrate on marketing foodstuffs, timber, firewood, and craft goods and use those profits to pay for indios de plata.[12] Thousands of Indians worked to supply Potosí. In 1603, aside from the mingados employed in the mines and mills, more than a thousand natives (including some women) hauled wood and other fuel for the refining mills; another thousand supplied the salt needed for amalgamation; over three hundred *chacaneadores* provided llama teams to carry ore from the mines down to the mills; a thousand Indians made charcoal; and two hundred made candles to illuminate the deep shafts. Indeed, in the early seventeenth century one hundred thousand llamas arrived at Potosí each year loaded with goods for the city to be slaughtered later to feed the workers and provide raw materials for the candle makers.[13] Many more natives lived by marketing foodstuffs and chicha or serving the city's upper and middle classes. Thus, the mita indirectly mobilized, often in unexpected ways, a much larger indigenous population than just the Indians who worked in the mines.

A few villages, such as Tiquipaya in Cochabamba, even resisted supplying indios de plata. Assigned to send eighty-four mitayos in 1617, Tiquipaya, abetted by the local Spanish corregidor because he profited from keeping the workers at home, sent neither workers nor money.[14] Of course, what was true in one village in 1617 did not necessarily suggest broad practice. A change of corregidor could force a recalcitrant ayllu into compliance with the mita. In addition, conditions might change for those ayllus that had previously managed to gather enough money to provide indios de plata. At a later date, a more rapacious governor or priest might siphon off the village's commercial surplus, hindering its ability to supply indios de plata rather than efectivos. As the repartos de mercancías became more onerous in the eighteenth century, they made it more difficult for ayllus to save enough to provide indios de plata.

The mita depended on the stability of the indigenous population, yet such stability was a forlorn dream. According to Peruvian historian Scarlett O'Phelan Godoy, the mita impeded the ayllus' ability "for production and reproduction since they could not rely on an important percentage of their adult males."[15] Families had to uproot themselves and trudge off to Potosí. Many never returned to their home villages. Factors beyond the state's control, such as epidemic disease, rapidly killed off a large percentage of the population, and mita-caused migrations may have contributed to the spread of epidemics. As the population declined, workers had to return to Potosí more frequently than the seven-year rotation stipulated by Toledo, or the state had to accept a reduction in the size of the levies. Azogueros balked at attempts to cut the size of the mita drafts, although the colonial state eventually made them accept modest reductions. As other sectors of the colonial economy developed, they also required labor and began to compete for the pool of available Indians in the mita provinces. Spanish landholders hired workers and sometimes tried to hide them from census takers and mita captains. Choosing to become a peon on a Spanish plantation or ranch, however, often meant cutting ethnic ties to one's ayllu and losing one's freedom of movement. As the population dropped in the mita provinces, the state reclassified Indians in an attempt to increase the number liable for mita service. In the census carried out in the 1680s under direction of the viceroy, the Duke of Palata, forasteros were reclassified as tributaries in their new place of residence and thus liable for mita service. But Indians recognized that they could regain forastero status simply by moving again.

Of course, those who remained on their ayllu lands and tried to preserve their culture and resources had to endure the mita. Indeed, some carried their mita service as both a grievous burden and a badge of royal honor. During Inca times, an ayllu secured its right to land under the Inca through its tribute and labor service to the state. Indians maintained the same perception following the conquest: the Spanish king rewarded their payment of tribute and mita labor with the right to hold and use land. By sending its annual levy of mitayos to Potosí, an ayllu gained a special status vis-à-vis the king. Mitayos occasionally carried their understanding of this relationship with the king even further. In 1801, for example, a contingent of mitayos headed to Potosí from San Martín de Chupa caused an uproar outside Oruro, seizing food and animals from local Indians and Spaniards on the grounds that the goods were necessary for their royal service. Witnesses claimed the mitayos said their service made them "worth as much as the king." Because they were on a royal mission, they deserved the prerogatives of the monarch himself.[16] Some ayllus departed for Potosí armed with traditional weapons, as though serving in the Inca royal army.[17]

The struggle between azogueros and mita workers intensified during the eighteenth century. Mine and mill operators faced a dilemma. Ore quality was very poor, and most of the material they consumed, such as mercury, timber, and candles, had fixed or rising costs. In addition, they lacked new technologies to improve significantly either the extraction of ore or its refining. Predictably, they cut their costs by extracting even more labor from the mitayos. This chiefly meant increasing the quota of work they demanded. Viceroy Toledo had decreed that the conscripts work only one week in three as mitayos and that they not be forced to produce a quota, but in the 1700s the azogueros ignored those laws. The state increased the mitayos' work period to every other week from every third week. Quotas were a constant temptation to the mine owners: without them, mitayos had little incentive to work. Thus, by midcentury, mine owners required apiris to carry out twenty or thirty loads of ore per shift. When they failed to meet the quota (*palla*), the mine owners cut their meager wages and required them to complete the task, without pay, during the "rest" week. Workers went up to the mines on Monday morning and did not return until Saturday evening. They typically worked two ten-hour shifts back to back and then rested for ten hours before enduring another double shift. In general, apiris had to work seven ten-hour shifts during a five-day period. In five and a half days there are 132 hours, and the mitayo worked 70 of them. Intendant Pedro Vicente Cañete y Domínguez aptly described the conditions for the mitayos laboring as ore carriers:

> For these poor wretches all the nights are extremely bad. They climb and descend overloaded with a hundred pounds, through caverns filled with horror and risk, that seem to be the homes of demons. The mineral vapors afflict them to such an extent, that together with the fatigue of these heavy tasks, as well as their copious sweat from the underground heat, and the excessive cold they encounter when leaving the mines, dawn greets them so languid and mortal that they appear cadavers.[18]

By the late 1700s, a mitayo needed the help of his whole family to meet his work quota.[19] This meant that his wife and children were occupied in helping him satisfy his quota when they otherwise would have been working to supplement the family income. In the refining plants, ore was ground continuously. Although the mills probably offered greater opportunity for rest, mitayos there had to put in nine ten-hour shifts per week.

In Brazil, where most miners were slaves, workers had more freedom than might be expected. Many slaves worked as prospectors (*faiscadores*), panning for pay dirt with little oversight from their owners. Faiscadores usually paid their masters a weekly quantity of gold, and the quota was set according to whether the worker had found rich diggings or not. Two or three grams per week were the usual expectation unless prospects were especially promising. Master and faiscadores often lived together in crude huts. The work was hard: Slaves were half submerged in cold rivers and half blasted by the sun's intense rays as they panned. Many miners were crippled by spending months and even years bent over while panning for gold. Respiratory disease, dysentery, and other maladies took their toll, limiting a slave's life expectancy in the mines to ten or twelve years.[20]

Faiscadores enjoyed surprising freedom, especially in contrast to plantation labor. They roamed the countryside searching for gold-bearing alluvium because the typical owner preferred to let his slaves go out and prospect as long as they paid him an agreed-upon income. Some slaves found enough gold to pay their masters and have some left over to buy goods, including the purchase of their own slaves, and even freedom for themselves.[21] In 1719 the governor of Minas Gerais, Dom Pedro de Almeida, Count of Assumar, expressed his disgust with the laxity of slavery in the mines: "The manner in which they live today cannot be considered true slavery but may more appropriately be termed licentious liberty."[22] Assumar's comment reflected the astonishment felt by visitors from Brazil's sugar-growing regions when they saw the slaves' independence in the mining districts.

Brazilian mining labor, with its surprising "liberty," promoted a more racially egalitarian society than was true on the colony's sugar plantations. Slaves and free men mixed more readily in the goldfields than on sugar plantations.[23] In Minas Gerais the gold rush spawned a racially mixed society, the result of heavy immigration by white males and their slaves combined with widespread miscegenation. As was true in mining districts throughout colonial Latin America, the number of men, both free and slave, who went to the goldfields far outnumbered female migrants. Among slaves, men probably outnumbered women by four to one in Minas Gerais, and few white women braved the frontier conditions. Labor demands meant that miners preferred to buy male workers, but they also believed that women from Mina in Africa possessed a special knack for finding gold. Due to both superstition and passion, miners took Mina women as mistresses, hoping to ensure the discovery of pay dirt.[24] Even without such prospecting abilities, however, the gender imbalance in the gold and diamond fields meant that mine owners took slave women as concubines. Whether sanctioned by marriage or not (and most were not), these relationships yielded a mushrooming population of illegitimate mulattoes. André João Antonil, the cleric who observed and wrote about early Minas Gerais, penned a scathing indictment of the miners and their women:

> There is no thing so good that it cannot be the occasion of many evils, . . . the greater part of the gold that is taken from the mines passes in dust and coins to foreign kingdoms and the lesser remains in Portugal and the cities of Brazil, except what is used on necklaces, earrings, and other adornments, of which today the mulattas of evil life and black women are loaded down, more so than the ladies.[25]

In 1734, more than 90 percent of the fines imposed by the Inquisition in Sabará were for the sin of concubinage.[26]

Forced labor at Potosí had always destabilized life in the Andes, and the mita's pernicious impact intensified as the colonial era wore on. Not surprisingly, hatred of the Potosí mita became a rallying cry for the Indians during the Great Andean Rebellion that convulsed the central Andes between 1780 and 1782 and took as many as one hundred thousand lives. In 1777, José Gabriel Condorcanqui, kuraka of Tungasuca and Pampamarca, traveled to Lima from his home in Tinta province to assert his claim to the marquisate of Oropesa, a title of nobility reserved by the Spanish Crown for a descendant of the last Inca ruler, Tupac Amaru. Condorcanqui also carried petitions from other kurakas in Tinta asking the government to exempt their people from service in the Potosí mita. The petitions argued that Indians from Tinta should no longer have to provide mitayos because creation of the new viceroyalty of the Rio de la Plata the previous year placed Potosí in a rival jurisdiction. Tinta lay in the viceroyalty of Peru, Condorcanqui insisted, and thus his men should not have to labor in the mines of the other viceroyalty. Colonial authorities rejected his argument. To have done otherwise would have threatened the mita's survival, as many of the mitayos were drawn from outside the new viceroyalty. Nonetheless, Condorcanqui's actions against the mita were, it turned out, only his first act in a drama that eventually exploded into a violent attack on forced labor at Potosí as part of the Great Andean Rebellion.

Frustrated by the government's denial of his claim to the marquisate and its refusal to grant the exemption from the mita, Condorcanqui returned to Tinta. By then he had dropped his surname and called himself José Gabriel Tupac Amaru. Once back home he became involved in a dispute with the local governor, Antonio de Arriaga, over the collection of tributes and reparto debts. Supported by disgruntled Creoles, including the bishop of Cuzco, Juan Manuel Moscoso y Peralta, who had feuded with Arriaga for years and had even excommunicated him, Tupac Amaru seized the governor, placed him on trial, and executed him in November 1780. Dressed in traditional Inca clothing, the kuraka announced to the crowd assembled for the execution that he would lead a movement to free the people from the oppression they suffered from corregidores and peninsular Spaniards and their mitas, tributes, and repartos.

Meanwhile, violence related to the mita had already erupted in Chayanta province, just to the north of Potosí. There the local Spanish corregidor, Joaquín Alós, appointed mestizos as kurakas of Macha, displacing the legitimate lords, Tomás Catari and Isidro Acho. Although Catari and Acho accused Alós of several abuses and crimes, one of their chief complaints related to the Potosí mita. Macha traditionally used part of its village lands to grow foodstuffs to feed its mitayos. The recently appointed illegitimate kurakas forced the ayllu to work the lands but diverted profits to themselves and to the corregidor, leaving Macha's mitayos to fend for themselves. As the dispute unfolded, Spanish officials in Potosí supported the suits of Catari and Acho to protect the mita. For the Macha villagers, resentment erupted not because they had to fill the hated mita, as they had traditionally done, but because Alós and his confederates were making it nearly impossible to do so.[27] Catari even traveled across the continent to Buenos Aires, seeking and obtaining redress from the viceroy, but the audiencia in La Plata refused to enforce these edicts. Divisions among the Spaniards combined with mounting hostility among the Indians as bloody violence erupted.

Despite smoldering resentment against forced labor at Potosí, the rebel leaders initially did little more than talk about abolishing the mita. Tupac Amaru made only a halfhearted effort to end it. He needed Creole support if his rebellion was to succeed, but many Creoles benefited economically from mita labor. Despite playing upon popular resentment against the mita at the outset of the rebellion, he soon moderated his position, not wanting to alienate his nonindigenous sympathizers.[28] In Chayanta province, Tomás Catari worked to preserve his village's resources rather than eliminate the mita.

In fact, it was the rebel rank and file that made the strongest demand for elimination of the mita. As the violence intensified, the rebels pressed Tupac Amaru and other leaders to eliminate the Potosí mita. Unlike Tupac Amaru and Tomás Catari, Tupac Katari, who headed the uprising around Oruro and

La Paz, made elimination of the mita one of his main objectives. Upon his return from slaving in the Potosí mita, Katari's brother Martín joined the rebels and pressed urgently for its abolition.[29] Katari received strong support from the indigenous populace in Sicasica, Pacajes, and Omasuyos provinces, all of which had to send mitayos to the mines. Yet many Indians refused to support the rebellion, even though they also were subject to the Potosí mita, an indication that forced mine labor was not sufficient by itself to generate revolt.

Successful rebellions require solidarity, but ethnic divisions at Potosí hindered cooperation and unity among the workers. The ayllus lived in separate parishes at Potosí, reinforcing the cultural separation. The Lupacas ayllu, for example, lived in San Martín to the west of Potosí, while yanaconas, who had lost their ethnic affiliation, resided in San Roque. Colonial officials had established ethnic "parishes" so that when mitayos arrived, they could connect with ethnically related workers and have the support of a social network that would help them adjust to the demands of mine labor. Throughout the colonial period, the parishes provided an ethnic anchor for the transitory workers, a cultural refuge that slowed Hispanicization and preserved ethnic differences. Strong ethnic animosities helped undermine the Great Andean Rebellion, when some kurakas sided with the colonial state rather than support indigenous leaders from other ayllus.

It is not clear how many mingados stayed on permanently in Potosí's mines. Much free Andean mine labor was temporary rather than permanent. Mingados worked part of the year in their fields and went to the mines to supplement their incomes. This was typical of mine workers in Oruro, which had no mita.[30] Even though labor there was voluntary, it did not produce a proletariat because workers generally stayed for a few weeks or months and then returned to their farms. Those who remained permanently in Oruro usually gave up mining to work as artisans, rather than miners, in the city.[31] Andean miners often grew their own food, which they carried with them to the mines to avoid paying the high prices in the isolated mining camps and cities. But this also reduced inflationary pressure on salaries. Because these workers supplied part of their own food, mine owners could pay them less than would have been true had they depended only on wages for survival. The temporary nature of their mine work also blocked their proletarianization, because they never became fully dependent upon their mining wages for survival. Income from the kajcheo and trapiches also impeded any attempt by the mine and refinery owners to reduce their workers to a proletariat.

In Brazil, mine laborers faced even greater coercion than did the Andean mitayos, but the slaves in Brazilian mines sometimes had surprising liberty. Gold deposits were not renewable and were soon exhausted. It made economic, if not humanitarian, sense for the owners to work their slaves as long and as hard as possible, purchasing new chattels to replace those who died in the process. Perhaps they managed to do this in the lavras, but relentless coercion was not feasible with faiscadores. They often knew more about prospecting than the owner, who found that if he abused his slaves, gold output dropped rather than increased. Owners had to negotiate work conditions with these skilled slaves, giving them a share of the gold or granting them freedom after a specified term of service if they had worked diligently. Even so, slaves stole and smuggled gold, checked only by "their own personal loyalty to their masters—or, more probably perhaps, some profit-sharing arrangement."[32] Although some slaves accommodated themselves to bondage, others resisted by fleeing to the *quilombos* (communities of runaway slaves). Successful flight was not rare. Around midcentury in the diamond fields, for example, nearly a quarter of concessionaire João Fernandes de Oliveira's six-hundred-man slave gang had escaped.[33] At least 127 quilombos dotted the province of Minas Gerais, testimony to the lack of effective control over the slaves.[34]

Occasionally slaves rebelled, with the most notable examples occurring in 1711, 1719, and 1756. The rebellion of 1719 was potentially the most serious. Slaves from the African region of Mina launched the conspiracy and attempted to recruit Angolans. They planned an uprising for the Thursday night before Easter, anticipating that the Portuguese would be at Mass. The slave conspirators intended to break into the masters' homes and seize weapons and then kill all the Europeans, "beheading them without mercy" in the words of the governor reporting to the king.[35] After the slaughter, the slaves aimed to establish their own kingdom in Brazil and had gone so far as to choose a king, prince, and military officers before the Portuguese discovered the plot. Disputes between the Mina and Angolan conspirators over who would be king and prince led some of those involved to betray the scheme to the Portuguese, who arrested the chief plotters before the rebellion exploded. The 1719 rebellion was typical of other slave conspiracies in that it failed in the planning stage. The different African ethnic groups found it difficult to trust one another enough to cooperate and could not count on support from Brazilian-born slaves.

Ethnic and cultural differences divided the slaves from one another. One division was between Creole (a slave born in America) and *bossale* (a

slave born in Africa). Torn out of Africa, slaves arrived in Brazil as merchandise, usually with no family or other social support. Once in the goldfields,
they gravitated toward their own ethnic groups, if any were present, where
they could speak their native language and obtain comfort. Bondsmen who
spent most of their time with members of their own ethnic group were
slow to learn Portuguese because they typically conversed in their African
tongue.[36] Such ethnic bonds impeded a slave's assimilation into colonial
culture and worked against solidarity among slaves. Those from Mina and
Benin disdained Angolans, for example, and animosity between the groups
undermined the rebellion of 1719, although it is also true that certain Central
African cultural practices and beliefs survived long after slaves from that
general region arrived in Brazil.[37] In this the slaves were not much different from the paulistas and emboabas, who fought for control of the goldfields around 1708, or from the Basques and other Spaniards and Creoles,
who in Potosí waged a three-year battle against one another in the 1620s. In
Minas Gerais the Africans displayed greater solidarity because their ethnic
ties were stronger. This made them more dangerous in times of trouble than
the Brazilian-born slaves, who showed little unity.

The mining slaves' acculturation to the norms of Portuguese colonial
society was slow.[38] In frontier regions such as Minas Gerais, slaves vastly
outnumbered Europeans and as noted above often worked with little supervision from masters or overseers. In the mining districts the surprising freedom enjoyed by the bondsmen perhaps also worked against the rebellions.
Furthermore, the quilombos provided a social safety valve because the most
rebellious and independent slaves could more easily flee to them than organize and carry out a successful rebellion.

Although cities such as Ouro Preto and Diamantina existed on mining
profits, the gold and diamonds were predominantly extracted in rural areas.
This meant that the Portuguese government struggled to control those who
held mining concessions or claims and their slaves. Furthermore, quilombos
of runaway slaves resisted Portuguese authority in the mining region. The
quilombolos themselves often did some prospecting and mining. Garimpeiros
(illicit prospectors who lacked royal authorization) also prowled the rural
hinterland. Many were probably freedmen who lacked the resources and connections to obtain mining concessions. They worked outside the law, invading prohibited regions such as the tightly regulated diamond fields. Fearful
of smuggling, the government tried desperately to establish control around
Serro Frio and Tejuco (later Diamantina). It outlawed stores in the mining

camps or within two leagues of them and prohibited anyone from purchasing diamonds from slaves. But potential profits were too great to dissuade garimpeiros from seeking their fortune, even if prospecting placed them outside the law.[39] When Brazilian output caused European diamond prices to drop, the Portuguese government banned production altogether in 1734. Five years later the state took the diamond fields as a Crown monopoly, to be worked by a single concessionaire.[40] Such policies challenged the garimpeiros' ingenuity but did not eliminate them.

Although there were coercive elements to colonial Mexican mining, such as the repartimiento, debt peonage, and some use of slaves, labor there did not endure the institutionalized oppression found in the Andean mita or in the widespread slavery of Brazil. Colonial Mexican mine workers had not become proletarianized, but they were further along that path than was true for the Andeans. Mexican miners were less likely to retain agricultural lands in indigenous villages, in part because many of the northern mines lay in regions where there had been no dense sedentary Indian population. In the north, in fact, mestizos and mulattoes made up much of the labor force at the mines. To cut operating costs, many Mexican mine owners had farms to grow food for their mine workers, who otherwise would have had to purchase it on the local market.

If anything worked against proletarianization, it was the partido, or tradition of ore sharing, which the workers protected at all costs. It is not surprising, then, that owners tried to eliminate the pepena as both a way of increasing profits and of gaining better control over the workers by making them more dependent on their daily wages. One of the most famous events in Mexican mining history occurred in 1766, when Pedro Romero de Terreros, owner of the Vizcaína vein at Real del Monte near Pachuca, tried to abolish the partido. When combined with other worker grievances, his action provoked laborers to organize and strike in 1766.[41]

By investing hundreds of thousands of pesos to dig a drainage tunnel, Romero de Terreros had gained access to deep, previously flooded parts of the Vizcaína vein. A determined entrepreneur, he then set about exploiting his bonanza with an eye to enriching not only himself, but also the Crown. He requested more and more workers, and the government authorized him to use recogedores to round up idlers and press them into service at Real del Monte. Convinced that their set wage plus the partido ore gave the workers more than a fair share of the mine's profits, he cut wages and began to manipulate the partido. He increased the quota of ore miners had to produce before they were entitled to a partido bag. Suspecting that the miners reserved the richest ore for their own partido bags, Romero de Terreros then required them to mix all the ore together before taking the partido. In the summer of 1766, when the miners learned they could not be present for the mixing and selection of the partido ore, they angrily concluded that the managers intended to keep the best ore and give them the poorest for their partidos.

Driven to action by the owner's selfish innovations, some workers began meeting secretly to discuss ways of protecting their livelihoods. The recogedores' oppressive tactics heightened popular discontent. On July 29, several hundred miners stopped work and met at the Pachuca treasury office to protest Romero de Terreros's changes. Dissatisfied with the response of local authorities, they had a sympathetic priest draw up a new petition, which they presented to the viceroy, the Marquis of Croix. Discontent festered, then small riots broke out in the following month until Francisco de Gamboa, appointed by the viceroy, arrived at Real del Monte to mediate a solution to the crisis. Already famed for his commentaries on the royal mining ordinances of Mexico, Gamboa clearly understood both sides of the dispute. He knew that miners could not be allowed to cheat the owner by filling their partido bag with the richest ore. Nor could Romero de Terreros and the managers be permitted to take all the good ore, leaving the miners in poverty. His mediated settlement sided with the workers but required them to mix the ore so that owner and miner received the same quality.

This temporarily defused the partido dispute, but Gamboa was less successful in cleaning up the aftermath of the riots, in which a local official and a foreman had been killed. The violence left Romero de Terreros fearing for his life, and Mexican officials worried that the entrepreneur might abandon Real del Monte.[42] To mollify Romero de Terreros, whose capital and energy were crucial to Real del Monte's prosperity, Gamboa decided to inflict exemplary punishments on the strike leaders. Viceroy Croix, fearful the arrest and punishment of the strike leaders would reignite the violence and disrupt mining, recalled Gamboa and proceeded cautiously.

Made Count de la Regla in 1767, Romero de Terreros campaigned for permission to abolish the partidos altogether. He won powerful supporters, including José de Gálvez, the visitador general of Mexico and future secretary of the Indies, and his lieutenant, José Antonio Areche. Yet Viceroy Antonio de Bucareli refused to allow the count to eliminate the partido. Bucareli concluded that the partido was a traditional privilege enjoyed by nearly all Mexican miners. To tamper with it was to invite "general revolution" and economic disaster.[43]

The workers' actions at Real del Monte were, however, extraordinary. Elsewhere, resistance to management's demands rarely resulted in worker solidarity and united action such as a strike. At Potosí, mine owners groused about the kajchas and trapiches but received little support from the government when they tried to suppress this indigenous competition. The colonial state feared the Indians' silver production could not be replaced. Even at Potosí and Huancavelica, where exploitation and oppression were truly staggering, laborers failed to unite. By investing the mita with its authority and power, the government made it impossible for workers to attack the Andean system of forced labor without also challenging the colonial system itself. At Real del Monte, on the other hand, the strikers could aim their grievances at Romero de Terreros and his foremen without defying Spanish colonialism directly. The Real del Monte strike did not pose such a revolutionary threat.

The degree of proletarianization also affected miners' solidarity. It is unclear how much of Romero de Terreros's labor force comprised a proletariat: that is, workers who depended completely on what they earned from mining as compared with peasants who spent only part of the year at Real del Monte. If many were full-time miners, this would help explain their solidarity in face of Romero de Terrero's attempt to reduce their incomes. Andeans, on the other hand, tended to be part-time miners. Mitayos went to the mines, but they were generally peasants who worked their fields back in their home provinces when not mobilized by the mita. Their understanding of conditions at the mines must have differed from those who toiled permanently in the mines and refining mills. Although azogueros at Oruro tried to secure a mita for their mines, they never succeeded and had to depend entirely on wage laborers. Even there, a proletariat did not emerge during colonial times because the miners spent only part of the year producing silver and the remainder in their villages farming. They went to the mines to earn enough to pay their tribute, reparto debts, and a little extra to supplement their crops and livestock. A large-enough number needed those extra monies that Oruro had sufficient labor, if not a surplus.[44]

Colonial mining depended to some degree on pre-Hispanic labor systems, whether the Andean mita or the southern and central Mexican coatéquitl, that region's pre-Hispanic system of rotating forced labor. Mine owners and refiners needed workers, and it would have been surprising had they not resorted to such indigenous methods to mobilize labor. The Spaniards preserved important parts of the indigenous administrative apparatus, such as kurakas and *tlatoque* (rulers of Mexican indigenous communities), to facilitate relations between the conquerors and the vanquished. Local chieftains provided workers on orders of the new state, just as they had obeyed earlier imperialists prior to the Spaniards' arrival.

To serve as mita captain or kuraka was, in fact, a precarious endeavor. Caught between the competing interests of the village and the mining industry, the indigenous leader also had to protect himself. Some valiantly tried to shield their ayllus from abuse and organized the village to produce food-stuffs and other goods to sell so the community could more easily pay to fill its quota when potential workers died or ran away. Others behaved tyrannically, serving the demands of colonialism and their own lust for enrichment by stripping resources from the villagers. Pressures from the mita heightened tensions within indigenous villages.

Colonial forced labor contrasted qualitatively with the Aztec coatéquitl and the Andean mit'a. Toil in the mines proved far more arduous than pre-Hispanic building projects, agricultural labor, and mining had been. Of the coatéquitl's communal nature, historian Charles Gibson remarks on "the sense of contribution, the 'merriment' and 'great rejoicing' that attended it." Under colonialism, however, "labor tended thus to move from the social, moral and spiritual categories, in which Indians had placed it, into the economic or physical categories of Europe."[45] A cynic might wonder if the "rejoicing" that accompanied the pre-Hispanic communal labor of the coatéquitl did not, after a few hours or days, give way to a sense of drudgery and toil. Indians soon understood, however, that colonial forced labor such as the mita, rather than strengthening the community, undermined and destabilized it.

Forced labor, even brutal deadly labor, became the lasting image of colonial mining especially in the viceroyalty of Peru, as well as in Brazil's goldfields. In his *Crónica moralizada*, Augustinian friar don Antonio de la Calancha offered an assessment of Potosí's effect upon the Indians who worked there:

The mills have ground more Indians than ore, for each peso that is coined costs ten Indians, who die[;] in the entrails of the mountain resound echoes, from the blows of the pry bars, that with the voices of some and the groans of others, resemble the horrible sound of hell.[46]

Potosí officially produced nearly 900 million pesos of silver during the colonial period, and by the Augustinian's measure would thus have killed nine billion Indians. Calancha's charge is therefore an obvious exaggeration, although work in the mines and refining mills of colonial Potosí was certainly dangerous and often brutal. Another critic of the mita and Spanish actions in the Americas claimed more modestly, although he still exaggerated, that as much as eight and a half million Indians died in the mines and mills of Potosí.[47] Modern guides tell tourists to Potosí that the Spaniards used Indian slaves to dig the mines and process the ore. That image is partially accurate and also incomplete. At both Potosí and Huancavelica, the two great mita centers, wage earners worked alongside the mitayos. Peter Bakewell, who has studied colonial mining in the Andes and Mexico, concludes that free labor constituted about half the labor force at Potosí and in the parts of Mexico where the repartimiento existed.[48] In Brazil, African slavery predominated, but of a peculiar sort. Owners forced their chattels to produce gold but permitted many slaves a surprising degree of freedom in doing so. Meanwhile in northern Mexico, where free labor prevailed, mine owners and refiners managed to control workers to some extent through debt peonage and impressment by recogedores.

Mining clearly caused major demographic dislocations, reshaping colonial society as a result. The mita uprooted villagers and forced them to trek off to the mines. Many never returned home. Some Indians avoided service by emigrating to non-mita provinces. Even more striking was the forced movement of Africans to Brazil, then to the gold and diamond fields of the interior. Tens of thousands of Africans, mostly slaves, migrated to the mining districts. They and their descendants helped produce the racially diverse populations of Minas Gerais, Mato Grosso, and the other mining provinces. In Mexico, workers moved to the mining districts in the lightly populated north, where a semi-nomadic workforce evolved. Word of a bonanza elsewhere enticed miners to pull out of poor workings and migrate to the new site. Cities sprang up in direct response to demand created by the mines. That the city of Potosí came into existence at all bears clear testimony to the power of colonial mining to move peoples in response to market factors and state coercion. Potosí's population of 150,000 in the early 1600s made it the largest city in the New World, and it dominated the economy of Spanish South America.

Although mining was crucial to the colonial economies of Spanish America and Brazil, it would be wrong to assume that the mining labor force was large compared to the overall population. In the late eighteenth century, the Mexican industry probably employed fewer than fifty thousand workers, whereas a 1799 census for the mining population of the Peruvian viceroyalty found less than nine thousand.[49] Yet riches from the mines increased demand for foodstuffs, clothing, and other manufactured goods. Of his travels in the colonies, the great German naturalist Alexander von Humboldt remarked, "In all the places where veins of ore have been discovered, in the most uncultivated parts of the mountain ranges, in isolated and desolate plains, the exploitation of mines, far from impeding cultivation of the soil, has exceptionally favored it. . . . Without the establishments formed by the exploitation of the mines, how many sites would have remained deserted, how many lands unopened to cultivation!"[50] The circulation of silver and gold traveled through farms and ranches, in the packs on traders' mules, and into the holds of merchant ships.

Although mine owners sometimes complained about labor shortages, what they usually meant by "labor shortage" was a lack of cheap workers. Even the mitayos were not necessarily averse to working in the mines: They,

> however, would cooperate with their kurakas only as long as their wages, right to kapcha, and rescates were sufficient compensation for their hard work; and they would remain in the pueblos as long as the benefits of residence there outweighed the obligations. Indeed, when the Indians' own profits at Potosí again fell below an acceptable level, the Crown, the azogueros, and even the kurakas discovered just how difficult it was to make them work against their will.[51]

Mexican miners clearly responded to economic incentives, as did the mingados of Potosí.

The question remains, however, as to what degree mining prepared colonial society to flourish with the arrival of independence. American gold, silver, and diamonds did not necessarily generate self-sustaining economic growth in the colonies. Although New World mines helped transform social relations in Brazil and Mexico, they had less effect in the Andes. By the early 1800s, with independence on the horizon, Potosí was a faint shadow of its early colonial grandeur. Its population had dropped to a few thousand inhabitants, and much of the silver registered in its treasury office came from mines elsewhere in the province, rather than from the Rich Hill itself. The challenges Potosí confronted as Bolivia rose from the ashes of war show both the difficulties of breaking out of the colonial socioeconomic system and the potential that mineral wealth offered the new nation.

CHAPTER 5

New Nations Resurrect
Their Mining Industry

> Mines that, as they say here, are too poor to pay, too rich to quit.
>
> —Wallace Stegner,
> *Angle of Repose*

✦ BETWEEN 1808 AND 1825, INDEPENDENCE FREED THE LATIN AMERICAN colonies from Iberian domination and promised to liberate the mining industry from colonial modes of exploitation. In some places, however, colonial mining institutions, legal practices, and working conditions survived through most of the nineteenth century. The Nuevas Ordenanzas de Minería (New Mining Ordinances), adopted in Mexico in 1783 and transferred with little modification to the Andes shortly thereafter, provided the legal underpinnings of the Spanish American nations' approach to mining until the late 1800s. In terms of state controls, technology, labor systems, and capitalization, mining changed only slowly in the decades following independence.

Lack of resources prevented the new governments from giving the extraordinary support that Spain had provided to mining in the late Bourbon period, support that in some ways undercut other sectors of the colonial economies and propped up mines, whose costs of production would have been too high to compete in a free market. In the decades following independence, however, changes in the world economy created demand for nonprecious metals, and this eventually affected mining in Latin America. Even though Latin America's mining industry continued to emphasize gold and silver throughout most of the nineteenth century, industrialization in Europe and the United States diversified this sector by producing markets for copper, tin, and other industrial metals. By 1900, Latin American mining was transformed by the North Atlantic's appetite for such metals; by the application of new forms of energy, such as steam power and electricity, to ore extraction and refining; and by metallurgical innovations, such as the use of cyanide and flotation processes, which greatly improved the profitability of refining low-grade ores. In some countries, proletarianization and class consciousness among miners began to emerge, but these trends did not occur at the same rate everywhere.

Their wars of independence harmed, sometimes seriously, mining operations in Mexico, Peru, and Bolivia. The rebel and royalist armies destroyed machinery, killed draft animals, and damaged mines and refineries. In Mexico, more than a decade of war devastated mining. The hostilities created such economically risky conditions that many investors withdrew, depriving the industry of vital capital. When fighting forced mine owners to stop work, their diggings flooded, and the cost of draining pits was enormous. Workers fled, either for personal safety or because there was no employment. Many of those who did not flee found themselves drafted into one of the contending armies. At Taxco, for example, a royalist commander conscripted the miners to fill the ranks in his forces.[1] In many places, Spaniards involved in the industry had to emigrate, taking their skills and capital with them. The destruction and disruption at Guanajuato was so acute that annual output dropped from 5.3 million pesos in the first decade of the nineteenth century to only one million pesos annually in the 1820s.[2] Rehabilitating the industry proved a slow and costly process. Foreign capital would eventually underwrite the ensuing mining recovery, although early foreign investments proved surprisingly unrewarding. Nonetheless, mining continued to have a far-reaching economic impact in Bolivia, Peru, and Mexico, less so in Brazil, and for the first time the industry began to transform Chile.

Latin America, where per capita income exceeded that of British North America in the early 1700s, fell far behind the United States after independence. The gold and silver mines were in disarray, and high transportation costs impeded the export of most other products.[3] Bulky agricultural goods were expensive to export except from coastal or island locations. From the interior, only precious metals, gemstones, and dyes such as indigo and cochineal had high-enough value relative to their bulk to compensate for transportation costs. Spanish American nations that during the 1700s had depended on the export of silver and gold for economic growth lagged after independence as they continued to promote mining. Partly to blame was the retention of colonial-style policies that restricted the industry and drained it of profits.

Independence brought an influx of foreign capital, especially from Great Britain. The ink had barely dried on the new constitutions of Bolivia, Peru, and Mexico when British investors, in a speculative mania, created in 1824–1825 at least forty-six stock companies to exploit the new opportunities in Latin America. Some of these hoped to resurrect the Latin American mining industry. But too many of these enterprises aimed "to obtain precious metals from the Andean cordilleras, where there were few workers, no fuel for the fires, and no roads for the vehicles; technicians and machinery were hurried off in utmost ignorance of the almost impenetrable mountains and matted jungles that awaited them."[4] Fantasies about easy profits to be made in El Dorado bedeviled nineteenth-century investors, just as they had the sixteenth-century conquistadores.

Mining and the Repercussions of Independence

Among many companies born of such enthusiasm was the Potosí, La Paz, and Peruvian Mining Association, formed in London in 1824. The following year, its directors sent representatives to Bolivia to reconnoiter and purchase promising mining claims. They also shipped supplies and machinery to Arica, where they were to be hauled up to the mines. Among those sent was the company's secretary, Edmond Temple, who sailed from Falmouth, destined for Buenos Aires. He then headed overland to the Andes, enduring with good cheer the primitive trailside inns and their meager fare. Finally, in his journal for March 19, 1826, Temple recorded:

> Suddenly there appeared before me, in the distance, a high mountain of a reddish brown colour, in the shape of a perfect cone, and altogether distinct in its appearance from any thing [*sic*] of the kind I had ever seen. There was no mistaking it: it was that . . . mountain, incapable of producing even a blade of grass, which yet had attractions sufficient to cause a city to be built at its base, at one time containing a hundred thousand inhabitants;—it was that mountain, whose hidden treasures have withstood the laborious plunder

of two hundred and fifty years, and still remain unexhausted . . .
it was the celebrated mountain of Potosi.[5]

He rode on and entered the Villa Imperial.

When Temple reached Potosí, its abandoned buildings and ruined mills
bore silent testimony to the decadence of its mining economy and the travails
inflicted by late colonial rebellions and the wars of independence. The largest city in the New World in the early 1600s, Potosí housed only about ten
thousand inhabitants when Temple arrived. The city's already much dimin-
ished population had declined by half over the twenty-year struggle for independence. Where Indians and miners had once lived, large neighborhoods
lay abandoned. Mining continued, but on a much reduced scale. Of forty
refining mills operating in the late colonial period, Temple found only fifteen still grinding and refining ore in 1826.[6] Patriotic forces from Argentina
had occupied Potosí in 1810, executing Francisco de Paula Sanz, the energetic
and enlightened Spanish intendant who had kept Potosí's silver mills operating for more than twenty years.[7] Thereafter, marauding royalist and patriot
forces looted, vandalized, and ruined the azogueros' industrial infrastructure:
"Their expensive machinery has been wantonly destroyed by the enemy; their
extensive ingenios have been plundered and dilapidated; their mines, from
having been so long abandoned, have crumbled in, filled with rubbish or with
water, and their [financial] capitals, exposed to the arbitrary contributions
of military chiefs, have been reduced to a pittance."[8] Overall, the azogueros
were refining a little more than fifty thousand marks of silver per year, and
indigenous smelters nearly the same amount. Together, it came to only half of
Potosí's output immediately prior to the wars.[9]

Despite the crisis afflicting Potosí's industry, the British were confident
that their capital and technology would turn the fabled silver mines into
a bonanza for the association's investors. Coupled with the directors' ill-
founded naïveté and their overconfidence in Anglo-Saxon know-how, the
challenges of Bolivian mining almost immediately overwhelmed the association's resources. Back in London, the *Morning Chronicle* sarcastically
reported that Potosí was "all in an uproar, with the competition of English-
men for pits full of water."[10] Lavish spending ate up all the association's
capital before Temple and his colleagues even arrived in South America.
Creditors placed liens against the supplies and equipment in Arica, valued
at thirty thousand pounds, most of which never reached Potosí.[11] Temple
estimated that it would have taken at least three thousand mules to carry

everything up to the mines, if indeed the heavier machinery could have been transported at all.[12] Although the association bought rights to some of the more promising mines, nothing came of its efforts. This led inevitably to the company's bankruptcy, an event that made British investors wary of further Bolivian adventures. The only lasting result of this episode of British speculation turned out to be Temple's narrative of his journey to Potosí.

Several decades passed before foreign capital again became available for Bolivian mines; meanwhile, the industry stagnated. One historian wrote of Potosí: "Condemned to underdevelopment, without any sort of industrial infrastructure, with a population that had disintegrated even before the war, the city that had awed the Europe of Philip II was on the path of transforming itself into a peripheral mining settlement."[13] Other Bolivian mining districts faced equally dismal prospects. Oruro's mining infrastructure had suffered terribly during the Great Andean Rebellion of the early 1780s, and during the remainder of the colonial period, its output remained at half or less of what it had reached before Tupac Amaru II and Tupac Catari unleashed their revolts against the colonial state. By the 1820s, Oruro's mines lay flooded and abandoned, with no pumps to drain the promising deep pits.[14] Throughout Bolivia the scarcity, high cost, and irregular supply of mercury also hampered attempts to resuscitate the once rich industry. Huancavelica's paltry mercury output went to nearby Peruvian refiners, while the rest of Latin America had to obtain quicksilver from the Rothschild monopoly, which controlled the European supplies from Almadén and Idrija.

In addition to the dearth of capital once the British bubble burst, Bolivian mining confronted a thicket of other intertwined challenges, including a scarcity of labor and mercury, a primitive transportation infrastructure, and debilitating fiscal policies on the part of the government. Industrialization began to revolutionize mining, but Bolivia's difficulties hindered its adoption of modern technologies.

And Bolivia's mining was not alone in facing these daunting challenges. Of all the regions of Latin America on the eve of independence, Mexico seemed the most prosperous, largely because of its silver mines. Yet its mining industry had been in decline even before the wars began. Desperate for funds to fight its wars against revolutionary and Napoleonic France, Spain forced Mexican ecclesiastical institutions to lend it money through the Consolidación de Vales Reales beginning in 1804, which intensified an already severe specie drain from the colony. Operating capital that might have gone to the mining industry flowed instead to Europe. Then, in 1810 the struggle for independence erupted. Miguel Hidalgo's peasant army devastated the great mining district of Guanajuato, and violence spread to other mining areas. The result was disaster for the Mexican mining industry:

> Raids destroyed mine towns, the workings, the mints, and the archives. Transportation of bullion and supplies was hazardous at best. Mines filled with water, timbers rotted, shafts collapsed, roads fell into disrepair, and isolated mines were forgotten while prospectors left off their work. Finally, the Peninsular-born Spaniards and wealthy Creoles . . . , who held the best mines and most of the capital, were either expelled from Mexico by discriminating laws passed by the new government or confirmed in their predilection for landowning. "Mexico's greatest fount of wealth" had ceased to flow.[15]

Silver production in the 1820s was only 45 percent of what it had been during the first decade of the century. Forty years would pass before Mexican silver output returned to late colonial levels.

The silver crisis hampered the domestic economy, limiting Mexicans' ability to import and depriving the government of revenue.[16] The scarcity of silver heightened competition between internal consumers, who needed coins to pay workers and extend credit, and the external trade sector because silver remained Mexico's main export. The late colonial specie drain, which afflicted the mining industry, became worse after independence.[17] This situation in turn made it difficult to maintain the credit networks serving the mining industry. These had been far better developed than had credit mechanisms in the colonial Andes. But the silver drain out of Mexico meant there was less and less capital to underwrite the new nation's mining industry.

As was the case at Potosí, one new source of capital was Great Britain. British investors rushed to exploit the newly independent Mexican mines but had little more success there than they experienced in Bolivia. One British observer in Mexico complained of "the total ignorance of every thing [sic] connected with the New World, under the influence of which most of the capital, now employed in mining speculations there, was invested. . . . Vast sums were embarked in schemes, of which the very persons, who staked their all upon the result, knew literally nothing, except the name."[18] Most British investors, such as the Anglo-Mexican Mining Association and the United Mexican Mining Company, which tackled the rehabilitation of the Valenciana and Rayas mines at Guanajuato, struggled to generate any profits.[19] As a result, the speculative soon bubble burst in London before many could make serious attempts to resurrect the Mexican mines.

A few investors began operations, the most notable being the Real del Monte Company, which continued for a quarter century. It imported five steam engines to run pumps to drain the Real del Monte mines near Pachuca and another to power a stamp mill for ore-grinding, hauling machinery weighing fifteen hundred tons in from the coast. The British company ordered this mining equipment to be constructed in small components that could be bolted together at the mines. Even so, it was no small matter to haul the equipment from the coast to Pachuca. The company imported 150 British military wagons that had been used during the Peninsular War in Spain and 760 mule harnesses. It then took several months to improve the road inland from Veracruz so that the road could handle the wagons, and difficulties in acquiring sufficient mules and horses caused further delays. This setback meant that company employees were still on the coast during the summer months, when yellow fever typically afflicted the Veracruz region. Twenty of the 120 English workers died from the disease, along with uncounted Mexican laborers. Fighting off yellow fever at Veracruz, the British engineers and managers and their Mexican mule drivers slowly struggled inland, climbing more than nine thousand feet as they went from Veracruz to Real del Monte (of course, such an altitude would have been almost nothing in the Andes). The arduous trek required seven hundred mules and between seventy and one hundred workers and took five months.[20] Nonetheless, the company succumbed to a variety of ills, including the Mexican government's ban on foreign ownership of mineral rights, which national leaders had derived from the colonial mining code of 1783.[21] In fact, foreigners could not own land, which hindered the company's development of secure sources of mining inputs, such as fuel for the smelting ovens, timber for fortifying tunnels and pits, and food for its workers.[22] Before the discovery of mercury in California in the 1840s, the high price of mercury, three times more than it had cost in the late 1700s, limited amalgamation to only the richest ores: "Heaps of silver lie abandoned, because the expense of acquiring quicksilver renders it wholly unprofitable to extract it."[23]

Furthermore, foreign and local investors failed to understand that long-worked late colonial mines produced great quantities of silver not because the ores were still extremely rich but because they contained vast amounts of low-grade ore. In Mexico, which produced three million marks of silver annually on the eve of the wars of independence, each one hundred pounds of ore contained perhaps 2.5 ounces of silver. Because of the destrution caused to the industry during the wars of independence, investors in Mexican mining in the 1820s and 1830s had to rebuild a huge productive infrastructure to extract and process the ore:

> horse-whims, (Malacates,) magazines, stamps, crushing-mills, (arastres,) and washing-vats; to purchase hundreds of horses for the drainage, and mules for the conveyance of the ore from the mine to the Haciendas, (where the process of reduction is carried on;) to make roads, in order to facilitate the communication between them; to wall in the Patios, or courts, in which amalgamation is at last effected; and to construct water-wheels wherever water power could be applied.[24]

And in addition to all this, the flooded mines had to be drained and rehabilitated.

Guanajuato, Mexico's greatest silver producer in the late colonial period, suffered horribly during the wars of independence. When the British-backed Anglo-Mexican Mining Association and the United Mexican Mining Company began operations there in 1825, the companies found the task of restoring the mines overwhelming. Both the Rayas and Valenciana mines were flooded, and it took several years to drain and rehabilitate the underground workings. The English assumed "that *water* was the only obstacle to be overcome, and that the possibility of surmounting this, by the aid of English machinery, was unquestionable!"[25] At that point, British managers and investors discovered to their chagrin that the pits showed few signs of profitable ores and that they would have to undertake costly explorations if they hoped to find the bonanzas they had envisioned. To complicate matters further, Mexican mining law prevented them, as foreigners, from owning the mines. They consequently had to act as managers and capital-suppliers under long-term agreements that depended on Mexican frontmen with connections to Mexican politicians. Labor shortages also hampered work at Guanajuato because many miners migrated to Pachuca and Real del Monte, where prospects seemed brighter. The British attempted to impose new labor regimes on the workers, particularly to eliminate the partido. The miners resisted by refusing to work, although in 1834 tensions reached the point that the company persuaded the government to send military forces to impose order. Not until the 1860s were the mine owners able to limit, although not eliminate, the size of the partido taken by the miners.[26]

Peruvian mining recovered more quickly from the ravages inflicted by the wars of independence, but with its colonial character largely intact. According to British consul Charles Milner Ricketts, Peruvian mining in 1826 posed the same challenges to British investors and engineers as they had encountered elsewhere in the former Spanish colonies. Ricketts wrote of the "imprudence of their projects," the investors' failure to develop rational strategies for resurrecting abandoned mines, and their tendency to pay excessive salaries to managers and engineers, who were often foreigners, and to import heavy machinery that was nearly impossible to haul to the mines. He did note, however, that silver production in Peru had not dropped off as much as in Mexico. Such was due, he believed, to the fact that Mexican output was centered in several great sites that had largely been brought to a halt during the wars, whereas Peruvian silver came from many comparatively small mines, most of which had operated continuously.

In both Mexico and Peru the industry suffered from the sometimes forced exile of foreigners (in the Peruvian case, Spaniards, Argentines, and Chileans) and the disinclination of British investors to risk more capital in Peru once the initial speculative bubble had burst. The British considered the Cerro de Pasco Peru's most promising silver district, but many of its mines were flooded with water seeping in from surrounding lakes. In 1816, Peruvian investors had imported four British steam pumps to drain mines of the Cerro de Pasco, using coal from nearby deposits that were available at an economical price. They spent up to a million dollars to purchase the pumps, transport them high into the Andes, and finally install them at the mines in 1820. Initial results were very promising, although corrosion ate at the pumps and marauding armies damaged them. After independence, British interests hoped, without much result as it turned out, to claim the pumps as partial payment on the debts still owed by their original purchasers.[27]

Despite initial British failures, Peruvian silver production quickly recovered its late colonial levels. Output had declined precipitously from about 600,000 marks per year around 1810 to a quarter of that during the independence struggle. By 1840, however, Peru's annual production had again reached a half-million marks. Both the decline and revival were heavily influenced by the crisis and recovery at Cerro de Pasco, although Hualgayoc, Morococha, and other mining districts contributed sizable portions.[28]

Whereas in Spanish America independence provoked economic dislocation, such was not the case with Brazil. The wartime destruction, capital flight, and need to reorient foreign trade that Bolivia, Mexico, and Peru experienced did not affect Brazil. It remained an agricultural nation whose gold mining had already declined from the heights reached during the first half of the eighteenth century. Most of its exports continued to flow to Portugal and Great Britain, as was already the case during most of the preceding century. Nor did independence cause the violent political turmoil that wracked Spanish America.

Nonetheless, independence did provide the opening for some changes in Brazilian mining. In the 1820s, the lure of Brazilian gold attracted British capital, but as in the case of Spanish America, most of those early investments failed. Although the constitution of 1824 allowed foreigners to obtain mining concessions, Brazilian law subjected them to higher taxes and forced them to offer stock to Brazilian investors. In 1834, the London-based St. John d'el Rey Mining Company acquired rights to the Morro Velho mine, the only deep-shaft Brazilian gold mine to survive over the long term, under British direction. In at least one respect the company retained a colonial character: slavery. Although England actively sought an end to the slave trade, the St. John d'el Rey Mining Company was unable to obtain sufficient free labor and "reluctantly" turned to slaves. Indeed, the company eventually became the largest slave owner in Minas Gerais, the province with the largest slave population in Brazil. This practice brought the operation into open conflict with British antislavery foreign policy and public sentiment.[29] To ensure stability in its force of fifteen hundred slaves, the St. John Company gave them "rewards ... to encourage marriage, procreation, and good behavior."[30] With labor tranquility foremost in mind, the company's Protestant directors even worked to convert their slaves to Catholicism, in keeping with Brazil's dominant religious culture.

Meanwhile, Brazilian independence opened new mining opportunities in addition to gold. Despite Brazil's rich iron ore fields, Portugal had blocked its colonists from creating an iron industry. The second decade of the nineteenth century witnessed three attempts to establish an iron industry in Brazil. The first to produce iron, in 1812, was a small-scale factory established at Congonhas do Campo, Minas Gerais, by the German Baron Luis Guilherme von Eschwege. Hired in 1803 by the Portuguese Crown to run the national iron factories in Portugal, he had moved to Brazil with the court when it fled the French invasion of 1807. He assumed responsibility for reinvigorating the gold and diamond mines and establishing the iron industry. The second attempt to establish an iron industry, funded by the government, was in Minas Gerais at Morro do Pilar, where there were rich ore deposits but little wood to produce the charcoal needed to fuel the ovens. The venture soon failed as a result. The third attempt was at São João do Ipanema in São Paulo, and the area produced into the twentieth century. It initially operated under the direction of Swiss technicians while Brazil struggled to acquire the technological expertise needed for the new industry. Eschwege claimed to have established thirty iron mills altogether but bemoaned the future of iron production in Brazil. The ore deposits lay in the interior, making it necessary to provide costly transportation either for the raw materials or the final product, to make the iron accessible to its markets. Furthermore, he found little reliable free labor and experienced very high labor turnover rates. To solve that problem, he swallowed his scruples and bought slaves, complaining "it is almost impossible in Brazil for an industry to prosper when it depends on the labor of free men."[31] Its heavy reliance on foreigners for technology and industrial knowledge also handicapped the industry.

Brazilian independence brought few changes to labor in the new nation's mines, and the same was also true for workers in Spanish American mines, with the principal exception being the abolition of the mining mita. Even in Mexico, where foreign capital was perhaps most prevalent, colonial modes of mine labor persisted after independence. For example, the Real del Monte mining and refining complex relied on poorly paid, often coerced laborers, free and skilled wage workers, and salaried technical and administrative personnel until the mid-1800s. Mining of silver ores was chiefly the task of skilled workers, including barreteros, who drilled holes and set gunpowder charges to dislodge ore; timbermen, who fortified the underground tunnels and workings with wooden buttresses; mechanics, who operated the steam pumps needed to drain water from the pits; and blacksmiths, who sharpened tools. These workers were assisted by unskilled peons (equivalent to the colonial apiris at Potosí) who hauled the ore out of the pits to the surface, where it could be transported to the refining mill. None of this was much different from how it had been before independence.

Given the desperate conditions of the industry in those early years after independence, few mine owners could afford free labor, and the new government showed less inclination to coerce workers than had been common during colonial times. At Potosí, abolition of the mita inflicted a crippling blow on the traditional subsidy enjoyed by the azogueros. Mine operators and refiners no longer could rely on cheap forced labor or the cash paid by "silver mitayos" to make their operations profitable. Although the Great Andean Rebellion of the early 1780s had only briefly disrupted the migration of mitayos to Potosí, the mita received a death blow from the wars of independence. With royalist and patriot forces fighting over Potosí, the mitayos fled. To win indigenous support for the patriot cause, Juan José Castelli, commander of the Argentine forces that briefly "liberated" Potosí in 1810–1811, abolished the mita, but the effect of his decree expired when royalists drove Castelli and his army from Upper Peru. In 1812 the liberal Spanish Cortes abolished the mita obligation, and the decree reached Upper Peru by late 1813. The region's azogueros resisted its implementation, however, and a somewhat reduced mita seems to have survived until 1819. Simón Bolívar declared the end of forced indigenous labor in Peru and Bolivia in 1825.[32] Throughout all the tumult, the Indians regarded the abolition with great suspicion. On one hand, payment of tribute and labor in the mita had guaranteed their right to village lands, and they feared that the government, whether royalist or patriot, might use the end of the mita to threaten their traditional fields and pasture rights. On the other hand, while the struggle for independence remained in doubt, the Indians had no guarantee that the mita might not be restored, with local officials punishing the villages for not sending their levies of mitayos in the interim. The Englishman General John Miller, who fought for the patriotic forces to liberate the Andean region, noted: "Although these poor people had become entitled by law to the privileges of citizens, such was their distrust of the cruel whites, that they considered the abolition of the tribute and the *mita* to be some kind of trap to ensnare them into the commission of a fault."[33] The psychological burden of the colonial mita did not die quickly in the Andes.

Prodded by the complaints of silver refiners, the government created a voluntary "mita" in 1829, on the condition that operators pay travel costs. In fact, many peasants were willing to work in the mines part of the year, but they soon found the azogueros' expectations were outlandish: for a day's wage, frequently paid in exorbitantly priced merchandise rather than money, a miner often had to work twenty to thirty-six hours.[34] To some extent, however, the laborers' meager wages matched the operators' scant profits. The "voluntary" mita ended in 1832.

Elimination of the mita increased the opportunities of free workers. Mine owners complained of labor's lack of discipline. After independence, the workers' behavior recalled the colonial mingados' turmoil and lack of restraint. Desperate mine owners and mill operators tried through the legal system to force mingados to work. The refiners' guild urged magistrates and police to survey the city's residents to determine which miners were idle, arrest them, put them in chains to prevent their running away, and then assign them for work in the mines.[35] Azogueros even offered to provide manpower for such a roundup.[36] Following independence, Bolivian mine laborers continued to demand and receive advances on their wages and all too often spent the money to drink themselves into oblivion on the weekends, with the mines suffering rampant absenteeism on Mondays. Religious feast days and public celebrations ate into the days available for work, leaving perhaps two hundred work days during a year. Carnival was the worst offender, bringing a week or sometimes a fortnight of drunkenness and ritual protest against the mine owners.[37] And working days were reduced further by other conditions that cut into production, such as the lack of capital and mercury. Even when workers were available, mines could not necessarily operate, and when other conditions were satisfactory, laborers were sometimes scarce. Such difficulties place the colonial achievement in clearer perspective: the state provided cheap mita conscripts and mercury at stable prices.

Because they often ran out of mercury or operating capital, most mine operators could not permanently employ workers. However, most workers (especially those employed to haul ore with their llama teams) were first and foremost farmers who went to the mines during breaks in the agricultural calendar to earn money to pay taxes and buy goods they themselves did not produce, such as coca and aguardiente (distilled cane or wine liquor). But they gave first priority to their farms. Even when mine owners had good ore, mercury, and operating funds, they could not count on having sufficient labor during the planting and harvest season. Worker culture and economic conditions militated against transforming these part-time laborers into a mining proletariat, devoted exclusively to life at the mines and dependent on the wages earned there for their existence. Few miners became part of a capitalist proletariat, dedicated exclusively to mining and dependent only on mining wages for their livelihood.

Kajchas, who worked mines on weekends and feast days on their own account, also continued to play a critical role at Potosí, just as they had during the final colonial century: "Even if the kajcha system had vast colonial antecedents, . . . only during the first years of republican life [did it] reach its greatest importance."[38] Perhaps half the silver produced at Potosí in the 1820s came from the kajchas. By the middle of the century, many Bolivian silver mines were worked exclusively by teams of kajchas, who split the ore they took from the pits with the mine owners. Such workers no longer merely supplemented their wages with plundering the best ores on the weekends: the kajcheo had become the principal labor system in the mines. If proletarianization was a modernizing trend, the kajcheo was a countervailing path. As in colonial times, the kajchas either refined their ore in trapiches or sold it to mill owners. The kajcheo expanded in the wake of the mita's abolition.[39] It meshed well with Andean agriculture, for workers could spend part of the year at the mines and still return home to plant and harvest. Whether it be the kajcheo in the Andes or the partido in Mexico, ore sharing between mine owners and workers remained a feature of the Latin American industry.

Besides dealing with labor problems, silver refiners also had to tackle the shortage of mercury and sometimes devised new technological remedies. At the Cerro Rico, the Ortiz brothers devised an amalgamation machine to stir the crushed ore and mercury, thereby eliminating the labor costs of the *repasiris*, who had traditionally mixed the materials with their naked feet. Elsewhere in the province, where mercury costs were even higher than at the Rich Hill but where fuel was more readily available, refiners developed a refining method of mixing ore, mercury, and boiling water in copper

Figure 6. The patio process.
A worker uses horses and mules to tread the muddy mixture of ground ore
and mercury, a process essential to amalgamation. From T. A. Rickard,
Journeys of Observation (San Francisco: Dewey Publishing, 1907).

cauldrons. With this process, amalgamation took hours rather than the days or weeks required by the "cold process" traditionally used at the Cerro Rico and had the additional benefit of expending less quicksilver.[40]

Another obstacle to the recovery of the silver economy was the lack of capital. Mines were flooded and caved in, and refining mills were in ruins from a decade of destruction. High-grading or picking through colonial tailings for bits of rich ore often proved more profitable than trying to work old mines. Without the necessary capital, operators could not afford pumps to drain the mines or cut adits capable of draining the deep pits. Lacking funds to buy sufficient stocks of mercury from the Rothschild monopoly, refiners could not rest secure in their ability to process their ores. Everyone needed working capital to continue operations until richer ores could be discovered. Capital was not immediately available from local sources, and the speculative bubble of the mid-1820s discouraged foreign investors.

In this regard, Chile was an anomaly. Although Chileans had exploited gold, silver, copper, and mercury mines during the colonial period, they were the poor stepchildren of the Peruvian and Bolivian mining centers. Indeed, Chilean wheat and viticulture fed what vitality the regional economy enjoyed. But in the 1800s Chile quickly became a major mining player. Three factors aided its emergence: Chile was endowed with rich copper deposits, the deposits were located where they could be easily exported, and foreign capital was able to play a crucial helpful role. As a consequence, Chilean copper production exploded.[41] Indeed, Chile quickly emerged as a dominant producer, providing 40 percent of the world's copper output in 1852. Industrial demand for copper rose dramatically in the North Atlantic economies, and this stimulated more British and Chilean investment. One result was the construction of the first railroads in Chile to serve the industry. Yet Chile's mining code was based on colonial precedents and used the mining industry as a source of government revenue, placing an onerous tax burden on the copper miners.[42] Meanwhile, copper mining expanded rapidly in the United States, which imposed a tariff on Chilean copper imports in the 1860s to stimulate greater domestic production. By the next decade, U.S. technology had surpassed that available to the Chileans. In the 1880s, U.S. producers began to dump excess output in Europe to drive out Chilean competition. Although they had initially sent part of their ore to Britain for smelting, Chileans eventually built domestic smelters but had to import coal from the British Isles to fuel them. Stiff competition from the United States, which benefited from lower transportation costs due to its growing network of railroads and canals, and Chile's comparative technological backwardness dropped the South American nation's share of the world market to 5 percent by the end of the century.[43]

Chile's mining economy compensated for the decline of the copper sector with rapid expansion in nitrate mining. British, French, and even U.S. agriculturalists needed fertilizers, and the Atacama desert of northern Chile, southern Peru, and western Bolivia had vast deposits of sodium nitrates, which were also an essential component of gunpowder. Chilean interests began mining and exporting sodium nitrates in the 1840s. Meanwhile, Peru was exporting millions of tons of guano, a natural fertilizer consisting of bird droppings that had accumulated in tremendous quantities (on the Chincha Islands guano occurred in layers hundreds of feet thick). By the 1870s the guano boom had run its course, supplanted by Chilean nitrates. Competition led to the War of the Pacific (1879–1883), during which Chile defeated Peru and Bolivia and seized the nitrate fields of Tarapacá from Peru and those of Antofagasta from Bolivia. This gave Chile possession of the greatest nitrate deposits in the world. Even before the conflict, Chileans and their foreign partners had invested capital and labor in the nitrate region. Following the war, what became known as the Gran Norte underwent rapid development, with European investors helping build the necessary infrastructure. English companies controlled the industry, which was "a foreign factory, with Chileans deprived of all but a small portion of the enormous profits derived from nitrates."[44] The English completely dominated Tarapacá, while limited amounts of Chilean capital helped develop the Antofagasta fields. John T. North, the "Nitrate King," and others formed combinations or cartels to limit the companies' output and thereby support higher prices.[45]

For four decades, from 1880 to 1920, Chile nearly monopolized the supply of nitrates to the European market. The Chilean state imposed export taxes of 30 to 70 percent of the domestic nitrate price, and these revenues provided a major portion of government revenues. Market prices rose and dipped according to fluctuations in demand for fertilizer by European buyers. World War I and its demand for gunpowder drove nitrate demand to dizzying heights. When demand was high, there was often a scarcity of workers in the arid but nitrate-rich Atacama; when demand dropped, companies laid off workers, causing great social distress.

While Chile flourished, the mining industry in other Latin American nations found the going more difficult. Nowhere was this truer than in

Bolivia. Decisions by its government hindered rather than stimulated the industry's recovery. Although the tax on silver was lowered to 5 percent, half of what silver refiners had paid in the late colonial period, other factors added substantially to the burden imposed by the state. With the economy nearly moribund and with Indian tribute having been abolished, the government was desperate for funds. It turned to a traditional source of revenue, the silver mines. The government required that refiners sell all their silver to the state, at, it turned out, a price below market value. The difference between official and free-market silver prices cost producers an additional 10 or 12 percent in income. And that was not all. Upon receipt of the silver, the government minted it into debased coins that were worth less than 90 percent of their face value, then forced the mining industry to accept them at full value as payment for the silver. Thus, the cumulative cost of the official tax, the below-market price, and the debased coinage amounted to about 28 percent of the silver's market value.[46] These government-imposed costs drove silver production underground and prompted refiners to smuggle silver.

Despite all these problems, Potosí's Rich Hill continued to produce silver at low levels. Combined with production from the surrounding region, the level was sufficient to make the province of Potosí Bolivia's leading source of silver and provided the new nation with nearly its only means of participating in international trade. The city itself remained the foremost commercial center of the high Andes, drawing goods from northern Argentina, southern Peru, and Bolivian agricultural centers such as Cochabamba. Indeed, Potosí's silver monetized the regional economy, breathing life into the weakened traditional trading patterns that survived from the colonial period. English cloth and other manufactures flooded into Potosí, quickly saturating the market and supplanting many of the indigenous textiles.[47]

Only around midcentury did Bolivian silver mining begin to recover. By that time producers had managed to import steam-driven pumps that drained some of the old mines at Potosí's Cerro Rico and at Oruro and Corocoro. In the late 1840s mercury dropped in price due to the discovery of major quicksilver deposits in California (at the New Almaden and New Idria mines). This new source broke the long mercury stranglehold that European suppliers had enjoyed. Lower mercury prices, of less than half of what they had been earlier, made it possible to refine Bolivia's lower-quality ores.[48] Output began to rise modestly after 1850, especially following 1872.

Whereas mercury and other refining expenses contributed three-fourths of the cost of production before 1850, cheaper mercury helped reduce these expenses to less than 40 percent by the 1870s.[49]

Structural Change and Technological Innovation

For the first half-century following independence, Latin American mining retained its colonial roots, with the exception of developments in the Chilean industry. Few technological innovations emerged to transform mining, which generally remained focused on precious metals. After mid-century, however, embryonic changes began to transform mining in much of Latin America. First was the shift from gold and silver to nonprecious metals. Although silver and gold remained important, industrialization in Europe and the United States brought more and more demand for copper, lead, and tin. Second, productivity rose when mining companies invested in new forms of energy to supplement or replace the wind, water, and animal power and human labor on which the industry had long relied. In the early 1800s, miners hesitantly imported steam engines to run pumps. Later, they used coal-fired steam engines to grind ore in the refineries as well. Railroads, in turn, made it far cheaper to transport ore and finished products to ports for overseas export or, in the case of Mexico, directly to the United States. In the late 1800s the companies became great consumers of electricity to light the mines and run machinery. They also provided cargo for the railroads, which had been built in large part to serve the mining industry. Third, new technologies began to transform the refining process. The use of new reagents such as cyanide had as profound an influence on the industry's future as amalgamation had for silver production three hundred years earlier. All of this innovation had implications for labor, although changes in that area had to wait until the following century.

Latin American mining needed technological changes that led to greater productivity if it were to compete in the world economy and at the same time improve its workers' well-being and its stockholders' profits. Foremost among the innovations to affect mining productivity was the railroad, which could swiftly carry large heavy loads at relatively low rates.[50] Copper mining triggered construction of the earliest operating line: between 1849 and 1851 American entrepreneur William Wheelwright laid fifty miles of track in Chile to link the port of Copiapó with the copper mines of Caldera. The iron roads eventually opened remote areas for mining and

Figure 7. Tanks used at Guanajuato for cyanide processing of silver ores. Refining by cyanide replaced amalgamation in the late nineteenth century. From T. A. Rickard, *Journeys of Observation* (San Francisco: Dewey Publishing, 1907).

reduced transportation costs. They also made it possible to move large heavy machinery.[51] Their impact proved crucial as Latin American mines began to produce nonprecious metals such as copper and tin for the industrializing nations of the North Atlantic. In Brazil, before 1900 railroads had little impact on the mining industry, even though by that time the country possessed twenty-thousand kilometers of track.[52]

In Chile, railroads made possible the large-scale mining of nitrates and copper. Chileans laid track linking nitrate deposits with the coast, with the first such completed in 1868. Construction sped up after victory in the War of the Pacific. British capital built and controlled most of the lines, providing outlets to the nitrate industry. The most famous was the Nitrate Railways Company, operated by "Nitrate King" John North.[53] Constructing the railroads employed thousands of workers in sufficiently large force to compete with mining for labor and sometimes requiring the recruitment of laborers from Bolivia. Although railroad construction temporarily drove up mining wages by draining labor from the mines, over the long haul the iron horse lowered mining costs.

When Porfirio Díaz seized the presidency of the country in 1876, Mexico had only four hundred miles of track, two-thirds of which lay between the capital and Veracruz. About seventy miles of it lacked steam locomotion, the power there being supplied by mules.[54] The Díaz regime granted concessions to two U.S. groups, the Mexican Central and the Mexican National, that proposed to build lines linking central Mexico with the United States to the north. Their lines stimulated Mexican mining and enabled copper interests to export ores to refineries in the United States.[55] In a symbiotic relationship, profits from mining helped subsidize the railroads, and the trains made possible the Mexican smelting industry and determined the location of the smelters.[56]

Similarly, in the 1870s the Peruvian government awarded Henry Meiggs, an American who had helped build lines in Chile, contracts to the Central line, which ran from Lima to La Oroya, and to the Southern line, from Mollendo to Arequipa and on to Cuzco. Meiggs employed more than twenty-five thousand workers from Peru, Bolivia, and Chile, at times offering stiff competition to Peruvian mine operators for labor.[57] These railroads opened up rich ore deposits in the Peruvian highlands and helped revive Peruvian mining. The Central Railroad enabled large-scale copper mining at Morococha and stimulated silver production at Cerro de Pasco.[58] Foreign corporations controlled most of the mining and refining operations, just as they did the Peruvian railroads.

Nineteenth-century Brazilian railroad development served the expansion of coffee planting and export and in so doing also aided the internal economy by creating domestic markets.[59] Although Brazil's vast iron reserves were known, they remained largely unexploited; the country imported most of its track and locomotives. One railroad venture mounted in 1866 specifically to serve mining interests in the central region of Bahia province, where diamonds had been discovered, was the Paraguassú Steam Tram-Road. But it failed in 1869. By the time the British-capitalized Imperial Central Bahia Railroad assumed the concession in 1880s, the diamond boom had already ended.[60]

Railroads replaced tremendous amounts of human and animal power with energy generated by steam locomotives burning coal. Another revolutionary change was the introduction of electricity. It transformed refineries, illuminated mine shafts, drove pumps to drain the pits, and eventually made transportation both within and outside the mines more efficient. Mexican mines and refineries were first to experience the modernizing impact of electricity, introduced in the 1880s to light the mines. Thereafter, Mexican mining companies began to replace their Cornish steam pumps with electrical

Figure 8. Electric engine for pulling ore carts. Around 1900
electricity had begun to replace brutal human effort in modern
mines but required a heavy capital investment. From T. A. Rickard,
Journeys of Observation (San Francisco: Dewey Publishing, 1907).

ones and to use electricity for hoisting and moving men and materials and
for running air compressors and mill machinery. By 1910 electricity had
become a standard source of energy in nearly all major Latin American
mines. Electricity was critical to the large-scale exploitation of low-grade
ores and reduced labor costs. Electric companies and mines became inter-
dependent, and some mining companies operated their own power plants.[61]

Refineries also profited from the invention of new processes that made it
possible to extract minute bits of metal from huge quantities of low-grade ore.
Potosí and Bolivia again lagged behind, not only with relation to Australia
and the United States but even other Latin American nations. Australian
and British engineers and chemists invented the cyanide process and began
to use it to treat ores in the Australian goldfields by 1888. Refiners in Mexico,
which were in general foreign-owned companies, introduced it by 1894. The
process depended on the solubility of gold and silver in potassium-cyanide

Figure 9. The *tiro grande*, or central shaft, at Guanajuato's La Valenciana mine. Used to haul water out of the mine for drainage, it measured 33 feet across and traveled down 1,730 feet. Originally, horse-turned whims brought the buckets to the surface, but horses and whims were eventually replaced by electric motors. From T. A. Rickard, *Journeys of Observation* (San Francisco: Dewey Publishing, 1907).

and sodium-cyanide solutions. Refiners ground their ores into a fine powder, mixed it with water in a large vat to create a "slime," then added a diluted cyanide solution. Workers stirred the mixture, and the cyanide formed a compound with the precious metal, which could later be broken down by adding zinc dust. The refinery then precipitated out the gold or silver and melted it into bars. Compared to amalgamation, the cyanide process was inexpensive and permitted the processing of lower-grade ores than amalgamation made possible. Despite its use of a deadly poison, the process posed fewer environmental risks than might be supposed. Sunlight rapidly broke down the cyanide, although the cyanide compounds could last in tailings ponds for several years. By helping to eliminate the need for hand-sorting and concentrating of ores, the new technology enabled companies to introduce mechanized mass mining.[62]

The cyanide process marked a clear technological break with the colonial era, when mercury amalgamation offered the best means of refining low-grade ores. First in Mexico and then elsewhere in Latin America, gold and silver refiners shifted to cyanide. At Guanajuato the colonial patio process had not only survived but dominated throughout the nineteenth century, but by 1907 all but two of its refining plants had switched to the cyanide process.[63] By 1910 the process had become the dominant method throughout Mexico, with the cyanide imported from German producers.[64]

The cyanide process marked only part of the technological shift in refining ore. Suitable for precious metals, it did not meet the needs of mine operators producing copper, zinc, and lead, which increased in demand as industrialization gathered steam. When taken from deep mines, these were often low-grade complex ores (sulfides, for example).[65] They were difficult, if not impossible, to refine profitably with earlier methods that relied on the principle of specific gravity: the differences in the specific gravity of the mineral and the waste rock were used to separate the two. In the 1890s, however, metallurgists began to develop a flotation process that treated ores by "taking advantage of the surface tension of liquids and the adhesion of liquid films to the surface of the minerals."[66] Flotation added to the trend started by the cyanide process: huge quantities of low-grade ore could be profitably refined, making skilled pickmen less important to the extraction process than great earth-moving machines.

Different minerals had affinity for different oils and acids. The refiners put crushed ore into a large vat with the appropriate oil or acid and then forced air into the vat with big beaters. Bubbles clinging to the mineral rose to the surface, forming a frothy mixture that paddles skimmed off the surface. The waste rock, or gangue, did not attach itself to the bubbles and thus remained at the bottom of the vat for removal. Ores containing several minerals could be treated with a series of oils to remove each mineral. Flotation complemented the cyanide process, which remained the preferred method of refining simple ores.

First used in Australia, flotation spread to Mexico only in 1908 and became widespread among U.S. copper companies in Mexico by 1920.[67] The flotation and cyanide processes also had a momentous impact on labor. Companies no longer concerned themselves as much with ore selection and concentration during the mining phase. Mechanized extraction and transportation became the norms at many mines, rather than the traditional reliance on skilled miners to select high-grade ores. Engineers, geologists, and metallurgists, most of whom were foreigners, directed operations.

Compared to their Mexican counterparts, Bolivian refiners lagged behind technologically. They were still clinging to amalgamation at the end of the century, whereas the cyanide process, leaching, and electricity had transformed silver production in Mexico and the United States. Foreign companies, in fact, often chose to ship their ore out of Bolivia to refining plants in the exterior, where it could be processed much more cheaply. Such ore exports first helped pay for a cart road linking the highlands with the railroad on the coast in the mid-1880s and eventually for a railroad line itself. The exports reflected not only the technological backwardness of Bolivia's refining infrastructure but also the degree to which foreigners and their Bolivian associates controlled the mining industry.

Despite its backwardness, even Bolivian mining had recovered by the 1870s. First came a recovery of the traditional silver sector, with a rise in silver production in both the highlands and along the coast in the country's narrow corridor to the Pacific Ocean. Mining there in the coastal Atacama desert was not new: at Huantajaya, colonial miners had exploited tremendously rich silver deposits. The discovery in 1870 of silver lodes at Caracoles followed in that tradition.[68] In the highlands, silver mining experienced a brief renaissance, much of it attributable to new mines in the province of Potosí, such as Huanchaca and Colquechaca. Their output far surpassed that of the great Cerro Rico itself, which could not reclaim its colonial glory. This silver mining recovery peaked from 1873 to 1895. It had resulted in part from technological change, but capital was also crucial. Believing that commercial growth depended on greater silver output, Bolivian merchants and entrepreneurs such as Gregorio Pacheco, Avelino Aramayo, and Aniceto Arce began investing in silver mining in the 1840s in the hope that it would invigorate Bolivian trade.[69] Silver output grew. This made Bolivia more attractive to Chilean and European investors. Chilean money largely underwrote the Bolivian National Bank, which along with the Bank of London and South America provided capital for many mining operations.

The capital enabled Bolivian companies to import technology, although they lagged behind the United States, Mexico, and Australia. By the 1860s, steam pumps had become cheap enough to permit Bolivian mining companies to use them to drain old colonial diggings. Created in 1873, the Huanchaca Company had foreign funding, including a one-third ownership by expatriate Bolivian investors. Probably the most technologically innovative mining enterprise at the time in Bolivia, the company began using steam engines in its milling operations in 1878.[70] Steam engines also began to replace water mills for grinding ore. Their use at Huanchaca in the late 1870s, for example, led to a 9,000-percent increase in the plant's capacity. A railroad connecting Bolivia with the outside world had to wait to be built, but some mining companies constructed cart roads between the mines and refining plants. Carts represented a great improvement over the llamas and mules used since early colonial times.

In the history of Bolivian silver mining, 1873 proved a crucial year because the government ended its monopoly over the purchase of silver. Local mining interests and their foreign investors had gained enough political power to force the change. An additional offshoot of that clout was the government's decision to stop issuing debased coinage. Meanwhile, down in the Atacama desert, the Antofagasta Nitrate Company began construction of a railroad linking its mines at Salar del Carmen with the port at Antofagasta. This eventually resulted in the extension of tracks up into the Andes that connected Bolivia to the coast for the first time by rail. The tracks reached Oruro in 1892. These developments came long after the construction of railroads to serve the mines in Mexico and Chile but represented a tremendous achievement for the Andean industry, which could now easily transport mineral exports.

Bolivia seemed at the dawn of a new age of silver, made possible by changes in governmental policy, availability of foreign capital, importation of technology, and discovery of better-quality ore. Yet this prosperity proved remarkably short-lived. After decades of generally stable value, the international price of silver began to decline. The first shock occurred when Germany opted for gold over silver as the standard for its coinage in 1871. Two years later, it began selling off its silver stocks. Other nations followed the German lead, culminating in 1891 with the U.S. decision for gold. Although demand for silver remained strong in the Orient, the demand fell significantly in the industrialized West, undercutting mining's profitability in Bolivia and elsewhere.

When the industrialized world abandoned silver for the gold standard, the change had grave consequences not only for Bolivia but also for other silver producers such as Peru and Mexico. Peru's currency, the *sol*, was based on the price of silver, yet silver's value declined rapidly against gold. This precipitated a flight from silver, affecting all Peruvian economic transactions with the outside world. Within Peru, the prices of consumer goods and basic necessities were increasingly pegged to gold, yet wages continued to be paid in silver.

Even the rich, who were more likely to buy imported merchandise, saw their purchasing power decline, based as it was on silver. Urged to switch monetary standards, the Peruvian government at first resisted because it lacked both gold stocks and international credit. Yet each day its revenues dropped in value as citizens paid fiscal obligations in silver. Peruvians believed the nation possessed goldfields, especially in the province of Arequipa and at Carabaya, but estimations of their potential proved exaggerated when the silver crisis of 1893 provoked a gold rush in the ensuing years. The declining value of silver also led Peruvian miners to shift their attention to the nation's copper deposits. At Cerro de Pasco, for example, operators had earlier ignored copper, but in the late 1890s they began to exploit the deposits as silver values fell. Coal-fired smelters processed the copper, and llamas and mules carried it over a sixty-six-mile trail to the railroad terminus at La Oroya, from which it went to El Callao for export.[71]

Transformation of Mining Labor: A Beginning

Independence may have revolutionized the political landscape in Latin America, but it did little to change conditions of mining labor for most of the nineteenth century. Conditions in the mines and mills remained abysmal. Underground work remained arduous and unhealthy, in many respects resembling what mitayos and mingados had endured during colonial times at Potosí's Rich Hill. In Bolivia as late as the 1890s, for example, the Huanchaca Company's mines at Pulacayo employed young boys to carry ore to the railheads.[72] They earned a pittance, and the deadly dust soon filled their lungs, promising an early end to their lives. Although miners' families had some opportunity for education and medical care, wives and children spent much of their time toiling as high-graders (palliris) in the ore dumps for a pittance in wages, there being little else they could do in the mining towns to supplement family income. Indeed, labor shortages plus the need to have workers pick over ore dumps for whatever bits of silver might be rescued led companies to hire more and more women as palliris in the nineteenth century. Sometimes 30 or 40 percent of the workforce in Bolivia was female, just as was true during colonial times. Thereafter, however, their proportion began to decline as silver gave way to tin and mechanization of the extraction process made high-grading less necessary than it was at the silver mines. Only in times of emergency, such as the Chaco War (1932–1935), did companies permit women to work underground, where the men feared a feminine presence would anger the Tío, the deity who controlled access to rich ores and could protect or harm miners.[73]

Colonial-era production relations prevailed, with relatively little proletarianization of the workforce. Proletarianization, whereby mine workers lost their economic ties to their villages and to agriculture, implied that workers would become completely dependent on mining wages for survival. They would no longer have access to village agricultural lands, nor would they receive a share of the ore through the partido. Personal and even institutional and cultural links that had previously brought owners and labor together would disappear, to be replaced by the wage. This would lead to a growing cultural and psychological gulf between employer and miner. By the late nineteenth century, proletarianization coincided with mechanization of the workplace, stripping many jobs of artisanal or craft skills. The extraction and processing of huge quantities of earth and low-grade ore required a relatively few skilled machine operators and mechanics, plus many unskilled laborers. Yet by making workers dependent on their wages, proletarianization in the mines also tended to throw workers together and instill in them a greater sense of solidarity. They came to understand that they could only protect their interests through collective action. Return to peasant life was not an option. This situation eventually motivated them to form labor unions.

Meanwhile, owners also began a transformation of labor culture at the mines. They pressed the Catholic clergy to move midweek feast days to the weekend and tried to prohibit the sale of alcoholic drink in mining districts from Sunday evening through the work week. Workers often drank themselves into oblivion on Sunday, and as a result the mines suffered rampant absenteeism on Monday. Little by little, Saint Monday succumbed to the mine owners' pressure, and by the end of the nineteenth century, laborers typically showed up for work on Monday morning. Those who arrived late lost half the day's wage. In 1856, management in Potosí and Oruro created mining police and charged them with rounding up workers and sending them off to the mines and refining mills on Monday morning. A perhaps more impossible dream was the task of preventing miners from becoming drunk on workdays.[74] Some managers tried to ban alcohol from the workplace altogether. As companies gained better control of their labor force, they had to rely less and less on ore-sharing arrangements such as the kajcheo.

With the industry's prosperity in the 1860s and 1870s, even Bolivian miners and refinery workers and their families benefited from the relative good times. Companies built schools and hospitals to serve their labor forces. The better capitalized companies also paid higher wages and reduced the length of the workday from the abusive demands earlier in the century. Nonetheless, the higher wages paid by the companies had only a marginal effect on economic conditions in Bolivia because mining employed only a tiny portion of the population, perhaps 1 percent. Furthermore, only the most prosperous companies, such as the Huanchaca Company, could afford such generosity. Small and middling operations survived hand-to-mouth, with primitive technology.

Modernization of the refining mills also had social repercussions. Technicians oversaw the refining process and supervised large numbers of unskilled laborers. The technicians, as well as administrative personnel, were frequently foreigners brought in by foreign-owned companies or by domestic firms seeking to upgrade their engineering and metallurgical expertise. Employees in such staff positions usually constituted an enclave living in social and cultural isolation from the rest of the workforce. They and their families often had difficulty adapting to the new climate and culture, and it is not clear that their technological expertise always surpassed that of the locals they replaced.

Labor shortages bedeviled mining operations everywhere, and proletarianization of the mining force proceeded irregularly. Mine operators and politicians adopted a variety of tactics to provide workers for the mines: the *enganche* (labor recruiting, often through unscrupulous and coercive means) flourished in Peru and Chile, Mexican authorities permitted debt peonage, and at times mine operators persuaded their governments to send convicts to the mines to work off their sentences. These tactics were suitable for supplying unskilled labor but less useful for providing barreteros and other skilled workers. Coercion rarely proved successful over the long term, however, and conditions in other sectors of the national economies often pushed workers into the mines more effectively than the blatantly coercive methods. In Chile, for example, the copper mines and nitrate fields lay in the northern unpopulated regions of the country, far from Santiago and the major urban centers. Mines there could not depend, as could mines in Bolivia and Peru, on seasonal migration of peasants to the mines. What attracted Chileans to the mines were the wages and the alternative employment they offered to peasants who were expelled from lands in the central valleys, where agriculture concentrated more and more on export markets. To find work, many had to migrate to the northern mines. Wages, rather than coercion, drew workers to the Atacama.[75] In Mexico and Peru, proletarianization of the workforce proceeded very slowly in the mines because the workers remained tied to their agricultural roots. Villagers retained rights to share in the communal lands and consequently worked at the mines on a temporary basis. Once the Díaz regime began to attack the ejidos (communal land holdings) in the final quarter of the nineteenth century, it forced more people to move permanently to the mines, as they no longer had access to village lands. These large economic changes finally made it possible for a large full-time workforce to evolve at the Mexican mines, whereas Peruvian and Bolivian mining companies still had not managed to cut the ties between the workers and their agricultural villages.

Nevertheless, miners' wages were high on average, compared with what agricultural workers earned. Silver miners' wages included payment in money, goods, and a share of the ore. The percentage received in coin varied from place to place and time to time but probably amounted to one-third to two-thirds of the wage. Companies often forced workers to accept part of their pay in chits redeemable at the company store (the infamous *tienda de raya* in Mexico), a prime tool for leading the workers into debt and using the money they owed to force them to stay at the mines. Barreteros, or facemen, generally garnered some share of the ore they produced (the Bolivian corpa, Peruvian *huachaca*, or Mexican partido), although these payments were more common at silver mines than in camps where copper or tin were mined. Workers and company managers struggled and negotiated over rights to such ore sharing. On the one hand, when ores were rich, workers insisted they were entitled to it, and companies resisted them on the grounds that the company lost too much profit. On the other hand, when ores were poor, a share had little value to the workers who preferred a set wage, but companies insisted the miners accept the partido or corpa as part of the wage so that the workers had to shoulder part of the cost of low profitability. Wherever ore sharing flourished, however, proletarianization was retarded in its development. It also meant that workers did not depend solely on their wages for survival but were shareholders in the mine.

For this reason, the partido and its Andean equivalents constituted a major obstacle to the proletarianization of the mining workforce. Barreteros were risk takers, willing to gamble that they could find and extract profitable ores, as long as they received a share of their findings. Only when rich ores were gone did the barreteros submit to suppression of the partido. This foreclosed opportunities for risk taking and entrepreneurship by individual barreteros or small teams headed by a faceman in the large mines.[76] Such attitudes continued to flourish in small mines, where *buscones* (prospectors) and barreteros found and produced much of the ore.

As proletarianization continued to develop, worker solidarity began to spawn strikes, protests, and other signs of militancy in some, particularly Mexican, mining districts. The famous strike and riots at Pachuca beginning in 1766 established a heritage of worker protest in Mexico that was largely missing elsewhere in colonial Spanish America. The partido or ore-sharing arrangement behind the 1766 strike continued to afflict labor-management relations following independence. Mexican miners hired by the British-owned Real del Monte Company in the mid-1820s demanded that management reinstitute the partido as part of their payment and in 1826 went on strike to secure their demand. They insisted on a daily wage of four reals plus an eighth of the ore they produced. In response, the company offered to pay a piecework wage (*destajo*) according to the amount of ore the worker or team of workers extracted. Work teams would also have to supply their own tools and blasting powder. As the strike dragged on, the company relented, largely acceding to the workers' demands of late 1826, including restoration of the partido. It also agreed to provide equipment. The result was "probably the first formal labor contract of the Mexican mining industry."[77]

The strikes of 1766 and 1826–1827 heightened the solidarity of Pachuca–Real del Monte miners, and over the nineteenth century they banded together several times to oppose managers' attempts to abolish the partido, reduce wages, and lay off workers. Even after the British company turned control of Real del Monte over to Mexican investors in 1849, the district remained a hotbed of labor agitation and violent protest. A labor union was emerging, ably organized and led by barreteros such as Juan Rangel. The workers insisted "with the greatest insolence that they were owners of the Mines because they were in their locality and they had worked them."[78] That assertion, and the workers' claim on the partido whenever ores were rich enough to make it worthwhile were the chief bones of contention. By 1874, facing exhausted pits and poor ores, the Real del Monte Company tried to cut wages and force the union to accept the partido again. The miners went on strike for nearly a year. Workers at Pachuca and Real del Monte united, but in the end the company's precarious economic position forced them to accept the partido. The union dissolved, and many miners moved away to more prosperous mining districts. Soon thereafter, the rise of the Porfirio Díaz dictatorship made labor organization and strikes more difficult and dangerous.[79]

Subject to international prices for copper and nitrates, Chilean mining passed through booms and busts, which in turn wreaked havoc on Chilean miners and their families. Nitrate miners, thousands of whom had migrated to the arid wastelands of the Atacama desert, suffered tremendous hardships when foreign-owned companies laid them off during downturns in the world nitrate market. These same conditions in the nitrate and guano fields of Tarapacá provided ample opportunity for proletarianization of the workers. The region's pitiless desert ("It lacks water; it lacks soil and vegetation. There is only guano, living rock, and sand.") meant that almost no one lived there aside from the miners, and to exploit nitrate and guano, the companies had to recruit laborers from other parts of Chile, Bolivia, and Peru.[80] Wages were high, perhaps three or four times what the workers would have earned elsewhere, although offset to some extent by the great expense of living in the desert, where nearly all goods were imported. Workers became a real proletariat when they moved to Tarapacá, depending completely on their wages for survival. They had no family gardens or village resources to fall back on, as would have been the case among many miners in Bolivia and Peru, and the nitrate and guano fields were so distant that it was difficult for them to return to their original communities.

With the workers' mobility thus restricted by geography, the companies found it easier to make them adhere to work schedules and rules. In these conditions, a mining proletariat evolved in Tarapacá, and with it a sense that solidarity among the miners was the sole means of protecting themselves against the ups and downs of the mining cycles and exploitation by the foreign companies. The economic panic of the late 1800s cut into world demand for nitrates, and companies laid off workers and cut the wages of those they retained. The resulting tension heightened the workers' determination to defend themselves. When striking port workers at Iquique called on the miners in mid-1890 for backing, the miners provided violent support, unleashing Chile's first general strike. It contributed to the Chilean Civil War of 1891. The miners' oppressive treatment at management's hand led to increasing worker radicalization and Chilean socialism.[81]

Thus, during the century following independence, the colonial legacies of Latin American mining clung to the industry, but by 1900 its transformation had begun. Mines and refining plants damaged during the wars of independence were slowly rehabilitated, and capital from foreign and domestic sources made possible the expansion and modernization of the industry. Only after 1850 was there notable technological transformation, particularly with the construction of railroads to serve the industry and the introduction of new metallurgical processes that made refining of low-grade ores more cost-effective. By 1900 silver lost its dominance as nations switched to the gold standard for their monetary systems and the need for copper, tin, and other industrial metals surged.

The new economic realities imposed changes on the industry. One change was the mining of copper, tin, and other industrial metals to satisfy the industrial world's voracious appetite. Another was the drive to increase mining's productivity, regardless of whether the output was precious or base metal. The industry could raise outputs per worker by discovering richer ores, developing new extractive and refining technologies, utilizing more efficient equipment, and intensifying the exploitation of labor to maintain or increase production levels with a reduced number of workers. Just as the output of nonprecious metals had already begun by 1900, so to a certain degree had the march toward higher productivity. Before management and shareholders could achieve even greater productivity, however, they had to discipline mine workers and transform their culture. This obviously threatened the miners' way of life and inevitably led to bitter and sometimes violent resistance by the miners. In some regions proletarianization began, although its progress was uneven.

CHAPTER 6

The Technological and Social Dimensions of Modern Mining

Mineral economies are capable of generating vast wealth, and much of the frustration of societies dominated by them derives from their inability to tap this wealth and use it for other national productive purposes.

—John Hillman,
"The Emergence of the Tin Industry in Bolivia"

✣ SIMÓN I. PATIÑO RECALLED MANY YEARS LATER HIS ANXIOUS WAIT for the assay results of ore from his first mine, La Salvadora: "I believe that I never had a greater impression of discouragement. I didn't want silver. If it had been silver, it would have upset all my projects."[1] Given Bolivia's fabulous history as a silver producer, these were remarkable sentiments from one of its legendary miners. Yet in 1900, as Patiño waited, he prayed for tin rather than silver. Both his workers and even the assayer initially believed the samples to be silver ore. The following day the assayer announced the results: of the three samples, one was 47 percent tin, the second 56 percent tin, and the third 58 percent tin.[2] Patiño and his workers had discovered an incredibly rich vein of tin, perhaps the richest in the world; thus began the meteoric rise of Bolivia's greatest tin baron, a man who became one of the world's wealthiest men.

By the end of the nineteenth century, Latin American mining was undergoing a profound shift. In the 1890s silver lost value when the wealthiest industrializing nations abandoned it in favor of gold as a monetary standard. Miners turned increasingly to the search for base metals such as copper and tin that were in high demand in the industrializing nations of the North Atlantic. Meanwhile, Bolivia's first railroad, inaugurated in May 1892, arrived in Oruro, linking that city with Antofagasta. This opened new possibilities for the mining industry.

Patiño was the most dramatic human example of this transformation. A mestizo from Cochabamba, Patiño moved as a young man to Oruro, where he worked for a commercial firm before obtaining employment as a clerk for the Huanchaca silver-mining company in southwestern Potosí province. His experiences at Huanchaca infected him with a serious case of the mining bug and gave him an apprenticeship in the industry's possibilities and challenges. Returning to Oruro, Patiño worked for the Herman Fricke Company, which purchased ores to refine from miners and provided them with supplies and credit. In 1895, Patiño met Sergio Oporto, a miner who was working the La Salvadora mine near Uncía, in northern Potosí department and southeast of Oruro. A series of hopeful prospectors had worked the mine for at least a quarter century, but Oporto had found only low-grade tin ores, nothing to satisfy his dreams. To continue work, he needed funds and consequently entered into a partnership on August 26, 1895, with Patiño, who, obsessed with mining, invested his personal savings.[3]

Oporto oversaw operations, while Patiño decided to remain with Fricke until La Salvadora yielded better profits. The partners struggled on, finding no ores rich enough to compensate for their labors. After two years, Oporto gave up and sold his share to Patiño, who then left Oruro and moved to the mine itself to oversee its meager operations. He faced a bleak future. Although three other operators were exploiting tin deposits with some success lower down the Espiritu Santo mountain, La Salvadora lay high up, at an altitude of over fourteen thousand feet. Work there posed the same physiological challenges that miners had earlier faced farther south at Potosí's Rich Hill: frigid climate, oxygen-scarce atmosphere, barren landscape, and an isolated mining camp that had to import all its supplies. Finally, in 1900, Patiño's workers struck a rich vein of metal that they believed was silver, a disappointment for Patiño, who had convinced himself that his and Bolivia's future lay in tin rather than silver.

Tin had, of course, been mined for thousands of years; when alloyed with copper, it produced bronze. The early 1800s brought the discovery that cans made out of tin-plated steel did not corrode, nor did they emit harmful substances to contaminate food.[4] Tin cans made it possible to preserve perishable foods for distribution to national and even international markets. By the late nineteenth century, world demand for tin had increased dramatically. In addition to tin plate, tin was used in solder, alloys, and other chemical processes. Meanwhile, traditional European suppliers, such as at Cornwall in Britain, were largely played out, replaced by producers in Malaysia, Indonesia, and Thailand.

Bolivia had produced tin since Incan times. Although the viceregal market was small, colonial miners smelted some tin. They generally regarded it a nuisance that complicated their quest for silver, and dumps at colonial silver mines were filled with tin ores. After independence, tin output grew slowly, chiefly through exploitation of the old dumps near silver mines, rather than through the construction of expensive shafts for new ores. With the rise in international demand after 1850, however, interest in Bolivia's tin potential increased. By 1852, English tin smelters had begun to purchase Bolivian tin ore concentrates for processing in Great Britain.[5] Because these shipments had to go by mule or llama to the coast due to Bolivia's lack of improved roads, efforts to expand the industry were seldom successful. Mining costs in Bolivia's underground mines also tended to be higher than in those of Southeast Asia, where alluvial deposits were more easily extracted by dredging and gravel pumping. Nonetheless, as Patiño gained his precarious foothold at La Salvadora, Bolivia began to emerge as a major player in the world tin market. Around 1890, Bolivian mines produced about one thousand tons of tin per year; by 1905 output had increased to fifteen thousand tons.[6]

With his expertise gleaned at Huanchaca and his years at Fricke, Patiño understood how to take advantage of tin's prospects. He hired an engineer to run the mine and concentrated on marketing the ore and financing expanding operations. International investment capital enabled him to build his own modern concentration mill and install electric power. By 1905 he was the largest tin producer in Bolivia. Patiño then began expanding his mine holdings, purchasing the nearby Uncía mine and several other properties. Neither charcoal nor coal was available near La Salvadora to smelt tin, and consequently Patiño exported his ore to Europe for refining, but transportation remained a severe bottleneck. Mules and llamas were still used to carry out the ore concentrates and bring back necessary supplies. Recognizing this obstacle, he joined with other operators to fund the construction of a road to ease the transportation headache. Final resolution had to wait until 1921, however, when he completed a railroad spur to link the Salvadora-Uncía mines with the Antofagasta-Oruro line. This facilitated the importation of equipment and, more important, the export of concentrated ores.

Meanwhile, Patiño complemented his Bolivian holdings with expansion overseas. Perhaps because of his early association with the Fricke company, Patiño initially sold his concentrates to the German Zinnwerke-Wilhelmsburg smelters and eventually bought a part ownership in the refinery. When World War I erupted, he began selling all his ore to the British firm of Williams, Harvey & Company, which owned the largest tin smelter in Europe. To enhance his position and create a vertically integrated industry, Patiño maneuvered to gain control of Williams, Harvey. He joined with the U.S.-based National Lead Company and announced its intention to build a new smelter unless the Pearce family, which owned Williams, Harvey, agreed to sell. The British company gave in to his pressure and allowed Patiño and National Lead to purchase a half-ownership. Later, they bought the remaining half. Back in Bolivia, Patiño purchased the competing Llallagua Tin Company, located near his Salvadora-Uncía holdings. He then founded the Patiño Mines and Enterprises Consolidated, Inc., on July 5, 1924, with headquarters in the state of Delaware in the United States, close to the American capital, and where, he hoped, his company would be less subject to the vagaries of Bolivian politics. At that time his operations produced 49 percent of Bolivian and 11 percent of world tin supplies.[7] By the 1940s, his Siglo XX mine reportedly had seven hundred kilometers of galleries and eighty kilometers of railroad track underground. He generated more electricity for the mine and refining plant than was produced for the rest of Bolivia.[8]

Patiño played a critical role in the formation of the international tin cartel, the Tin Producers Association, and was elected its president in 1929. The Great Depression that began that year cut demand for tin and plunged Patiño and tin mining into crisis. In response, the association established the International Tin Control Scheme in 1931 to limit the tin supplies that reached the international market and thereby raise prices. Bolivia reaped generous benefits from the scheme. Its quota was larger than that of other producers relative to their potential productive capacity. By maintaining higher prices, the cartel enabled marginal underground Bolivian tin mines to remain in operation, despite their comparatively high production costs.[9] Economic

Figure 10. Mansion built for Simón Patiño in Cochabamba, Bolivia. Patiño never lived there, residing instead in Europe and the United States. In old age he tried to return to Bolivia, but poor health and death intervened to prevent his arrival in the Andes. The mansion and other buildings are now used by a foundation and research institute funded by his wealth.

conditions favored the cartel's success. Few countries produced significant amounts of tin, which was an essential industrial metal, and tin profits were crucial to those governments, which consequently were willing to cooperate in the cartel.

By the time he died in 1947, Patiño, the once-humble *cholo* from Cochabamba, was one of the world's five richest men. He lived grandly in Paris and on the French Riviera until the outbreak of World War II, when he moved to New York and took up residence in the Waldorf Astoria. In his eighties, Patiño tried to move back to Cochabamba, but ill health kept him in Argentina until his death in 1947, when his remains were moved to his homeland. Although Bolivia had other important tin producers, Simón Patiño was clearly the *rey de estaño* (tin king). Through his drive and genius, he expanded his stake in La Salvadora into a horizontally and vertically organized tin empire. In cooperation with other producers, especially in Southeast Asia, he had also organized a tin cartel that with some success controlled world prices by controlling output, foreshadowing later attempts to prop up export prices by cartels such as the Organization of Petroleum Exporting Countries (OPEC).

What was the impact of Patiño and tin on Bolivia? Many Bolivian workers around 1950 considered him, along with the other tin barons, a parasite who had stolen national resources for his own enrichment and left little for the Bolivian people. Mine workers resented the fact that he lived outside Bolivia, in their eyes siphoning off riches to his own and foreign pockets. Without a doubt, he and his fellow tin barons began a transformation of Bolivian labor. In the opinion of a Bolivian historian of mining,

> [t]he transition was brusque. In a brief lapse of time, it passed from the stone quimbalete to diesel motors, from hand work, slow and heavy, to electricity, from transport on llama back to the railroad. . . . This violent change did not give time for the gradual adaptation of thousands of peasants that in less than a decade traded the wooden plow for the mechanical drill.[10]

Although it is obvious that some of these changes were under way in silver mines before Patiño and the tin boom took center stage, the early twentieth century marked a new phase in Bolivian mining and hence in the Bolivian economy. Foreign capital and Bolivian capital that moved overseas predominated in the mining industry.[11] With the modernization of the industry, labor became more and more proletarianized. This transformed the traditional relationship between the miners and the rural communities from which they came. Simultaneously, workers for the great mining companies began to organize themselves into unions. Strikes provoked violent responses from the companies and the state, which led to further worker radicalization. Bolivian miners helped carry the revolution of 1952 to victory, and the resulting government responded by nationalizing the largest mines and creating the state-owned Bolivian Mining Corporation (Corporación Minera Boliviana, or COMIBOL). This ended the tin barons' control over the mines but failed, as we shall see, to solve the industry's problems.

Meanwhile, a similar process was unfolding in mines elsewhere in Latin America. Whether in Bolivia or Mexico, Peru or Chile, the industry underwent structural and cultural changes. Technological innovation led the way. At Bingham Canyon in Utah, Daniel C. Jackling, a mining engineer and metallurgist, saw profits to be made through open-pit extraction of vast quantities of low-grade copper ore. He used great steam shovels to remove the overburden or non-ore-bearing layer, then used the same machines to fill railroad cars with ore, which contained at most only 2 percent copper. Trains hauled the ore to a concentration plant, where the new refining technology of flotation made it possible to process the low-grades ores. By substituting huge machines, explosives, and open pits for human laborers tunneling away underground, profits could be made from low-quality ores.[12] Foreign and domestic capital vied for control of the mines, and corporations faced mounting resistance from leftist organizers and labor unions to their control of the workplace. Proletarianization changed women's economic and cultural role at the mines. The adoption of new technologies and machinery at the mines and refining plants confronted cultural resistance that companies tried to overcome by importing foreign managers and technicians, whose higher wages and better housing caused envy and xenophobia among the local workers.

Modernization of Latin American Mining Labor

Transformation of the mining industry had profound consequences for the industry's workers. Proletarianization was one result, as is clearly seen in the nitrate and copper mines of Chile. As the twentieth century dawned, the mining of nitrates continued to fuel the Chilean economy, but copper reemerged as a vital export. The former boomed until the end of World War I, then fell prey to the postwar depression and the development of synthetic nitrates. Meanwhile, radical nitrate workers formed organizations to press their claims for better working conditions. Chile had seized Tarapacá from Peru and much of Antofagasta from Bolivia during the War of the Pacific but faced difficult challenges in supplying labor for the nitrate fields. The Atacama's sparse population forced the nitrate companies to depend on migrant labor that came chiefly from Chile but was supplemented with Peruvians and Bolivians.

Most nitrate workers were single men from rural regions who migrated to the caliche (saltpeter, or potassium nitrate) fields of the Atacama desert. Many were former inquilinos, tenant farmers who worked the landed estates of the Chilean elite, or *rotos* (literally, the "broken"), impoverished itinerant laborers who wandered in search of employment. In Bolivia and Peru, miners had considerable mobility through maintaining ties to their villages and peasant culture. This worked against their proletarianization, which came more rapidly in Chile in part because its miners had no home villages to which they could easily return. In the nitrate fields, the caliche lay like a thick blanket five or ten feet below the surface of the desert. Companies based pay on piecework, according to the amount of caliche the miners extracted. Workers also toiled in the mills, crushing and grinding the ore and then dissolving and drying it. The companies provided primitive barracks-like living quarters and brought in food and drinking water, which they sold in the firms' pulperías, or shops. They paid workers in chits that were redeemable for high-priced goods at the company stores. To get money, the worker had to sell his chits at a discount, thus reducing his effective wage. Even so, real wages were higher than elsewhere and thus attracted laborers.

From fifteen hundred workers in the 1880s, employment numbers in the caliche fields rose to thirty thousand by the end of the century. Work was not steady, however, because in times of depression the companies simply laid off the laborers, who found themselves adrift in the desert with nowhere to go and no way to survive. The waves of unemployment caused by the intermittent crises caused great suffering and labor radicalism. Workers protested the companies' attempts to reduce piecework rates and their use of scrip redeemable only through the pulperías as a way of cutting workers' wages. Socialist and anarchist labor organizers found the Atacama's workers fertile ground for their organizing efforts.[13] They helped miners press for better wages and working conditions and for the creation of social networks and cultural activities. Key to early worker solidarity was the *mancomunal*, part proto-union and part self-help society. Anarchist and socialist organizers helped the maritime and railroad workers who serviced the nitrate fields establish *mancomunales* and then turned to the caliche fields, where the wild fluctuations in employment made miners receptive to the mancomunal.[14] In late 1907, labor leaders called for a general strike at Iquique, a main port in Tarapacá province for the export of nitrates. After several thousand strikers assembled in the yard of the St. Mary School, managers from the nitrate companies refused to negotiate unless the strikers returned to work. Government officials initially tried to mediate but soon convinced themselves that the strikers might turn violent and endanger public safety. Mayor Carlos Eastman and Interior Minister Rafael Sotomayor decided to launch a preventive attack to remove such a threat. They instructed local military commander General Roberto Silva Renard to use whatever means necessary to break up the strikes. On December 21, soldiers opened fire on the workers, who were still densely packed in the schoolyard. Machine guns killed hundreds and perhaps a thousand strikers in a horrific massacre, the worst brutality in Chile's history of organized labor.[15] Because the corpses were buried in mass graves, the total number of deaths is unknown. Government reports carefully accounted for the handful of military casualties but said nothing about the number of dead strikers.[16] With its leaders dead, imprisoned, or driven into exile and the rank and file traumatized, the Chilean labor movement took years to recover.

World War I tortured the nitrate industry with wild fluctuations in demand, and miners suffered intensely during the downswings. The war pitted Germany and Britain, the two biggest consumers of Chilean nitrates, against each other. In 1914 and 1915 the conflict disrupted shipping, cut Chile's ability to export nitrates, and idled thousands of workers, perhaps half the workforce.[17] Demand for fertilizer dropped, but once shipping resumed in 1916, Chile was able to recall many workers to produce nitrates for the manufacture of gunpowder. That boom died with the end of the war, however, and during the postwar depression unemployment soared. To defuse a potential popular explosion, the Chilean government began to provide housing for the workers in the early 1920s.

By the mid-1920s, the Chilean nitrate industry began to decline. The belligerent nations in World War I had bought huge quantities of nitrates for explosives, but with the end of hostilities, the boom faded. Furthermore, German chemists invented synthetic substitutes for the Chilean nitrates. The foreign-owned nitrate companies responded by laying off workers and cutting miners' pay. Anarchists and communists organized strikes against the companies, and labor became more radicalized.

Growing labor unrest meshed with Chilean political turmoil to create the conditions for another massacre of workers in Antofagasta province at Marusia and La Coruña in 1925. The nitrate companies were anxious about Bolshevist influences among the workers and also feared that Peru, Chile's foe during the War of the Pacific, was fomenting discontent in the nitrate fields. When workers called for a general strike, the companies persuaded the governor to arrest union leaders and close the communist and anarchist newspapers. Tensions mounted. In early June 1925, two policemen were killed when they tried to break up a meeting of labor organizers at Alto San Antonio, a town in the nitrate zone. Furious company and government officials were determined to avenge the deaths. Meanwhile, anarchist and communist activists worked to turn any repression into further radicalization of the miners. It took little to escalate the violence. At Marusia, miners used dynamite to kill several soldiers from a detachment that tried to occupy the mining community. Workers from

Figure 11. The great open pit at Chuquicamata in northern Chile.
Around 2000, this mine was the largest copper producer in the world.

Marusia and surrounding nitrate towns armed themselves but also sought to negotiate a peaceful end to the conflict with the companies and the government. The Chilean government's response came quickly. A large military force invaded Marusia, with weapons firing. Several hundred men, women, and children died. The state inflicted similar atrocities at La Coruña.[18]

Although nitrate mining's importance to the Chilean economy declined, that of copper had grown since the beginning of the twentieth century. Burgeoning demand for copper in Europe and the United States helped resuscitate Chilean mining. Nature had endowed Chile with great copper deposits in the nation's central and northern regions. In 1903, William Braden secured an option on what became El Teniente copper mine, a little more than fifty miles south of Santiago, and began to exploit it in 1904 through the Braden Copper Company, which was backed by funds from the Guggenheim family's American Smelting and Refining Company trust. Braden applied Jackling's open-pit method to Chuquicamata and some other Chilean mines, although El Teniente remained an underground operation. Over the twentieth century, Chuquicamata produced more copper than any other mine in the world.[19] With the decline in the importance of Chilean nitrates by the 1930s, development of the great copper mines by American capital reoriented the Chilean economy away from Europe toward the United States.[20]

The copper mines faced problems similar to those confronted earlier by the nitrate companies: scarcity of labor due to geographic isolation, a workforce composed largely of single men, and radical labor organizations. Geography again impeded labor recruitment for these large mines, especially those in the Gran Norte, such as Chuquicamata. Like labor in the nitrate fields, copper miners had trouble retaining ties to the countryside, and this sped proletarianization. Even El Teniente, located little more than fifty miles southeast of Santiago, lay at high altitude where labor was scarce. On the other hand, the new mining and milling techniques used large machines to handle massive quantities of low-grade ore and were more capital- than labor-intensive. The American companies needed smaller numbers of permanent semiskilled workers, rather than the large numbers of transitory unskilled laborers that were necessary in the earlier era.

One solution was for the company to build a town to house its workers. This provided workers with a place to live and also tied the miners to the company because they depended on it for the homes they rented. From 1916 to 1956, for example, the American Anaconda Company built towns in Chile's arid Gran Norte at Chuquicamata, Potrerillos, and El Salvador. The town at Chuquicamata had a population of thirty thousand. Company towns had a company store, with all the principal streets leading to it as the "social focus of the town." Such towns reflected the social hierarchy that prevailed at the mines, with the best section reserved for the foreign managers and technicians and physically separated from the miners' houses. Often, foreign workers received their pay in U.S. dollars and enjoyed social clubs, special seating in the movie theaters, and superior schools for their children.[21]

The foreign staff at Toquepala, a copper mine in southern Peru, found the amenities in the 1950s comfortable:

> Toquepala had a fine camp with an expatriate population of about 400. Well stocked supermarkets went far toward keeping folks reasonably content. There was a golf course with the most expensive golf carts—pickup trucks. There was a club house for frequent parties and a bowling alley and swimming pool. A theater with rotten acoustics provided more entertainment. . . . The town site was a source of many problems! At Toquepala there were some 745 single men and 1,456 married for a total worker population of 2,211. Campsite design was based on an average family size of six persons but that was a bad job of estimating. In addition to averaging more than four children

per household, the worker often invited other members of his family or even friends to come and live with him. This not only crowded the apartment, it made for the use of substantially more electric power, water and waste disposal than we had figured on. . . . Toquepala was an island of economic well being in a sea of poverty. Everyone who could get there wanted on the island.[22]

Toquepala was, of course, not a literal island, but it was an island of economic security and prosperity. The disparities between workers and managers and between the mining personnel and the surrounding population were obvious to the workers and created envy and bitterness. Meanwhile, foreigner engineers and technicians enjoyed their exotic Andean adventures in the secure comfort of the artificial town provided by the mining company.

In the company towns, management aimed to transform what it considered ill-disciplined, poorly skilled, lazy workers into responsible, semi-skilled miners and respectable husbands and fathers. The location of the mines worked against this objective, however, because the camps usually lay in isolated areas. Traditional family life had difficulty taking root; instead, a masculine culture of gambling, alcohol, violence, and prostitution prevailed. In 1917 at the El Teniente copper mine, for example, only 10 percent of unions between miners and their women had been sanctified by marriage. As in Bolivia, miners' excessive carousing on the weekends left them too drunk to work on Mondays.

To curtail such problems, companies rewarded those who cooperated and suspended or fired the recalcitrant. Companies required legal marriages of workers and gave housing only to those who had government marriage certificates. If they were discovered cohabiting with women outside the bonds of marriage, men lost their jobs. The companies raised wages and offered other incentives and bonuses to productive workers. They established schools, clubs, theaters, and other amenities. The goal was to help mining families flourish. Men with the responsibilities of a family, management's thinking went, would be less likely to engage in drinking, gambling, or illicit sexual unions. More important still, their concern for their family's security would make them less likely to confront company officials by striking.[23] Companies also provided opportunities for the men to obtain education and training that enabled them to rise vocationally and socially.

Mining towns also attracted women. Some found employment as laundresses and cooks; not a few became prostitutes. But the companies, with their conservative emphasis on marriage and stable families, made life difficult for single women. Many of them married miners, obtaining benefits and security but surrendering social and economic independence for dependence on their husbands and the company. Miners expected their wives to stay at home and perform domestic duties rather than seek employment outside. Daughters of mining families faced social boundaries. Their fathers generally did not want them to hold jobs outside the home because working single women were often assumed to be prostitutes. As a result, daughters commonly left home when they married, often before the age of twenty.[24]

Some individual successes occurred, and many miners joined the Chilean middle class, largely because of their higher wages, better dress, and the amenities of the company town. Yet the companies could not overcome the rebellious masculinity of the camps. Many miners abused their wives, gambled, drank, and failed to provide adequately for their families with their wages. They admired workers who defied company officials and demonstrated their masculinity not only through hard work and skill but also through rebelliousness. These miners also resented foreign managers and engineers, who lived in separate neighborhoods where housing, food, and other amenities were superior to those supplied to the Chileans. Such conditions heightened social tensions and labor militancy.

Proletarianization was also under way in Mexican mines and had led to militancy even before the twentieth century. As noted earlier, Mexican miners went on strike at Pachuca in 1766 and Real del Monte in 1826–1827. Their actions also contributed to the onset of the Mexican Revolution. In 1906 and 1911, work stoppages at the great Cananea copper mines in northern Sonora indirectly helped destabilize the regime of Porfirio Díaz, and once the Revolution began in 1910, miners striking for higher wages and better conditions added to the turmoil. As a result, Cananea proudly calls itself the cradle of the Revolution. Yet, as historian Alan Knight observes, "If Cananea boasted the most militant proletariat in revolutionary Mexico, the boast was more a comment on the moderation of the Mexican proletariat than on the militancy of Cananea."[25] The leaders of the famous walkout at Cananea in 1906 were desk workers, not underground miners.[26] Like their American counterparts just across the border in Arizona, miners at Cananea were more likely to unionize than to rebel. While copper prices were good, the regular pay and security offered in large mining camps usually sufficed to forestall revolt and political radicalism: "So long as work was available [miners] showed a distinct preference for work and pay over armed rebellion—even when proselytizing revolutionaries visited the mine."[27] An exception was the Avino silver mines near Durango, where poor management and insecure employment left workers more susceptible to revolutionary enticements. A few took up arms at Avino in support of the revolution in 1911, but even there the miners lacked ideological zeal and fought instead for better pay and working conditions.

Mexican miners thus provided a different window on the revolutionary spirit than Chileans did. Around 1900, mine labor in northern Mexico experienced significant gains in economic well-being. This did not mean that miners' wages were high relative to wages earned in the United States, for example, but compared to Mexican agricultural and industrial workers, they were making a good income.[28] Furthermore, their wages tended to be regular and reliable. All this undercut revolutionary sentiment among the miners when the Mexican Revolution erupted in 1911. During the Revolution, peasant violence sometimes disrupted mining, angering the miners and hindering a revolutionary linkage of the peasantry and the mining proletariat.[29] Unlike miners in Chile, Bolivia, and Peru, Mexican miners did not call for economic nationalism. The Constitutionalists, who emerged triumphant from the Revolution, aimed to exert more control over foreign-owned mines and garner more tax revenues from them.[30] In many cases the miners disliked, even hated, foreign managers and technicians, but they did not protest against foreign investment or ownership.[31] Neither the Constitutionalists nor the miners aimed to make radical changes in Mexico's mining industry.

Nonetheless, once it recovered from the great revolution of 1910–1917, Mexican mine work experienced a double transformation. Demands on workers intensified as the world's appetite for industrial metals grew and new technologies were introduced. Although foreign investment in the industry declined during the Revolution and its immediate aftermath, investment began to increase again in the 1920s. Between 1922 and 1925, foreigners controlled about 98 percent of Mexican mines, compared to 97 percent before the Revolution, and produced 95 percent of Mexican mining output.[32] Gradual technological improvements were introduced. Facemen began using pneumatic drills to extract ore, and mules and electric carts carried ores out of the mines. The flotation and cyanide processes introduced at the turn of the century remained the chief refining technologies.

Even so, traditional labor practices prevailed within the mines. Most mining continued to be underground work. Teams (*cuadrillas*) headed by drillmen contracted with the company to extract ore and were paid on a piece-rate basis.

When metal prices were high, the work teams sometimes managed to negotiate a share of the ore similar to the old partido. Such negotiations with management gave the cuadrillas an autonomy the workers would not have enjoyed as individuals and proletariats. The cuadrillas also trained and acculturated new workers not only in the skills needed underground but also in attitudes toward management. They were the bulwarks of resistance to managerial oppression and technological change ("a serious obstacle to technological innovations").[33] They resorted to work stoppages and slow-down strikes (*brazos caídos*). Their absenteeism sometimes masked resistance to management's pressures. Refinery workers continued to receive a customary fixed daily wage. Thus, little had changed in Mexico since the 1800s or even the colonial period with respect to the relations of production, except that the mining equipment and metallurgical techniques had improved.[34]

Nonetheless, provisions of the revolutionary constitution of 1917 both claimed subsoil rights for the Mexican nation, thereby protecting mineral and petroleum deposits from foreign ownership, and provided some protections to labor. Little by little, miners strengthened their position in relationship to management. When the foreign mining companies responded to the economic crisis of the 1930s by laying off workers, reducing wages, and increasing workloads, labor organized the Sindicato Nacional de Trabajadores Mineros, Metalúrgicos y Similares de la República Mexicana (National Mine and Metal Workers Union) in 1934. Through collective bargaining agreements, the union protected experienced workers from selective layoffs; forced the companies to include provisions regarding health care, retirement, safety, and life insurance; and secured wages that were among the highest in Mexico. To strengthen its bargaining position, the syndicate launched a general strike in June and July 1944, during which fifty thousand or more workers brought 105 foreign and national mining companies to a standstill.[35] Although it represented all mine workers, the union negotiated special provisions for individual groups, such as the drillmen and maintenance shops.

Nonetheless, the National Mine and Metal Workers Union could not resist two developments: *charrismo* and ongoing technological change. Charrismo was the slang term used for union leaders who sold out workers' interests through cozy relations with management and corrupt bargains with the capitalist class. No one epitomized charrismo more than Fidel Velásquez, head of the Confederation of Mexican Labor, the umbrella organization that included the National Mine and Metal Workers Union. For more than a half century until his death in 1997, Velásquez ruled organized labor in Mexico with an iron fist, keeping the unions in line with the dictates of Mexico's single ruling political party, the Partido Revolutionario Institucional (Institutional Revolutionary Party), or PRI. The mining industry needed to modernize its technology in order to compete internationally and used the state's political power to impose changes, despite worker resistance. Only the large mining companies, which usually represented foreign capital, large Mexican banks, and the PRI had the resources to make the necessary technological changes. These changes made their greatest impact in ore extraction, which shifted from subterranean galleries worked by skilled drillmen and their cuadrillas to pits gouged open by huge machines. Great rotary machines tore at the earth,

Figure 12. Huge truck for hauling low-grade ore. Such trucks are capable of carrying as much as four hundred tons. Compare this to the indigenous ore carrier of colonial times, who could handle at most seventy-five to one hundred pounds.

and mammoth loaders filled two-hundred-ton dump trucks. These innovations made the drillmen and their teams of ore carriers obsolete, although they survived in small and midsize mines. Small operations could not afford refineries to compete with the large companies and consequently had to sell their ore to the larger companies for processing. The effect of these changes on the workforce was monumental. It reduced the number of workers and increased productivity. It also completed the proletarianization of workers in the huge mining complexes. Unskilled peasant-miners no longer found a place there. "The machines and not the miner fixed the rhythm and intensity of the work. Besides the volume, size and weight of the new machinery, the worker's ability to control the danger and risk of his labors turned more difficult."[36] Companies needed educated, experienced workers who were able to operate and maintain the machinery. Labor at the mines became "more closed, limited, and stable."[37]

Proletarianization came more slowly in Peru and Bolivia's mines, in part because miners there maintained closer ties to their home village and agricultural lands. Even so, the technological transformation of Peruvian mining in the first half of the twentieth century disrupted the industry's links to the countryside, from which it customarily drew its labor. Throughout the Andes, mines had previously drawn workers temporarily from the peasant communities or sent them home in response to changing conditions. In colonial times they went because of the mita or because they needed money to pay tribute. Following independence, the peasantry continued to supply most of this region's miners, but they too spent much of the year on their village farms and worked at the mines primarily to earn tax money or enough cash to purchase a few commodities from the outside. Although mining companies often complained about the shortage of labor and its unreliability, the arrangement was also mutually beneficial: because of their agricultural roots, peasant miners had access to provisions (they even took food and animals to the mines with them), and the companies could pay them much lower wages than would have been possible if the miners had been completely dependent on their wages for survival. To attract and retain workers, Peruvian companies used *enganchadores* (labor contractors who enticed peasants with advances on their wages). Companies often advanced wages to workers and paid them in company scrip or tokens redeemable only in company stores in an attempt to tie them to the mines. But workers proved no more controllable than earlier generations had been and sometimes disappeared before working off the advances they had received.

The story of the Cerro de Pasco Corporation, the greatest mining enterprise in Peru during the first two-thirds of the twentieth century, illustrated
these generalizations.[38] Before 1900, many foreign capitalists had refused to
invest in the Peruvian mining industry because the nation's laws prevented
them from owning subsoil rights. Then, in 1901, the Peruvian government lib-
eralized statutes regarding mineral rights, permitting foreign ownership for
the first time. A mission of American geologists and mining engineers identified good investment opportunities in the central Peruvian Andes, and in
1902 U.S. investors established the Cerro de Pasco Investment Company. The
company then began to purchase small- and medium-size Peruvian mining
companies, focusing on silver and especially copper. In all, it purchased five-
sixths of the mines in central Peru and then modernized mining and refining technology to lower production costs and capture a larger market share.[39]
The company had difficulty, however, in attracting workers, even though the
Mantaro Valley region held a large population. Inhabitants of these indigenous communities generally owned small agricultural properties and lived
isolated from the coastal economy. With sufficient farm and pasture land
available to them, few immigrated to Lima and the other major Peruvian cities. Peruvian mining engineers, eager to see the mines prosper, lamented that
because of the Indians' "natural indolence, their tiny farms and small flocks
allow them to live more or less miserably without subjecting themselves to
the hard necessity of working daily for others."[40] Despite such ethnic stereo-
typing, most of the indigenous population of the Mantaro Valley had some
education, and illiteracy was lower there than in many parts of the Andes as
the twentieth century began.

The Company, as Cerro de Pasco Investment Company became known
in central Peru, resorted to enganchadores to marshal labor for its operations,
but breaking the peasantry's traditional ties to the land was difficult. Among
their tactics, enganchadores threatened potential miners with military con-
scription if they refused to sign up for a stint at the mines. The recruiters also
enlisted boys as young as ten or twelve, although the average age was probably fifteen to twenty, along with men as old as forty-five. Conditions underground were unhealthy and dangerous; between 1908 and 1920, for example,
the Company had 527 deaths due to accidents at its Pasco and Yauli mines.
This figure did not include the workers whose health was being stripped away
by silicosis and other work-related afflictions.[41]

Changes in Peru's infrastructure simultaneously undermined traditional
peasant existence and drove peasants into the Company's pits and mills.

By 1900, the railroad had arrived in the Mantaro Valley. Many native team-sters with their llamas and mules now found it hard to compete and turned to mining.[42] Despite the unemployment provoked by the railroad and the devi-ous methods used by the enganchadores, however, what normally played out was a ritual reminiscent of mine labor since colonial times: peasants went off to the mines for a few weeks or months to earn enough money for taxes, or to pay for village festivals, or to supplement the foodstuffs and other goods they produced on their farms.

Further change was on the horizon. In 1926, the Company opened its smelter at La Oroya, which badly polluted surrounding farms and pastures. Their lands contaminated, peasants now had to find other employment, and many ended up working for the Company, either at the smelter or at the mines. A few years later, after the Company installed new refining equip-ment to cut the pollution, it found itself in possession of valuable lands suit-able for ranching. These lands produced meat and milk, which the Company sold to its workers through its stores at subsidized prices.[43] The result of all this was, of course, to weaken the ties between mine laborers and their vil-lages. More than the enganchadores or railroad, contamination from the smelter caused the semi-proletarianization of the miners because by spoiling the village lands, the pollution made it impossible for the miners to obtain food and other necessities from their home communities. The Company provided subsidized, low-cost provisions and housing, hovels barely fit for habitation, particularly compared with the homes constructed for the engi-neers, managers, and technicians, many of whom were foreigners.

The Company had promoted the transition to a permanent labor force during the 1920s with the construction of houses, schools, hospitals, and other infrastructure for the miners and their families. In the villages, pop-ulation growth reduced the amount of per capita farmland available and supplied surplus labor for the mines.[44] By the 1930s, proletarianization had commenced in earnest: most miners worked permanently at the mines and smelters rather than moving there seasonally from their agricultural villages.

Company managers tried to prevent the workers from organizing, al-though protests, chaotic work stoppages, and other types of resistance rose. When Company representatives went to villages to hunt down runaways, workers who had taken advances from the enganchadores but had not worked off their debts, violent resistance sometimes erupted. Yet there was no real solidarity between the miners and the peasants. Growing tensions burst forth in December 1928 when a cave-in, caused by Company negligence, took the

lives of twenty-eight miners. The increasing proletarianization of the workers, the 1928 disaster, and the Great Depression that began less than a year
later fostered solidarity among the miners. Leftists, including Peru's leading
socialist activist, José Carlos Mariateguí, took up the miners' cause in newspapers such as *Labor*, and Peruvian communists helped them unionize. Until
the late 1920s, the miners had primarily pressed economic concerns, but they
then began making both political and economic demands. "Cerro [de Pasco
Corporation] miners seem[ed] the directive force of Peruvian workers, as a
sector of heightened workers' consciousness." They became "the prototype of
the proletariat in Peru."[45]

For a while the Company managed to impose its labor regime. The Cerro
de Pasco Corporation was the only Peruvian copper producer to continue
operations once the Depression began, although its output fell by more than
half. It responded to the crisis by laying off many of its workers and then
demanding more hours for lower wages from those still employed. In other
words, it intensified its exploitation of labor rather than introduce technological improvements to cut production costs. Yet these conditions did not result
in proletarianization of the workforce. To the dismay of union organizers,
many workers, who before the onset of the Depression seemed permanently
established at the mines and smelters, simply returned to their villages: "As
long as a return to the village economy continued to be a viable choice for
migrants, . . . their class loyalties . . . remain[ed] divided."[46] Demand for copper increased with the end of the Depression and the onset of World War II.
But Cerro de Pasco Corporation's dominance ended because new competi-
tors, such as Arasco, had more advanced technologies.[47]

As was true elsewhere in Latin American mining, technological change
forced large companies to replace the old labor system, both in the traditional underground as well as the modern open-pit mines. Heavy-equipment
operators needed to be educated. Skilled workers now used mechanical drills
instead of sledgehammers and hand drills to dislodge ore. Ore carriers gave
way to railways, carts, and electric engines. In 1956 the Company began to
exploit Cerro de Pasco by using the open-pit method to extract huge amounts
of low-grade ore, further reducing the need for unskilled workers. All this
weakened the bonds between miners and the indigenous communities from
which they had come. To secure permanent employees, management had to
provide higher wages because such workers could not maintain their links
to village agriculture. They thus became "full-time miners whose livelihood
depended on wages and commercial consumption," meaning that the nuclear

family housed at the mines had to rely on its own resources and the commercial market rather than those of its extended network of relatives back in their village of origin.[48] Miners began purchasing their supplies through the company stores and other commercial networks, cutting demand for village food and artisanal production. Work also required them to be able to read and write in Spanish, which weakened another cultural link to the village, where indigenous languages were the norm.

As in Chile, Peruvian mining companies tried to transform the miners' culture to adapt them to industrial-scale mining and to make them more docile. Companies provided schools for the workers, built housing, set up medical facilities, and taught modern hygiene. Such programs foundered on the rocks of resentment and unreachable aspirations, however. On the one hand, company-employed social workers tried to educate miners' wives in home economics and middle-class values. They taught the women how to make nutritious meals from prepared foods such as pasta, gelatin, and tinned vegetables and fruit. Each month the company inspected the miners' houses to make sure that the wives were keeping them clean and fashionable and that members from the extended family were not residing there. Instructions went so far as to include everything from "the 'proper' way to arrange calendar pictures on the wall to admonitions against the 'unsanitary' storing of vegetables in the wet, cool shower stalls," a practice adopted by the women who could not afford the expensive refrigerators recommended by the social workers. On the other hand, these campaigns of cultural indoctrination caused resentment because miners and their wives understood that the companies considered indigenous culture and traditions to be inferior. At the same time, families that adopted the middle-class values espoused by the companies were frustrated because these campaigns raised material and economic expectations but the company paid wages that were too low to allow the miners to achieve them. As a result, cultural education often added to labor unrest and radicalization.[49]

From one perspective, this cultural transformation helped create conditions through which miners' solidarity could emerge to challenge the companies and the state. As long as the workforce consisted primarily of peasants temporarily employed as miners, the workers tended to retreat to their villages when conditions at the mines became unbearable. But as the workers became more proletarianized, such retreat was more difficult, and they had no option but to organize and press for better working conditions, higher wages, and political clout. In Peru such agitation erupted, ironically enough, following the revolution of 1968, when reformist elements in the military seized power and began programs of agrarian reform and economic nationalism. Miners demanded that the government nationalize the great foreign-owned mining firms, such as the Cerro de Pasco Company. A wave of strikes placed the government in a difficult situation, because they hindered its attempts to attract foreign capital. Seeking to forestall class conflict within the industry, the state established both the Comunidad Minera (Mining Community), to mediate disputes over working conditions, wages, and other labor issues, and the Comunidad de Compensación Minera (Community of Mining Compensation), which was to invest 6 percent of net profits back into the industry in the name of the workers until they owned 50 percent of the industry.

Much of Bolivian mining remained underground rather than in open pits, meaning that it was more difficult to introduce the modernizing structural changes that transformed the industry in Mexico, Chile, and Peru. As they had done for centuries, Bolivian mine operators complained of labor shortages. What they really meant, of course, was a scarcity of labor at wages they were willing to pay. During the first half of the twentieth century, miners and their families never made up more than 3.5 percent of Bolivia's total population.[50] Consequently, many potential miners existed in what remained an essentially agrarian economy. But mining companies no longer had the mita to mobilize indigenous laborers, and most peasants were content to farm their village lands and herd their livestock rather than endure the rigors and dangers of mining. Mine operators had to offer wages sufficiently high to attract labor. At the high-altitude mines where few people lived, wages had to be higher than in mining districts with larger populations. Demand for workers fluctuated widely, depending on the world tin price. In the 1920s, for example, when prices were high, companies struggled to find enough workers, even recruiting foreigners. Most foreigners, however, were skilled miners rather than general laborers. With the onset of the depression of the 1930s, tin prices plummeted. Small mining operations, which employed few permanent workers, simply closed down. The large companies such as Patiño's struggled on but were forced to lay off as much as two-thirds of their workforce.[51]

In both good and bad times, some workers, chiefly mestizos and cholos, remained more or less permanently at the mines and received higher wages. These were skilled barreteros who dislodged ore and machinists who ran and maintained equipment both inside the mine and at the mill. Temporary labor was recruited primarily from among peasants and craftsmen in indigenous farm villages whose first priority was agriculture but who spent some weeks at the mines. They provided unskilled labor, hauling ore out from the mines in bags or pushing ore carts, digging trenches, dumping ore carts, building sheds, illuminating the mines, and performing other menial tasks.[52] Mining operations also employed Bolivian women and children. As they had for centuries, women toiled as high-graders, or palliris, digging through discarded ore to pick out any bits and pieces worth salvaging. An American mining engineer working at Potosí in the early 1940s described the high-grading operations:

> Old mine dumps were everywhere! Young Henry Rothschild, a recent emigre from Cologne, was in charge of the "kaachas." These were operations on old dumps, where maybe a man and his wife and children would work. The old dump would be worked over, piece by piece. As the man would fish out a piece of rock, his wife and kids would break it with a hammer and sort out the higher grade mineral. Henry would travel the Cerro each day astride his mule and leading a few burros. At each kaacha he would bargain for the kilo or so of concentrated cassitterite [cassiterite, tin dioxide] that the gang had accumulated.[53]

Just as their ancestors had done two centuries earlier, boys as young as ten or twelve carried fifty- or sixty-pound sacks of ore from the pits to adits and tunnels, where it could be loaded onto carts mounted on rails.

Men earned twice as much as women, and boys a pittance. To attract workers to high-altitude or very isolated sites, Patiño and the other tin barons set up company pulperías, stores where workers and their families could buy cheap supplies. Yet the companies provided as little as possible in terms of wages and housing. In the early 1900s at Cancaniri, for example, the Chilean owners invested virtually nothing in housing for their miners, who ended up living in caves and abandoned diggings. They had to drink water from the drainage ditches, and many became sick.[54] The companies also had to compete for labor with railroad construction and even distant Chilean copper and nitrate mines. In 1911, Bolivian tin mining employed about 15,000 workers, compared with 4,600 workers who were building the railroads. Meanwhile, Chilean enterprises also sought Bolivian workers and tried to hire them for work in Chile, offering them "new camps, conveniences, hospital, medicine, doctor and school, merchandise, groceries and provisions at wholesale prices," if they migrated.[55] Those who brought their families with them or who had carpentry or blacksmithing skills received additional benefits.

The Chaco War of 1932–1935 also caused serious labor shortages in the Bolivian mines. With many of the men in the army, mine owners had to take extraordinary steps to maintain tin production. At Patiño's Siglo XX mine, management even hired two hundred women for underground work. Many women had toiled, of course, as palliris, scrounging through the ore dumps to hand-pick any bits of profitable ore, but rarely as miners who worked the ore faces with sledgehammers and dynamite and who earned higher wages than they could as palliris. Mining culture even militated against it, with the men fearful that permitting women to enter the underground diggings would antagonize the supernatural forces that governed the miners' safety and prosperity. Most of the newly hired women were *carreteros*, however, pushing the ore carts out of the mines. Some of those women were intensely proud to be miners. One reported: "The girls sang and even danced on the elevator while they went to the upper levels in the womb of the mountains."[56] Once the men returned, however, the women were laid off and forced back to the ore dumps at lower wages.[57]

With the exception of setting up trade-based guilds, Bolivian miners had done little prior to 1900 to organize themselves to press for better working conditions or to exert political influence. A growing phenomenon in the early twentieth-century Bolivian mines was labor unionization, which reflected cultural changes occurring at the mines. Traditionally in the Andes, "the miners' peasant origins molded their social behavior at the same time it modified the trajectory of their proletarianization."[58] Peasants working temporarily at the mine combated oppressive circumstances by returning to their villages rather than by organizing unions to press for higher wages and better working conditions. But as the size of the permanent force grew, so did the call for unionization. Marxist labor organizers managed to organize workers at Patiño's great Llallagua mining complex that included the mines of Catavi, Siglo XX, and Uncía. In 1918, showing a nascent militancy, the miners went on strike. Five years later they formed a local union, the Federación Obrera Central de Uncía (Central Labor Federation of Uncía), headed by Marxist Guillermo Gamarra. Management and the government responded to the labor militancy by arresting Gamarra and other labor leaders. When the workers protested, military detachments opened fire on the miners, resulting in the "massacre of Uncía" in June 1923. This event heightened revolutionary sentiment among the workers. The Great Depression of the 1930s, with its resulting drop in tin exports and economic turmoil, as well as the Chaco War of 1932–1935, undercut the unions temporarily, but after the war ended, militant unionization began to reassert itself. Bolivian workers formed the United Labor Front in 1936 and excluded political parties out of fear they would coopt labor.[59] Unions also restricted membership to the more skilled and higher paid employees, barring many of the temporary workers and the palliris, with whom they felt little solidarity. These divisions among the workers made organizing mining labor difficult.

Once labor organization began among the miners, the nature of the mining camps reinforced and stimulated it, contributing to its combativeness and militancy. As their ties to their ancestral villages and to the peasantry weakened, miners found themselves increasingly confined to life in the mining enclaves. Class consciousness began, little by little, to develop. Writes E. P. Thompson, the eminent British labor historian:

> Class happens when some men, as a result of common experiences (inherited or shared), feel and articulate the identity of their interests as between themselves, and as against other men whose interests are different from (and usually opposed to) theirs. The class experience is largely determined by the productive relations into which men are born—or enter involuntarily. Class-consciousness is the way in which these experiences are handled in cultural terms: embodied in traditions, value-systems, ideas, and institutional forms.[60]

During nonworking hours, the workers socialized with their fellow miners. In addition to the geographic isolation of the mining camp, other factors added to the miners' solidarity and militancy. For one, they shared the dangers and risks in the mines. Their sense of Andean communalism, which they had brought with them to the enclave, added to their cohesion. Neighborhood councils and committees of homemakers also brought the miners and their families together.[61] All this gave them a shared sense, as miners, of occupational identity, yet they remained nationalistic and ethnic in their outlook rather than developing true class consciousness.[62] Even though many women worked at the mines, they rarely had much voice in the miners' unions. And although the male miners used the unions to press for better working conditions and higher wages, they did little to advance the interests of female workers, drawing a distinction between the needs of men, as heads of households and authentic miners, and the needs of women, as subsidiary labor.[63]

As the miners' unions grew stronger and more militant, they provoked violent responses from the companies and the government. To break strikes, company managers called on the government, which sent troops to the mines to arrest union leaders and force miners back to work. This led to brutality and massacre. One of the most infamous incidents occurred in late 1942 at Patiño's Catavi mine in northern Potosí province. Pressed by the United States, which was trying to build tin stockpiles for the war effort, the company feared a strike would prevent it from delivering the amount of tin stipulated in its contract with the North Americans. Management persuaded the Bolivian government to declare the strike illegal and to send in the army. Confronted by eight thousand demonstrators on December 21, 1942, the troops opened fire and allegedly killed hundreds.

The unions responded to the Catavi massacre by pushing for both economic goals and political power. When the media discovered that the U.S. government had tacitly approved the use of force against the miners, the Catavi massacre provided Bolivia's nationalist political parties with a rallying cry against the state and the tin companies. Most important among the parties were the Partido Obrero Revolucionario (Revolutionary Workers' Party) and the Movimiento Nacionalista Revolucionario (National Revolutionary Movement—MNR), which called for nationalization of the tin mines and championed the miners' cause in the aftermath of the Catavi bloodshed. Led by Victor Paz Estenssoro, the MNR courted the Federación Sindical de Trabajadores Mineros de Bolivia (Syndical Federation of Bolivian Mine Workers—FSTMB) and its leader Juan Lechín. The MNR worked to organize the disparate miners' unions into a political force that it could control for partisan political purposes. By this time, Bolivia's miners stood at the front of the nation's organized labor and pressed their demands through strikes and the occupation of mines. With the end of World War II, demand for tin dropped, and hard times beset the Bolivian economy. Another government massacre at Potosí in 1946 further radicalized the miners. The Catavi–Siglo XX mines laid off several thousand workers in 1947, including many labor organizers and agitators, in the "white massacre," so called because the miners lost their jobs rather than their lives. The next year, however, the government returned to outright violence in support of the company, when the army and the police killed more than eight hundred miners and their family members.[64]

During the twentieth century, the mining industry transformed itself to meet new economic realities in which silver no longer offered its traditional profitability and other metals promised better profits. Gold and even silver were still valuable, but the industry regained its economic health by producing copper, tin, and other industrial metals to satisfy the voracious appetite of the industrial world. Mining had to raise its productivity, regardless of whether the output was precious or base metals. In other words, the industry could increase the output per worker by discovering richer ores, developing new extractive and refining technologies, utilizing more efficient equipment, and intensifying the exploitation of labor to maintain or increase production levels with a reduced number of workers or by shifting more of the risks and costs of production to the workers themselves. Just as the output of nonprecious metals had already begun by 1900, so to a certain degree had the march toward higher productivity. For management and shareholders to achieve higher productivity, however, they had to discipline mine workers and transform their culture. This obviously threatened their way of life, and inevitably led to bitter and sometimes violent resistance by the miners. In countries such as Bolivia, Peru, and Chile, where mining remained a major part of the national economy, miners' unions demonstrated great power through their understanding of how to resist violently and passively the coercion of company and government forces. Technological and macroeconomic forces proved more difficult for them to withstand.

CHAPTER 7

Miners and Revolution

It is the soft drilled lung,
Beating and squeezing the millenarian rock
To tear out its heart of tin.

It's the dark blood torturing itself, flowing drop by drop on "Pacha Mama,"
on Mother Earth, mixing itself with her, bewildered
in spasms of anguish and misery.

But what does it matter? If they are left in reserve
As ten tons of lungs
and plenty of dark blood
for each ton of metal
that there is in the hidden entrance of the earth!

> —The Miner, by Hugo Patiño del Valle,
> from *Antología de poems de la revolución*

❧ IN APRIL 1952 THE MNR OVERTHREW THE BOLIVIAN GOVERNMENT IN
a bloody rebellion. To help defeat the Bolivian army in La Paz and Oruro, the
mine workers seized weapons and distributed them among the rebels. The
movement leaders promised great benefits to the mine laborers and to their
umbrella confederation of unions.[1] Once in power, the MNR established the
Central Obrera Boliviana (Bolivian Workers Central—COB), to unite all of

Figure 13. Monument to the Bolivian miner in Potosí. Holding a
rifle in one hand and balancing a pneumatic hammer with the
other, he symbolizes the militant legacy of Bolivian miners.

the nation's organized labor. COB in turn pushed the miners' agenda, including the nationalization of mines. Newly installed president of Bolivia Victor Paz Estenssoro quickly established a state monopoly for the sale and export of mining output. On October 2, 1952, he created COMIBOL to manage the mines that the state planned to expropriate. At the end of the month the government nationalized the Patiño, Aramayo, and Hochschild mines, "the tricephalic hydra," but left untouched small- and medium-size mines, whether owned by foreign or national interests.[2] Although the miners had urged the government to confiscate the largest mines without paying compensation, Paz Estenssoro and the MNR worried about going that far, in part out of fear of U.S. reaction. In fact, immersed as it was in the Cold War, the United States was alarmed about leftist influence among the Bolivian revolutionaries and saw the nationalizations as a threat to American economic interests.[3]

The upheaval in Bolivia was not the only time that Latin American miners supported revolution in an attempt to secure their political and economic goals. The great Mexican Revolution during the second decade of the twentieth century clearly had a long-term impact on that nation's miners. As mentioned earlier, the strike at the Cananea copper mines in 1906 had helped to destabilize the dictatorship of Porfirio Díaz and unleash the rebellion. Although mine workers did not play a significant role in the revolution itself, they benefited from the pro-labor policies of the government that it brought to power after 1917. Although much of the Mexican industry remained under the control of foreign, and particularly U.S., interests, the new government enacted legislation to raise miners' wages, provide fringe benefits, make the companies responsible for accidents, and limit the percentage of foreign managers and technicians. During the presidency of Lázaro Cárdenas (1934–1940), the state adopted a pro-labor stance that encouraged miners to strike in order to win concessions from their employers, who were required by law to pay workers' wages even while they were on strike. Although some Mexican miners toiled in small-scale diggings where conditions were primitive, at least 80 percent worked in larger operations with more modern equipment and methods. By the 1950s, these new technologies had raised the miners' productivity to a level four times higher than that of the typical Mexican worker and ten times higher than that of a Mexican agricultural laborer. At the same time, miners' unions were powerful and made it very difficult for companies to fire or punish lazy or incompetent workers. Of course, Mexican mine workers continued to be threatened by silicosis and accidents that made the industry dangerous everywhere, but they enjoyed high wages and good benefits compared to most other workers.[4]

In 1968, revolution headed by its military forces engulfed Peru. Emphasizing economic nationalism, the new regime promised to combat the exploitation of Peru by foreign corporations and encouraged labor communities that would spread the profits of the economy more widely among the workers. Peruvian miners rallied in support of the regime, expecting to receive better pay and work conditions. When such benefits failed to materialize, mine workers went on strike, causing considerable turmoil in the mining industry in 1971 and 1972. Although the regime talked of nationalizing the economy, which had obvious implications for mining since much of that industry was foreign-controlled, it delayed expropriation of the principal foreign mining companies. Only in December 1973 did the military government take over the American-owned Cerro de Pasco Corporation; then again, in 1975, it took over the Marcona Company, another U.S. enterprise. Having earlier formed a partnership with the Peruvian government, the Southern Peru Copper Company avoided nationalization.

Chilean miners and their unions played a major role in events leading up to the electoral victory of the Marxist Salvador Allende in 1970. Like their fellow miners in Bolivia, Chilean miners played a revolutionary role. In the 1960s, copper miners mounted more and more strikes against the U.S. companies that operated the largest mines. Once Allende had taken office, the miners rejoiced when Fidel Castro, the Communist leader of Cuba, appeared at the Chuquicamata mine in 1971 and asserted that through the miners the copper belonged to the Chilean people.[5] But after helping create the turmoil and the votes needed to raise Allende to the presidency, the miners made demands the socialist government could not satisfy. In a way, their actions should not be surprising. Miners' masculinity was defined in part by their rebelliousness and willingness to confront owners and government officials. Once the foreign companies were nationalized, the Chilean miners came to view managers installed by the new socialist government in traditional ways. Furthermore, copper miners held a privileged position within the Chilean economy compared to the rest of the working class. They earned above-average wages and therefore sought to preserve this elevated economic status rather than press for more universal leftist political goals. The miners also feared that the relatively inexperienced, more political managers and technicians sent in by the government to replace the foreigners it had removed by nationalizing the mines would undercut the industry's profitability and eventually endanger income and other benefits. Unable to meet the miners' wage demands and insufficiently radical to placate the unions' extreme left, Allende found himself faced with a mining strike that lasted from April to June 1973.[6] This strike was one of the chief factors that led to the military coup that toppled the Allende government later that year. Chilean copper miners who had supported Allende earlier but turned against him found themselves confronting a harsh and long-lived Pinochet-led military dictatorship.

Despite the promise of these revolutions and the improvements achieved in Mexico, benefits for the miners elsewhere in Latin America were slow to materialize despite revolutionary rhetoric. This was true in Peru and Chile and especially in Bolivia. In part, Mexico's exceptionalism resulted from the success of its revolution and the power the labor unions had within the institutionalized revolutionary government. Revolutions in the other mining nations did not have the long-term political impact on mining that helped miners in Mexico. An examination of labor in the mines of Bolivia and Brazil during the second half of the twentieth century shows how modernization and political change affected the miners.

The Bolivian revolution of 1952 had promised that agrarian reform and nationalization of the mines would improve the socioeconomic conditions of the peasants, the miners, and the urban workers, but hopes that it could solve the crisis of the mining industry soon faded. At the time of the revolution, world tin prices were high because of demand stimulated by the Korean War. When the war ended in mid-1953, tin prices dropped. Yet tin production costs rose, in part because of political and social factors. Miners' unions compelled the government to hire disabled workers and labor activists who had been fired before the revolution. The MNR further inflated the rolls of mining employees by forcing COMIBOL to reward political allies with jobs at the mines. Most of these political hires had no desire or intention to work underground and therefore swelled the list of the mining bureaucracy but contributed little to tin output. Overall, employment rolls increased 25 percent. In 1951, before the revolution, 55 percent of the labor force at Catavi had been inside the mine; by 1961, only 30 percent of mine employees worked underground, reflecting the increase in superfluous employment.[7] Production costs also rose because the miners demanded and received subsidized food and other goods from the COMIBOL commissaries in addition to wage increases. The miners' militias had played a key role in the victory of the revolution, and the MNR leaders feared to challenge them. Meanwhile, agrarian reform disrupted Bolivian agriculture and led to a drop in the volume of foodstuffs reaching market because the peasants now ate more of the food they grew on their new lands. This touched off a wave of inflation. COMIBOL employees, who obtained subsidized staples from the commissaries, discovered they could purchase food and sell it on the black market at a profit. This further undermined COMIBOL's financial position. City dwellers who now stood in long lines to buy food blamed the miners for the shortages and high prices.

The revolutionary government delivered short-term rewards to COMIBOL miners. Benefits increased by as much as 250 percent during the first year after the revolution, but mining productivity lagged and was down by 40 percent over the next decade. The quality of Bolivian tin ores continued to decline, as it had since the 1930s.[8] COMIBOL lost great sums of money rather than turning a profit, yet workers looked on their COMIBOL jobs as precious prizes to be passed on to their children.⁹ Max Ferrofino, a thirty-eight-year barretero, reported: "My father was killed in a cave-in in 1933 and I took his place, when I was old enough, 17 years ago. My son takes my place when I die. I have decided that it is better to die young with silicosis than to die hungry. A revolution is made so people won't die of hunger."¹⁰ Nonetheless, the competitive world tin market required that the industry cut labor costs by replacing workers with machinery. This solution offered the remaining miners the possibility of higher wages, but the union resisted it because the national economy offered the displaced workers little hope of finding satisfactory jobs elsewhere. Nor was there much incentive for the COMIBOL workers to increase their productivity. By 1964, the state considered COMIBOL an economic liability.

COMIBOL was only part of the Bolivian mining force. A pyramidlike hierarchy had evolved among the workers. At the top stood the employees of COMIBOL. By 1956, these numbered thirty-six thousand and included incapacitated miners who had been rehired and some union activists fired before the revolution. Because of COMIBOL's close ties to the political establishment, its employees were the labor elite—the best organized and most politically influential. The government built hospitals for them and schools for their children. They received subsidized food and merchandise sold in the camp stores and earned secure wages. COMIBOL workers jealously guarded entry to this privileged status, reserving it for their own children. Whereas COMIBOL members earned salaries, other mine laborers were paid on a piecework basis. Below the COMIBOL employees, the *veneristas* were concessionaires who formed cooperatives to work deposits they rented from COMIBOL. Although they sometimes received equipment from the state, veneristas received no wages or other benefits but earned only according to the amount of ore they produced. Lower in status than the veneristas, a third group, the *locatarios*, rented old underground mines and ore dumps from the government. They had to buy their own equipment, and their income depended on the amount of ore they extracted. Even lower in the pyramid were the *lameros*, slime workers who reprocessed tailings, and palliris, usually women who picked over mineral dumps, extracting by hand whatever small amounts of valuable ore they could find. Last were the *jukus* or *buhos* ("owls," because they could work in the dark), descendants of the colonial kajchas. They invaded mines at night, sometimes with COMIBOL permission and sometimes without it, to strip what rich ores they could find and smuggle them out before the government work teams returned to work in

Figure 14. Bringing ore out of a cooperative mine at Potosí's Rich Hill. Miners'
cooperatives began to exploit existing mines that were too poor for COMIBOL,
the state-owned mining company. Laborers dump the content of the car into a
walled-off sector that belongs to the coop partner for whom they work.

the morning. Sometimes COMIBOL miners worked as jukus, sneaking away
during their shifts. The jukus also sold their ores to the state.[11]

COMIBOL's profits and Bolivia's production depended on this mix of
wage workers and independents. On one hand, the locatarios and jukus
shouldered all the costs of producing the tin concentrates and had to sell them
to COMIBOL at a price fixed by the government. Profits from tin produced
by COMIBOL miners, on the other hand, were reduced by the miners' wages
and benefits, which often exceeded the value of what they had generated.

Locatarios and jukus scratched out a difficult living. A locatario, or
piecework tin miner, at Bolivia's Catavi mines in the late 1970s would arise at
6:00 a.m. and eat potatoes, rice, or pasta with broth and a little meat, if any
was available. The breakfast had to last, because his next meal was in the evening after he returned from work. Around 6:30 a.m., he and his companions

climbed on board a truck and traveled to the mine. There they spent a half hour or more chewing coca leaves to prepare themselves for the heavy work underground. Sometimes he worked in a difficult-to-reach section and had to crawl and drag himself seventy meters through narrow tunnels just to reach it. Once he was there, the area was so hot that he could only work for ten minutes and then had to rest for a couple of hours: "The heat seems like it is going to cook us, the air is used up and how many times will we have fainted, then, some companion helps us and drags us out."[12] As a locatario, he received no equipment from COMIBOL and had to furnish his own tools, explosives, and clothing. He could not afford a breathing filter to protect his lungs from the dust stirred up by the hammers and drills.

COMIBOL let locatarios work played-out sections of the mine, where it was unprofitable to use heavy equipment and the more highly compensated COMIBOL employees. These were often dangerous areas because COMIBOL did not maintain them and locatarios could not afford to maintain timbering or ventilation. The locatario scrounged for bits of low-grade ore. Some days he found nothing. Occasionally he discovered an ore pocket. He then had to haul both ore and dross back out through the claustrophobic tunnel, tying the sack to his foot and dragging it behind him. This was *tracción a sangre*, or bloody traction, when the miner was both the "means and the instrument of extracting and transporting the ore."[13] Outside, he concentrated the tin ores from what he had and took them to the mill to sell. His earnings depended on what he produced as an individual laborer and on depressed local prices.

The lower they were on the occupational pyramid, the less workers earned, with each declining level suffering greater economic desperation. Lack of employment in other sectors of the economy forced people into the mines, even when they earned only a pittance as lameros or palliris. The widows and abandoned wives of miners faced especially bleak prospects. They found themselves picking through ore dumps as palliris: "'We are paid $15 a month for this,' said Nellie Torrigo, a small, energetic woman in a black bowler hat and a discolored skirt, her hands and feet whitened with powdered rock. 'My husband died of *silicosis* at the age of 37, and I have six children. My older children help me work.'"[14]

At the end of the nineteenth century, women had made up as much as 35 to 50 percent of the labor force in Bolivia's principal mining districts.[15] Most worked at the ore dumps, where exhausting hours only added to time spent bearing and raising children, cooking and washing for the family, and caring for the home. Increasing mechanization of the industry, however, reduced these limited opportunities for women to work directly in mining. Even the need for palliris declined. More and more women found themselves restricted to the domestic sphere. In fact, one consequence of the miners' unionization efforts was a masculine "reconquest" of the mines from women.[16] Men and machinery purged the palliris and other female workers from mining. A miner's woman, it was said, needed to have three skills. One was the ability to sew and mend because labor underground tore a man's clothing and *copajira*, the mineralized, toxic liquid that dripped in the mine, ate at the cloth. The second was washing. A man returned filthy from his shift, his clothes encrusted with mud and stinking of copajira. His woman had to spend hours each week washing his work clothes. The third skill was cooking. She had to rise early, even before he did, and fix his breakfast of hearty soups, rice, potatoes, and pasta, so that he could leave for the mines before sunrise. His food also needed to be ready, hot, and filling when he returned from his shift.[17]

Family survival required more than domestic labor from the women. It sometimes included work related to mining, such as *juqueo* (stealing ore) and ore trading. But it often involved farming and herding and thus renewed the women's ties to the peasantry. Where possible, miners' wives planted gardens to grow food, both for their family's consumption and for the market. They made *chuño* (dried potatoes) and herded llamas and other livestock. Such activities were not always feasible at the mines and required women to herd or garden great distances from their homes. Sometimes they entered into sharecropping arrangements with peasants in nearby villages. Thus, whereas mining often drew men away from the culture of village life, the mining camps sometimes forced the wives and daughters to strengthen their ties with the villages and the agricultural-pastoral culture there.[18] Working as petty merchants rather than palliris, miners' wives also traveled in the countryside near the mine to buy potatoes and other crops from the peasants and to sell them sugar, coca leaves, and tobacco. To the Aymara peasants, such women were "ladies" (señoras) because they successfully mediated the cultural divide between the peasant village and the external world.[19] Women also knew how to press company and legal authorities for benefits: "They are firmly demanding but humble women. The best weapon they have is weeping. Tears in all and for everything."[20]

Nonetheless, the twentieth-century mines created a social and cultural gulf between the peasantry and the miners. An Aymara peasant might call himself *jaqi*, or person, but refer to someone who had abandoned the village for life at the mine as *q'ara* (someone stripped of his true identity and who had taken on a light complexion). The peasant-turned-miner quickly transformed his outward appearance and bearing, even if he could not erase his inner cultural moorings. He cut his hair and rid himself of the clothes that shouted "peasant." In short, he became a cholo, resented by the peasants and disdaining them in return. The cholo miner adopted a superior air to his relatives back home because they had "no money." At the mines the cholo and especially his children had opportunities for education that were lacking in the village. By the latter part of the twentieth century, most miners had some secondary education and some had even been to the university.[21] A peasant reported that q'aras were "bad (*malos*) because they had eyes (*layrani*) by which he meant they knew how to read and thus were powerful and ambitious."[22] Although both Quechua and Aymara speakers inhabited the region, only the former tended to work as miners. When Aymaras went to the mines, they generally did construction work or hauled materials rather than labor underground. Quechua miners were generally bilingual, able to speak Spanish but using their indigenous tongue among themselves and at home, whereas Aymara men usually lacked Spanish and resorted to Quechua when dealing with outsiders. The cultural gulf between the peasants and miners widened after 1952. Domitila Barrios de Chungara, a political activist from Siglo XX, remarked: "Most of us had been born in the mining community. It was the only life we'd ever known."[23] Yet some miners did not entirely dissolve their links to their home villages but retained some ties to the traditional culture of their villages.[24]

As the revolution and COMIBOL foundered due to corruption and inefficiency, worker militancy remained high at the Catavi–Siglo XX complex. The mines were huge, employing thousands of workers in difficult conditions. Despite some improvements, Bolivia's high-altitude mining camps remained bleak and forbidding, nearly unfit for human habitation:

> You must know a Mining Camp in Bolivia to discover how much man can resist! How he and his creatures hang on to life! In all the cities of the world there are poor neighborhoods, but the poverty in the mines has its own retinue; wrapped in an eternal wind and cold, it curiously ignores man. It has no color. Nature has dressed it in gray. The ore, contaminating the earth's womb, has turned it sterile. At four or five thousand meters high where not even tough grass grows is the Mining Camp. . . . Wealth is traded for misery. And there, in that cold, searching for protection in the mountain's lap, . . . are the

miners. Camps aligned with the symmetry of prisons, squat shacks, stone and mud walls, zinc roofs, dirt floors. . . . Hidden in those walls are the people of hunger and sick lungs. With neither past nor future, that misery enfolds everything. The Camp is simply there, lost in some corner; outside it, solitude; within, poverty.[25]

Most workers were semiproletarians. Their links to the countryside and their peasant roots had weakened. As a result, they could not fall back on agriculture to earn their bread and clothe their families. Even Catavi–Siglo XX's own economic difficulties fostered militancy by making conditions for the workers harder. And, of course, the workers imbibed the liquor of struggle and revolution brewed at the mines for decades.[26]

With the economy incapable of maintaining the revolution's hard-won gains, General René Barrientos overthrew Paz Estenssoro in 1964, repressed the militant miners, and favored the Bolivian peasantry. Barrientos outlawed the miners' union (the FSTMB), prohibited their strikes, and fired six thousand miners, claiming such measures were necessary if COMIBOL were to have any chance of prospering. At the end of June 1964, the army, rebuilt with U.S. aid, again massacred militant miners at Catavi and Siglo XX. The miners remained defiant, even though many of their leaders went into exile or were killed.

Looking back with nostalgia to the days when Patiño dominated Bolivian mining, some workers were "pleading with God that he [Patiño] return from the tomb, or that his son come and reclaim his patrimony."[27] In 1965, COMIBOL finally achieved a profit, but it took another three years for Bolivian mineral output to reach pre-revolutionary levels.[28] These achievements came at great human cost. Constantino Apasa, a miner at Siglo XX in 1966, earned only eighty U.S. cents per day to support a family of nine. He complained: "We now live worse than with Patiño. At least the old man understood that to get men to work you have to feed them decently, and there was plenty of cheap food in the *pulperías*. What we need is an armed uprising at the same time in all the mines."[29] The nationalized industry confronted difficult options. To compete internationally, COMIBOL tried to increase productivity by introducing new machinery, reducing the labor force, and cutting wages and benefits, and predictably harvested worker resentment and militancy.[30]

Despite its failures, the revolution did eliminate some aspects of the class system that had prevailed at the mines. Before 1952, a vast chasm separated the miners from management and engineers, who were generally foreigners. After 1952, Bolivians displaced the foreigners. But the economic and social gulf separating the mine laborers from the administrative personnel remained, and as noted earlier, the miners themselves were divided into several strata, from the COMIBOL employees to the veneristas, locatarios, palliris, and others down the pyramid of workers. Nor did COMIBOL provide sufficient housing for its employees; indeed, most mine housing dated from the Patiño era. Patiño's managers tended to hire single men out of concern that the company would have to care for widows and children of miners who inevitably died from silicosis and other job-related injuries and maladies. Thus, they did not provide houses designed for families. Only with the labor shortage caused by the Chaco War did they begin to hire men with families, but the construction of suitable living quarters lagged behind.

When COMIBOL took over the mines, it lacked resources to build housing for the workforce, creating the situation encountered by a team of Cornell University researchers in the late 1960s: At Colquiri, miners' families often had to accept a stranger in their home. The miners called it the "hot-bed system" (*sistema de cama-caliente*) because while one man worked, another occupied the house, depriving the family of privacy and often facilitating promiscuous relations with family members.[31] Even when the family had the house to itself, over sixty percent of miners' children had to share a bed with siblings.[32] Visiting a miner's home in the early 1970s, journalist Norman Gall encountered what he considered a typical housing situation:

> Nine persons sleep in two beds in one room. On one of the walls is an old soccer photo of Constantino with his teammates, and a wedding picture with a finely worked silver frame stands on the only table. A bicycle and a baby carriage hang from the ceiling of the room to economize in floor space. A broken window is stuffed with a burlap ore bag. Above that window outside the house two dried fish heads hang from a wire for good luck. As in most of the miners' houses, the kitchen is outdoors on the small porch that is crowded with wash basins and brushwood brought in from the *altiplano*.[33]

In Siglo XX miners' houses, built years earlier by the company, the COMIBOL families had electricity but shared showers and latrines. The houses lacked running water, which wives and children had to carry from the public spigots.[34]

Thus, by the 1970s Bolivian mining and its workers had experienced a profound transformation. The miners' militancy placed them in the front ranks of the revolution, but nationalization of the great mines proved to be no cure of the labor abuses. State ownership of the mines, in fact, created new challenges for the industry and the workers. In some ways, for the workers at least, conditions remained remarkably similar to what had existed since colonial times, even if the output had largely shifted from precious to industrial metals. To maintain cheap output levels, the government and the mines' owners shifted the risks and costs wherever possible to the workers themselves. COMIBOL lost money in the decades following the 1952 revolution because its workforce became inflated with salaried workers (almost a third in 1967 had desk jobs), many of whom were not even engaged in the extraction or refining of ore. Yet mine owners and the state were able to offset the decline in ore quality by paying piecework rates to veneristas, locatarios, lameros, palliris, and jukus, who produced as much as half the output. Owners and managers knew that miners worked harder when paid by the piece rather than on an hourly system. Four groups benefited from piece-rate pay: the government, COMIBOL, mine owners, and poor peasants who eked out small earnings from the mines to supplement their agricultural incomes.[35] There was no shortage of the last of these, for "when there are few alternative sources of employment, an old mine can keep people occupied forever."[36] Despite the poor conditions, Bolivia's mines continued to beckon to workers who could find no work elsewhere.

During the twentieth century, Brazilian mines represented the most modern and the most primitive conditions for workers. Mining made up a surprisingly small portion of Brazil's gross national product: 3 percent in 1983 compared with 14 percent for Chile and 19 percent for Mexico and Peru. Mineral production was substantially more important to the economies of Chile, Mexico, and Peru than to Brazil's economy, reflecting the importance of Brazilian agriculture, the success of its industrialization, and its comparative economic diversity compared with some of the other Latin American mining nations.

Nevertheless, the Brazilian interior held vast mineral resources, including huge reserves of iron (perhaps a quarter of the world total), manganese, tin, copper, bauxite, and gemstones. Yet access to these ore deposits was extremely difficult. Given the nation's lack of roads, the export of minerals awaited the construction of railroads. Compared to its Andean neighbors, Brazil's economy remained less dependent on mining, which consequently made it more difficult to secure the capital investment necessary to open the interior to exploitation. To do so also meant the transfer of labor to frontier regions. This had occurred earlier, of course, with the movement of slaves to the gold and diamond fields of the eighteenth century, but the abolition of slavery in 1888 meant that modern mine owners had to find other means of acquiring workers.

Before the 1940s, Brazil's mines produced minerals mostly for export, as the nation generally lacked the domestic industries to use the metals. In 1904, the Brazilian government had hired U.S. geologist Israel Charles White to head a commission to study Brazilian coal. The commission's findings, published in 1908, concluded that the coal deposits of Santa Catarina were unsatisfactory for coking. However, the country's pig iron industry relied on charcoal. As a result, Brazilian iron- and steelmakers imported coal until World War I made doing so impossible. They then began to develop the Santa Catarina coalfields more seriously and discovered that the much-maligned coal could be a viable energy source for the local steel industry.[37] In 1918, President Venceslau Braz discussed the need for a Brazilian iron and steel industry, referring to iron and steel as the "metals of civilization."[38] The nation's massive reserves of iron ore offered the possibility of such "civilization."

On the eve of World War II, the government of President Getúlio Vargas began negotiations with the United States to acquire capital and equipment to build a steel mill at Volta Redonda, in the Paraíba valley. In part due to Brazil's support of the Allies during World War II, the United States contributed equipment and funding for the Volta Redonda plant, which began operations in June 1946.[39] State intervention also helped establish the steel industry. The government set up the Companhia Siderúrgica Nacional (National Steel Company), and a U.S. ally took over German-owned iron-ore mines at Congonhas during the war, purchased coal mines in Santa Catarina, and arranged for transportation of the coal by railroad to the port of Laguna from whence it was shipped north to Volta Redonda. Brazil continued to be a major exporter of iron ore, but Volta Redonda created significant demand for the ore also. These developments had several important consequences for Brazilian mining. First, they stimulated internal demand for iron ore and coal. Second, they provided metal for Brazilian industry, including the growing railroad construction and production of automobiles. Third, the government continued to play an interventionist role in mining. Fourth, the postwar nationalist campaign of import substitution not only made the steel industry critical to Brazil's future but also was built, at least in part, on the optimism that the acquisition of Volta Redonda created. Mining was important both for the export earnings it generated and for its role in Brazilian industrialization.

State intervention in mining intensified during the two-decade military dictatorship that began in 1964. The generals and their technocrat advisers emphasized import substitution. If Brazil was to realize its economic potential and turn itself into a great nation, it had to industrialize. While working assiduously to attract foreign investment, the dictatorship created state-owned companies to compete with multinationals operating in Brazil. Such was also true in the mining sector. The military government carried out an extensive survey of the nation's subsoil resources in an attempt to determine the true dimensions of Brazil's mineral wealth. In 1965, the generals announced a ten-year plan for the mining industry. All this led to a massive increase in production. Brazil's output of iron rose from 16.8 million tons in 1964 to 143 million tons in 1984. Manganese production more than doubled, while zinc and gold production increased sevenfold. Bauxite production grew from 188,000 tons to more than 10 million tons.[40]

Brazil had fabulously rich reserves of these metals. Surveys from around 1990 concluded that Brazil possessed at least 48 billion tons of iron ore, 208 million tons of manganese, 2 billion tons of bauxite, and perhaps 450 million tons of nickel, in addition to sizable amounts of cassiterite (the chief source of tin, thus making Brazil a competitor of Bolivia), uranium, phosphate, lead, chromium, potassium, and zirconium. These reserves generally lay in the Brazilian interior and were often widely dispersed, thus requiring the most modern technology and highly mechanized methods to make extraction profitable. Massive state-owned mining projects such as the Great Carajás Program of the Companhia Vale do Rio Doce (Sweet River Valley Company—CVRD) exploited Brazil's mineral resources.[41] The Carajás mineral holdings covered a huge area (more than 10 percent of the national territory) in the valleys of the Itacaiunas and Parauapebas Rivers, a transition zone between the Amazonian forest and the savanna. It held huge reserves of iron ore (perhaps eighteen billion tons), plus large deposits of manganese, bauxite, gold, and copper. The discovery of these resources in the 1970s and 1980s seemed a bonanza both to international mining companies and to a Brazilian government desperate to open the interior to settlement, to stimulate export earnings, and to promote the nation's industrial base. CVRD began extracting the Carajás iron in 1985, moving massive amounts of earth in the process of excavating by the open-pit system. It built a 550-mile railroad to serve the mines and the Ponta de Madeira port to receive great ships for transporting the ore to Japan, Spain, France, Germany, and Italy. Much of Brazil's mineral production was exported, but the nation also had a growing industrial base that used a significant part of the country's mining output.

Brazil's great mining enterprises were highly capitalized and mechanized and employed technically skilled, well-paid personnel. CVRD, for example, announced intentions in 1998 to hire 896 additional engineers and engineering assistants.[42] At its Carajás mines, skilled workers ran huge machines that gouged open a great pit and loaded gigantic trucks, some of which carried as much as four hundred tons of iron ore. The trained truck drivers transported their cargo to the crushing plant, where machinery milled and sorted the ore. Because Carajás ore was typically 70 percent iron, workers did not have to put it through a concentration process. Instead, once it was crushed, they shipped it by railroad to seaports for export to international purchasers such as China. At CVRD's bauxite mines in the state of Pará, which produced aluminum for the domestic Brazilian market, the company employed similar mining technology and again needed educated, skilled workers to operate and maintain the machinery. By the early 2000s, CVRD employed twenty-five thousand workers, many of whom were well paid. Some were represented by labor unions. In what had previously been tropical wilderness, small cities sprouted near the mines to serve the miners, their families, and other company personnel.

Of course, not all workers associated with the Brazilian mining industry were highly skilled or well paid. Charcoal makers, for example, were the primitive side of the iron industry. Although much of the iron ore extracted in Carajás and other great mines was transported directly to the coast for export to overseas markets, some was smelted into pig iron (a brittle form of iron that is high in carbon content and typically requires further refining). Pig-iron smelting consumed tremendous quantities of charcoal. Poorly paid, nearly illiterate workers living in wretched hovels in the Amazonian wilderness built primitive ovens and filled them by hand with wood that they then burned to make charcoal. The "charcoal people" endured mind-numbing labor and their gaunt bodies reflected the destitute life of charcoal workers.[43] They earned little more than enough to survive for another day of toil. Labor recruiters enticed workers to the charcoal kilns, where they sometimes found themselves retained by debts in a form of peonage or quasi-slavery.[44]

Mining also had another face in the Amazon basin: it was the land of El Dorado, where Spanish and Portuguese explorers had searched for the mythical Indian chieftain whose servants sprinkled gold dust over his body each morning. Throughout the twentieth century, Brazil remained a gold producer. Output increased during economic hard times and decreased when the economy was healthy, in large part because garimpeiros, "furtive miners who wander along the mountain 'grimpas' (streams)," mined most of the nation's gold.[45] Their technology, except for a more widespread use of mercury for amalgamation and dredges for sucking alluvium off riverbeds, essentially resembled that used during colonial times. *Garimpagem* (extra-legal prospecting and mining) attracted workers unable to find employment elsewhere.[46] Some Brazilians lamented that compared to the inhabitants of other countries rich in mineral resources, their countrymen seemed to lack a real vocation for mining. They bemoaned the "frivolous enthusiasm of the garimpeiro," who had no real dedication to mining, but worked at it for lack of other economic opportunities.[47] Around 1980, geologists estimated that Brazil had a mere 2.7 percent of the world's gold reserves, and its output was only 2 percent of world's production.

Twentieth-century Amazonian gold mining was a scene more reminiscent of early Potosí than of the multinational or state-controlled enterprises that dominated most of Latin America. In the Brazilian states of Maranhão, Pará, Rondônia, and Mato Grosso, huge increases in the world price for gold during the 1970s touched off a wave of garimpagem. The gold rush drew into the Amazonian wilderness hundreds of thousands of garimpeiros, whose toil turned Brazil into the world's third largest gold producer, behind the Soviet Union and South Africa. The goldfields provided employment and a little hope for the poor of the northeast, Brazil's most destitute region. Garimpagem enriched some, left others bankrupt, and provided an income for thousands and thousands of agricultural laborers and urban poor.

Such prospecting was nothing new in Brazil, although its intensity fluctuated with the price of gold. In the eighteenth and early nineteenth centuries, for example, quilombos of runaway slaves in Pará and Maranhão often panned gold to trade it for manufactured goods and firearms. During the 1850s, the government destroyed the independent quilombos. Brazilian, Portuguese, and British companies then tried to develop mining operations in the region, but their capital and machinery failed. The descendants of the quilombos reemerged from the forests to reclaim control of the gold, protected in part by the local Urubú Indians' hostility to outsiders.

Thus, the region had a long history of informal mining prior to the 1970s. Nonetheless, in that decade several factors combined to produce a gold rush that ultimately surpassed the output recorded in California or the Klondike. One factor was the availability of surplus labor, desperate men unable to find work as the Brazilian economic "miracle" stagnated. Another was the rise in gold prices, which reached $850 per troy ounce in 1979. In addition, modern means of communication—radio and television—rapidly spread news of discoveries throughout the nation, and modern transportation enabled workers to mobilize quickly.

Word of a new strike, or *fofoca* (literally, gossip, about the strike), invariably spread quickly. The motivation driving the garimpeiros was often the thrill of discovery rather than wealth: "The happiness of the garimpeiro is not even to make his fortune. It is to find gold. So much that you can see: when one discovers gold in a new *garimpo*, he makes sure to inform the others, so all the world knows that it was he who found it."[48] Under Brazilian law, farmers and ranchers did not possess subsoil rights but were entitled to 10 percent of the mining production on their land. When a prospector discovered a new strike, the landowner generally accommodated the garimpeiros, parceling out claims (or *barrancos*) to them. The size of the barranco depended on whether the claimholder assigned to it had machinery or whether he worked it by hand. In either case, he would normally hire men to help him, either paying them a daily wage, for piecework, or giving them a share of the production. At especially rich garimpos, claimholders sometimes pooled resources or sought outside investors to underwrite mechanization and other costly improvements. This process also spread the risk if gold production did not meet expectations.

Prospectors discovered new strikes in remote sites that were nearly beyond the reach of the law and social infrastructure. Mutual need tended to organize the strike's initial chaos and tame the garimpeiro's extreme individualism.[49] Although highly independent by nature, garimpeiros often resorted to collective action when exploiting a strike. In most cases, the camps lacked stores where they could purchase food or hardware. Without nearby health services, the lone miner found illness or injury especially dangerous. Garimpeiros shared food and lent spare parts or idle equipment. When someone required emergency medical treatment, he could count on other garimpeiros to help transport him to the nearest clinic. In arduous conditions, the men recognized that they might suddenly need such assistance from other miners. Some camps even allowed a limited amount of state intervention.

Many claimholders and their workers came from similar social backgrounds. At the Gurupí district in southern Maranhão, a majority of each group had been smallholders before taking up garimpagem. The fathers of approximately two-thirds of the group had also been smallholders, eking out a bleak living by growing manioc and other subsistence crops. Nearly all came from Maranhão or the surrounding states. Those with claims tended to be older than the hired hands and had more experience in garimpagem. Usually, the employers had previously worked in other garimpos. Yet as laborers acquired experience and saved a little money, they could realistically hope to obtain a barranco somewhere, if they continued to work in garimpagem.

Life in a garimpo was hard and sometimes dangerous. Work normally extended throughout the daylight hours six days a week, perhaps with time for a nap after lunch. In barrancos worked by hand, human energy was employed to dig away and remove the dross in addition to extracting ore and carrying it to the processing area. The deeper the pit, the more labor was required to extract ore. As work levels went deeper in open-pit barrancos, dangerous cave-ins became more likely, and claimholders could gain access to the gold in the bottom only by removing great quantities of earth to widen the pit. During the rainy season, work in such pits was nearly impossible. The most dangerous type of garimpo, however, was extracting alluvium from river bottoms, especially along the Tapajós and Madeira Rivers. This required constructing a raft equipped with pumps to suck material off the riverbed. Divers worked shifts under water to direct the intake hoses and prevent them from becoming blocked with large objects. Broken or entangled air hoses, collapsed riverbanks, and decompression sickness (also known as the bends) caused by a too-rapid ascent from deep water, imperiled the divers. Almost all workers on the raft received a percentage of the profits because of the shared dangers.

Still, work in the garimpo offered upward mobility to those willing to work hard who were blessed with good luck. Capital and overhead costs were relatively low. Used machinery was often cheap because so many barranco owners either gave up or went bankrupt. They were the ones, after all, who carried most of the risk. Laborers received their wages whether or not the diggings yielded any gold and could leave when they desired.

Of all the gold strikes, the most famous was at Serra Pelada, in southern Pará. Opinions about Serra Pelada vary: "It has been variously portrayed as a place where people become fabulously rich overnight, or as a 'hellhole' where thousands work in semi-slavery for a pittance; as an escape valve for social tensions or as a powder keg of social tensions waiting to explode."[50] Although the state-controlled Companhia Vale do Rio Doce held mineral rights in southern Pará, it could do little to stem a tide of landless peasants invading and occupying land there in 1976. The next year, garimpeiros discovered traces of gold, touching off further extralegal exploration. Minister of Mines and Energy Shigeaki Ueki proudly announced to the nation that gold from the Amazon basin would pay off the nation's crushing foreign debt. Then, in 1980, rumors of fantastic gold deposits at Serra Pelada spread throughout the northeast. The story of its discovery is cloudy. According to some, the daughter of Zézinho, a peon of landowner Genésio Ferreira da Silva, found a nugget in February 1980. Others claimed that Genésio himself found gold while digging a post hole, or that Pedrão, another of his hired hands, discovered it while clearing Genésio's land. Whatever the truth of the legends that grew up around the origins of Serra Pelada, it was part of the rush to exploit the mineral wealth of the Amazon. As the rush to Serra Pelada gained momentum, the Brazilian media reported it, and gold fever infected the nation.

Soon thirty thousand men were digging feverishly at Serra Pelada. The site lacked any sort of infrastructure. Workers armed themselves to establish their own version of law and order. President João Figueiredo worried that wealthy investors from São Paulo and Góias were flying into Serra Pelada, illegally purchasing gold from the garimpeiros, and smuggling it out of the country. The government lost tax revenues in the process, just as the Portuguese colonial government had in the eighteenth century. This dismayed Figueiredo, because the Companhia Vale do Rio Doce had legal rights to the site and should have given the government a controlling interest over gold production at Serra Pelada. Yet the state could not afford to drive the garimpeiros away because Serra Pelada represented a safety valve for the socioeconomic pressures percolating in the impoverished northeast.

On Easter Sunday in 1980, a helicopter descended into the tumult. Aboard was Sebastião Curió Rodrigues de Moura, sent by Figueiredo to impose order and bring the garimpo under government control. He reportedly unholstered his pistol, fired it into the air, and announced that henceforth his gun spoke the loudest at Serra Pelada. The Brazilian military was there to back Curió's bravura, but he also mollified the crowd by proclaiming that the government was not going to remove the garimpeiros. Instead, he arrested the gold buyers, expelled women from the camp, and built infrastructure, including a health clinic, post office, telephone facilities, and a government store where workers could buy food and other supplies at cost.

Curió also established a tax office (Caixa Econômica Federal), where the garimpeiros had to sell all their gold. A police cordon around the site registered all incoming laborers and issued them a work card. The police also prevented gold smuggling by those who were leaving. By June 1980, Serra Pelada had officially yielded ten tons of gold.

Garimpeiros at Serra Pelada tolerated an unusual degree of state intervention in return for government acknowledgement of their extralegal claims. Curió headed the Coordenação, or Coordinating Committee, of federal police, national security agents, and representatives of the National Department of Mineral Resources. According to anthropologist David Cleary: "Each day began with a mass meeting in front of the office of the Coordenaçao, the singing of the national anthem, regimented calisthenics, and a pep talk from Curió before the crowd dispersed to start work."[51] Curió and his faction hoped to use Serra Pelada to launch social reform in the poverty-stricken northeast while also shaping the tens of thousands of workers into a voting bloc supporting Curió's own political ambitions.[52] In southern Pará, enthusiastic supporters named a town, Curiónopolis, for him.

Meanwhile, at Serra Pelada workers cut away at the hill by hand-carving an imposing pit. At its height, Serra Pelada employed eighty thousand workers drawn not only from the Brazilian northeast but from every state in the country. Most came from the marginalized segments of Brazilian society, especially downtrodden agricultural laborers and the chronically underemployed. Yet the allure of Serra Pelada's gold and the fever it provoked caused men from many backgrounds to abandon their careers and seek adventure in the garimpo. Barrancos were small, only a few meters square. Claimholders gambled that as they dug down, they would find enough gold to make operations profitable. Most workers had no claim but hired themselves out to those who did. Long lines of mud-covered workers, like tiny ants in a great pit, hauled sacks of ore and muck out on their backs. Better-equipped barranco owners used high-pressure hoses to dislodge earth and rock, and pumps to suck the material up and out of the pit through long tubes.

Given the huge workforce, per capita production was not great; estimates place it at three times the meager Brazilian minimum wage in 1984, when Serra Pelada's output was high.[53] A few, the *bamburrados*, made fortunes. Some, the *blefados*, lost them just as quickly through risky investments, dissipation, or bad luck. Those working for a percentage of profits sometimes did well. Even among the unskilled laborers working for a daily wage, economic conditions were not dismal during the bonanza years at Serra Pelada.

In addition to earning their wages, they received food and a place to hang their hammocks. This permitted them to save much of their money, if they exercised a little self-discipline. Serra Pelada thus attracted swarms of workers who left their families at home and went temporarily to the garimpo to supplement meager family earnings. Some stayed a few weeks, others stayed for the season before the annual rains made work dangerous in the pit, and still others never returned home. Work at Serra Pelada often made economic sense for the married worker but had debilitating consequences for his family, despite the money he sent home. His lonely wife was left to raise their children, and a sense of insecurity descended upon the home: fear for the man's safety, worry that he would abandon the family, and dependence on friends, relatives, and the occasional remittances of funds from the garimpeiro.

Garimpos such as Serra Pelada posed serious health and environmental concerns. Those working in the pit faced the constant danger of cave-ins. Teams using high-pressure hoses caused slides that killed workers below. Workers visited the pharmacies each Sunday to take an injection containing vitamins and antibiotics. This "cocktail," they hoped, would ward off respiratory diseases. At most garimpos, however, workers had no access to such medical services, and their isolation made injuries and illnesses difficult to treat.

Individual garimpeiros and small teams of workers fueled much of the new gold rush during its early years. They divided their output among themselves. Within a few years, however, a small group of investors, called the "Barões do Garimpo" (Barons of the Garimpo), gained control of more than three-fourths of production. Lacking the technological expertise and the equipment to exploit deep deposits, some garimpeiros hired themselves out to mining companies and prospected for new strikes. Most workers had to content themselves with wage labor. As one observer reported: "A proletarianization of the garimpo is clearly developing, with the introduction of wage earners, who sell their labor, the best example being the sack carriers (*formigas* [ants]) at Serra Pelada."[54]

By the late twentieth century, mining remained crucial to the economies of several Latin America nations, yet its structural changes created great diversity in the lives of the miners themselves. Some, such as the piece-rate workers in Bolivia's tin mines or the ore carriers in Brazil's Serra Pelada gold mines, endured harsh, primitive conditions. Some were skilled workers who operated great earth-gouging machinery in open-pit mines, such as Chile's Chuquicamata, earned good wages, and gained entry into the nation's middle class. Others toiled for a pittance. By the mid-1990s, Potosí's mining barrios had some modern utilities and conveniences, but the home of the average mining family of from six to seven persons was a humble structure, often consisting of one or two rooms. A majority of families owned their home, but a third rented. Nearly all had access to electricity, but only 80 percent had access to running water and sewage plumbing in the home.[55] Many of the women still worked as palliris. Although they claimed to be Catholic, women in the mining barrios still participated in traditional Andean religious practices. Nearly all spoke Quechua, but many also had some Spanish. An observer wrote:

> Bolivia is a member of a small group of African and Latin American countries for whom mining is the cornerstone of their economies; no other country of this group, which includes Chile, Peru, Guyana and Jamaica in the Americas, has been so dependent on mining over such a long period as has Bolivia. But nowadays, as in history, great mining wealth has brought only poverty to the average Bolivian; in no other country in South America is the standard of living so low.[56]

In many of the great mines, workers had become proletarianized, laboring permanently for the multinational, national, or state-owned companies, whereas others, particularly in Peru and Bolivia, retained economic ties to their home village and worked only temporarily in the mines. Throughout the mining industry, however, the coercion of workers that was characteristic of earlier periods gave rise to capitalist wage labor.

CHAPTER 8

Mining, Harmony, and the Environment

A grotesque figure occupies an important place in this system; seated within a grotto in the drilled rock, he shares in solidarity the daily labor of the miner. We have in mind the Tío, symbol of the mine's interior life.

—Javier Sangines C.

✤ TOO OFTEN, MINING HAS MEANT DESPOILING NATURE RATHER THAN living in harmony with the environment. Regardless of the size of the mine or refinery, processing ores with reagents poses some of the greatest environmental dangers. Indigenous miners smelted their ores. Colonial refiners turned to amalgamation. Even in colonial times, some of the dangers of quicksilver were well known. Observers called the Huancavelica mercury mines in central Peru a "public slaughterhouse" and considered labor there a death sentence.[1] Yet Andean silver refiners needed Huancavelica's output of mercury to amalgamate their ores, and the Crown consequently forced Indians to take turns working in the mercury mines and refining plants. In the early 1600s, as many as two-thirds of Huancavelica's workers perished from mercury poisoning and other illnesses and accidents at the mines.[2] Mercury easily accumulated in their bodies. They inhaled mercury-laden dust in the mines and absorbed the poison through their skin. Workers tending the primitive distillation ovens breathed in mercury gases as well. As the corpses of deceased Huancavelica miners decomposed, they reportedly left puddles of mercury in their graves. Exposure to mercury in its metallic form was poisonous and sometimes fatal, whether in colonial Huancavelica or Potosí or modern Brazil's garimpos.

Mining still pollutes the environment with mercury. In June 2000, a truck carrying supplies to the Yanacocha mines in the mountains of central Peru spilled two hundred kilograms of quicksilver en route, of which the company managed to salvage only a third. Villagers along the way recovered substantial amounts of the mercury in the mistaken belief that it contained gold. When they took it into their homes and burned off the mercury to recover the hoped-for gold, toxic fumes poisoned several hundred people.[3]

In the Amazon basin, prospectors and garimpeiros used mercury to refine gold and caused dangerous pollution. After removing as much gangue as possible with a sluice or shaker or by panning, the garimpeiros mixed the remaining ore with mercury to form a heavy amalgam. Further panning made it easy to separate the gold-mercury amalgam from the remaining dross, although workers usually washed away some mercury (perhaps 45 percent) in the process. To extract the gold, they heated the amalgam with a propane torch, vaporizing the remaining mercury. Such vapors could easily poison an unsuspecting garimpeiro. On average, gold miners expended 1.4 kilograms of mercury to refine each kilogram of gold, roughly the same rate that colonial silver refiners reached. Amazonian gold refiners polluted the environment with fifty to seventy tons of mercury each year.[4] Miners using primitive refining methods had little concern for the ecological consequences of their work. They had no permanent ties to the land and were only interested in the gold they could extract.[5]

Although environmentalists and the news media exaggerated the environmental threat posed by the mercury lost in metallic form through washing, the vapors released when the mercury was burned off the amalgam were very dangerous.[6] The vapors enter the food chain as methylmercury, a highly toxic organic form of the element. In the atmosphere, ultraviolet rays ionize the mercuric vapors and rain washes them into the swamps, streams, and rivers. There, microbes convert the ions into methylmercury, which is a hundred times more soluble than metallic mercury. This ionization and conversion occurs most readily in tropical waters, which are rich in organic matter, and thus the Amazon basin provides the perfect environment for contamination. Aquatic organisms such as plankton absorb the methylmercury and are in turn eaten by fish. This puts the methylmercury into the food chain. Once there, it is not easily eliminated. Compared to metallic mercury, animals excrete organic methylmercury with great difficulty, in part because the organic compound contains carbon, which bonds with the neurological system. Small fish eat plants containing the mercury and are in turn consumed by larger fish, and these poison the people who eat them. As a person eats more and more contaminated fish, the methylmercury, rather than being eliminated by the body, builds up in a process called bioconcentration and biomagnification. Thus, this bioaccumulation can expose humans to high levels of poison through consumption of only moderately contaminated fish.[7]

A powerful neurotoxin, methylmercury attacks the human central nervous system. Damage is particularly severe to the visual cortex and the infolded regions of the cerebellum. In its earliest manifestations, methylmercury poisoning afflicts its victims with the prickling or itching of paresthesia, tremors, blurred vision, emotional instability, and malaise. Even nonfatal high toxicity can cause permanent physical damage. The effects on humans are sometimes not evident until several months after exposure. Methylmercury poses severe danger to pregnant women because it enters the fetus through the placenta and damages the child's developing central nervous system. High rates of miscarriage result, and children are born with "smaller head sizes, cerebral palsy and loss of muscular control, shaking, seizures, and mental retardation."[8]

Brazilian environmentalists worked to raise public consciousness of the mercury danger. Areas near garimpos showed signs of contamination. Tests on fish caught in effluents of the Jamari River and at Porto Velho confirmed mercury concentrations of 2.70 parts per million (ppm) and 1.43 ppm, far above the maximum of 0.5 ppm permitted in fish by Brazilian law. The World Health Organization (WHO) defined mercury poisoning in humans as occurring at concentrations of 50 ppm, and some mining areas had pollution nearing those levels.[9] Even the president of the Amazonian garimpeiros' union, União Sindical dos Garimpeiros da Amazônia Legal (USGAL), attested to the ecological harm caused by gold prospectors and their mercury: "Wherever we go, a track of destruction is left behind. Mercury stays in the rivers and the soil is degraded. We corrupt the culture, the location, and the conduct of the areas where we arrive. We destroy everything."[10] Although natural processes release from two thousand to six thousand tons of mercury into the atmosphere each year, the WHO concluded that in air and water unpolluted by human intervention, mercury is barely detectable.[11] Thus, almost all mercury pollution in the mining districts of the Brazilian interior came from using primitive amalgamation techniques used to refine gold. The humidity, sunlight, mercury vapor, and biomass of the Amazon basin make it an ideal factory for methylmercury pollution. Contamination of a small area could produce highly toxic conditions even though the quantity of mercury expended is small relative to global emissions. "A silent catastrophe [was] in march."[12] Of course, the mercury affected both the miners themselves and the surrounding population, including indigenous tribes. Mercury's toxicological profile guaranteed an increase in birth defects in the contaminated populations.

Besides mercury pollution, mining had other important consequences for the environment. Forests succumbed to the demand for timber to shore up mines and for fuel for smelters. Railroads connecting mines to smelters and ports needed ties for the tracks as well. Rivers were dammed to provide water to turn stamp mills and later to power turbines that produced electricity for mines and refineries. By modifying the environment, mining caused changes in the flora and fauna. It contaminated the soil. Sewage and garbage caused more ecological change, and the human population had no immunity to the environmental damages.

Aside from the accidents workers suffered in mines and refining plants, they, their families, and the others living nearby had to endure polluted water and air. The dust from drilling, extracting, and grinding ore was pernicious, as was tainted water flowing out of mines and refineries and leaching out of tailings ponds, rubble, and ore dumps. Inside the mines, water mixed with sulfide ores to make highly acidic copajira or *agua de mina* (mine water), which is powerful enough to dissolve heavy metals:

> The mountain irritated by man wants to expel him. . . . In the adits the constant dripping of a yellowish and foul-smelling liquid called *copajira* burns the miners' clothing. Hundreds of kilometers away where there are rivers and fish, death arrives in the form of liquid poison coming from the sludge of the mills. The ore is extracted and cleaned, but the earth is made filthy.[13]

In ore dumps and tailings ponds, rain and snow leached out zinc, lead, copper, cadmium, arsenic, and other metallic contaminants.[14] Refineries also polluted rivers and lakes. Old ore dumps on Potosí's Cerro Rico contain almost no metals because leaching over the centuries has been so thorough. The leaching, of course, has released zinc, lead, mercury, and other metals into the Andean ecosphere. More than anything else, mining polluted water. Sometimes mining companies discharged untreated waste into nearby rivers or into the soil, from which it drained into the water system. At Oruro, for example, gastrointestinal illnesses caused high mortality rates, particularly among children, largely because of polluted water, and mining bore significant responsibility for the pollution.[15]

Given 450 years of exploitation, mining caused tremendous ecological damage at Potosí. When the silver rush began there in 1545, the site lay at an elevation above that typically inhabited by Andeans. Herders grazed their livestock there, and the foot of the Cerro Rico was covered with trees. The altitude made it unsuitable for agriculture or permanent residence. Silver and Europeans changed that and left a mountain pocked by mine entrances and scabbed with ore dumps. Miners soon cut the existing trees to build the first houses in the area and fuel their smelting ovens.[16] Today, the blue sky contrasts with the reddish browns of the Cerro and the grays and blues of the dumps. No vegetation softens the visage of the Cerro Rico; no greenery blots out the scars inflicted by centuries of mining. Only clumps of light brown icho grass still dot the hill. A small stream flows from refining plants down through the city, the sludge from the refineries giving it a sickly sheen. In the 1990s, thousands of small eucalyptus trees were planted around the Cerro; each was protected from voracious llamas and alpacas by rough circular stone walls.

Regardless of the environmental damage caused by earlier mining, the 1900s brought serious new challenges. Colonial miners would hardly have understood the economics and technologies of late-twentieth-century mining, when great machines dug and processed a ton of ore to extract two or three grams of gold. Such techniques created huge environmental problems and disturbed tremendous amounts of earth. Tailings from new refining technologies exposed heavy metals and poisons that endangered the environment on a new, greater scale. Used by garimpeiros to refine gold in the Amazon basin of Brazil, mercury posed ecological dangers when it polluted the rivers and entered the food chain. In addition to mercury, mining companies turned to other reagents to process ores. For nonprecious minerals, for example, refiners used cyanide and sulfuric acid to extract minute bits of metal from the massive amounts of ore taken from huge open-pit mines. At the Cananea copper mines of Sonora, Mexico, effluent from the refineries made local streams so acidic that their waters extracted copper from the rocks on the streambeds.[17]

The heavy metals and other pollutants threatened to contaminate not only workers in the mines and refineries but also all the people living in the region. In adults, lead contamination increased blood pressure and caused reproductive problems, irritability, and loss of memory. Lead contamination was even more serious for children, because it harmed their developing nervous systems. Children living in the polluted atmosphere near smelters suffered learning disabilities, reduced intelligence, and kidney damage. Lead in a pregnant woman's blood harmed her fetus. Arsenic, another pollutant from the smelting of many types of metallic ores, is a well-known poison. Chronic arsenic poisoning caused dermatitis, paresthesia, and arrhythmia of the heart, in addition to kidney and liver damage. A carcinogen, cadmium affected the liver, kidneys, and lungs; prevented normal enzymatic functions; and, ironically, given miners' reputation for masculinity, damaged the testicles. Mercury poisoning posed neurological danger.

One of the worst cases of pollution occurred at La Oroya, Peru, after the Cerro de Pasco Company opened its smelter there in 1926. The big smelter spewed poisonous smoke that contained sulfur dioxide, lead, and arsenic. Although the company installed new refining equipment to cut the emissions, La Oroya remained highly polluted. In the 1990s, the amount of lead detected in the town's air was more than seven thousand times higher than the World Bank's maximum permissible levels, that of arsenic was nearly as high, and levels of sulfur dioxide (easily converted into sulfuric acid) also far exceeded safe limits. Prevailing winds carried these contaminants down the Mantaro Valley to cause serious pollution as much as thirty kilometers away.[18] Around La Oroya itself, the sulfuric acid killed animals and vegetation, leaving a sterile wasteland for future generations. In 2006, the Blacksmith Institute, which attempts to eliminate pollution in the developing world, ranked La Oroya among the ten most contaminated places in the world and noted that virtually all of the children living there suffered very high levels of lead poisoning.[19]

The Cuajones and Toquepala copper mines in the Moquegua and Tacna departments of southern Peru also demonstrate modern mining's polluting effects. Winds carried poisons inland from the smelter near the port of Ilo. Located on the northern fringe of the Atacama desert, the driest place on earth, the surrounding region had few agricultural lands except in irrigated areas, and those were all eventually contaminated by the smelter's fumes. The coastal hills, green with vegetation from August to March due to the condensation of ocean mists, also became barren. Olive trees in the Locumba valley lost their leaves. The sulfur dioxide and heavy metals impeded crop germination. Heavy metals contaminated nearby coastal waters with concentrations of copper, arsenic, and iron that were far above acceptable levels, damaging the fishing and shellfish industry.[20]

Sometimes environmental damage came in a form more immediately catastrophic than the gradual leaching of poisonous metals or wind-blown clouds of heavy metals. In the 1990s, British-owned Rio Tinto and the Bolivian Compañía Minera del Sur (COMSUR) together operated the El Porco zinc mine west of Potosí. During heavy rains on August 29, 1996, the companies' improperly operated tailings dike broke. The dike was a dam built to create a reservoir to receive sludge and other refuse from the refining mill. When it failed, it released four hundred thousand tons of refining sludge containing zinc, lead, iron sulfide, cadmium, copper, and arsenic that flowed across peasants' fields and into the Pilcomayo River.[21] The cyanide and arsenic killed several children and poisoned untold numbers of other people living along the river.[22] Downstream as much as three hundred kilometers, the polluting muds continued to kill livestock and destroy aquatic life. The polluted river was dead and covered with a silvery sheen, the result of one of Latin America's greatest environmental disasters.[23]

Despite the public attention focused on them, great mining operations such as Rio Tinto and COMSUR were not the industry's only polluters. In fact, the World Bank concluded in a 1999 study that small companies and artisanal operations often cause more environmental damage than large transnational concerns, if the amount of pollution relative to the volume of mineral production is considered. New technology and foreign investment improved the environmental impact of large- and medium-size firms, but most small operations lacked the technical expertise and financial resources to store tailings and prevent acid rock water discharge.[24] Seepage led to oxidation of metal sulfides contained in mines and tailings ponds, making the water acidic. Unless a mining operation took great care, the acid-tainted water polluted nearby lakes and streams. Artisanal miners tended to work only when metal prices rose and returned to other jobs when prices fell. The diverse nature and irregular work of such mining activity made it difficult to monitor and regulate to ensure adherence to environmental safeguards. Chief among the artisanal and small-mining sector's environmental problems were "mercury disposal, direct dumping of tailings and effluents into rivers, improperly constructed tailings dams, acid rock drainage arising from the tailings dams or open galleries and the related problem of improper closure, river damage in alluvial areas, and erosion damage at the edge of highland areas."[25] The environmental record of Bolivian miners' cooperatives, which were usually made up of former COMIBOL workers and peasants from nearby villages, has been particularly bad. Often working old mines, they pay little attention to worker safety, maintenance of the mine itself, or proper disposal of tailings. This inevitably has led to serious pollution.[26] Yet technology was available to reduce contamination from small mines, sometimes at costs that would have permitted profitable exploitation.

Since colonial times prospectors, miners, and the throngs that followed them have transformed the ecosphere in the Brazilian interior. As one historian put it: "Ever since the first settlement of Minas Gerais, successive generations have burnt the trees and vegetation in order to clear the ground for mining or agricultural pursuits, which accounts for the desolate appearance of most of the countryside."[27] Rains have eroded lands denuded of their trees and underbrush. Great open pits such as the iron mines of the Quadrilátero Ferrífero in Minas Gerais and the Serra Pelada gold mines have devastated wilderness areas. Exploitation of iron ore deposits at Carajás northwest of Serra Pelada have defaced a vast territory. Raft-borne dredges have mined riverbeds. In 1990, five hundred dredges worked the Madeira River, many of them large enough to suck thousands of cubic yards of alluvium off the river bottom each day.[28] Dredging has destroyed the aquatic environment, but so have the mercury used to process the gold and the petroleum products, sewage, and other pollutants discharged into the water. Most types of ore refining need great amounts of water. Mining companies process millions of tons of earth and wash much of it into rivers, making the water so turbid that the normal life cycles of the flora and fauna are disrupted. Indeed, it was estimated "that [in Brazil] two cubic metres of sediments enter the watercourses for every gram of gold extracted from the *garimpos*."[29]

One consequence of Brazilian mining is widespread deforestation. Drawn into the Amazon by mining, millions of miners, their dependents, and people who otherwise served the mining industry needed food. They occupied land and cleared it for primitive farms. This added to deforestation that was already under way. Tremendous demand for charcoal to smelt ore into pig iron made the situation worse. By the late twentieth century, forests in the Rio Doce valley of Minas Gerais were so depleted by the voracious appetite of the iron industry that smelting operations were forced to relocate to the Carajás region. Such industrialization in the delicate ecology of the rain forest was, in the words of one ecologist, "nothing short of disastrous."[30] The government approved construction of nine iron smelters and planned for another eleven, in addition to two cement factories, which altogether consumed more than two million tons of charcoal each year. Nearly six million acres of forest were cut to supply these needs.[31] The plan made short-term economic sense but promised long-term ecological disaster. By the end of the twentieth century, government attempts to curb deforestation had only limited success; in large part they were undercut by the government's own development projects.[32]

Of course, the indirect impact of mining also had serious ecological consequences. Even though a large open-pit mine covered a comparatively small area, it indirectly required the burning of millions of acres of precious rain forest so the earth could be ranched or farmed to feed workers or to provide charcoal to smelt iron ore. By the late twentieth century, the great mining companies had become more sensitive to the ecological ramifications of their activities and worked to protect themselves from public outrage over the pollution and environmental devastation their industry.

Greed for metals spawned waves of migration, with its associated effects on the environment. Just as millions made their way to colonial Potosí over the centuries, the discovery of gold at Serra Pelada in 1980 touched off a huge wave of migration. The discovery began "the greatest and most disorderly occupation of the Amazon forest, marked principally by the inharmonious work among machine, man, and nature."[33] In the early 1980s, Serra Pelada held more than one hundred thousand people, whereas a decade earlier the site was unpopulated.[34] There had been perhaps fifty thousand garimpeiros in the Amazon before the opening of Serra Pelada in 1980. A decade later there were ten times as many.[35] Another 4.5 million people were linked to the garimpeiros as family members, merchants, farmers who produced food for the mining camps, and others. Garimpagem in more than two thousand sites sustained half the people in the Amazon. Of mining's impact on the Amazon, an observer wrote:

> The gold that mitigates the hunger of the migrant fleeing the misery of the great urban centers and the Brazilian Northeast and that warms the dream of rapid fortune is the same that sacrifices thousands of anonymous human lives, pollutes water resources and kills, silently, the greatest biological patrimony that the Earth has sheltered in the last millennia.[36]

Brazil needed to exploit the Amazon's mineral resources, yet the government was unable to control the environmental consequences such mining set in motion.

Modern mining's demand for great amounts of energy also has indirect ecological ramifications. CVRD needed electricity to exploit the deposits of iron ore, manganese, and other minerals in Greater Carajás. Beginning in 1977, Electronorte, a Brazilian electrical utility, dammed rivers to build the necessary hydroelectric projects. The facilities at Tucuruí and elsewhere lacked serious environmental planning and added to mining's indirect ecological impact on the area. To open space for a dam and the resulting reservoir, the company burned great swaths of forest. The conflagration produced so much ash that water in the reservoir became strongly acidic and, in turn, corroded the turbines and other metal equipment of the electrical plant. The sulfurous odor fouled the air as far as sixty miles away. Rotting vegetation stimulated growth of water hyacinths, which came to cover half the reservoir. Species of fish previously found in the river disappeared because planners had provided no way for them to get past the dams to spawn upstream. To clear paths through the jungle for electrical lines, workers sprayed sodium pentachlorophenate, a strong herbicide and carcinogen that also caused skin rashes, liver and kidney damage, and respiratory irritation. Many people were poisoned and several died, touching off a populist environmental movement.[37]

Mining also harmed the region's indigenous peoples. The Amazon basin was home to dozens of Indian tribes, some of which had only begun to emerge from primitive isolation in the twentieth century. Over the centuries, these peoples had adapted their cultures to the rain forest and lived by hunting, gathering, and slash-and-burn agriculture, particularly of plantains and manioc. They had little or no exposure to "Old World" diseases. The discovery of gold at Serra Pelada and elsewhere in addition to the development of the Carajás project stimulated encroachments on indigenous lands. In the 1980s, the Brazilian government made serious attempts to protect the tribes from garimpeiros, ranchers, and lumbermen. To minimize the impact of its Carajás project, CVRD worked with the Fundação Nacional do Índio (FUNAI), Brazil's Indian Affairs Foundation, which was created in 1967 (the year of the great Carajás mineral discovery) and charged with protecting the country's indigenous population. It tried, not always successfully, to minimize the mines' direct impact on indigenous lands.[38] FUNAI had responsibility for regulating indigenous land reserves and protecting them from external threats. Time proved, however, that such encroachments were nearly impossible to prevent. Laws and government policies had little power in the Amazonian frontier, where guns, greed, and aggression often trumped humanitarian concerns for indigenous welfare. Garimpeiros rushed to respond to great fofocas, whether the discoveries were on indigenous lands or not. By building roads to open the interior, the government gave migrants access to lands that had been the preserve of isolated indigenous tribes. Squatters arrived in the Amazon basin with a hunger for land and diseases that threatened the very survival of the Indians.[39]

In their search for gold and other mineral riches, garimpeiros invaded FUNAI-established indigenous reserves. The Indians often welcomed the intruders in the beginning because they were few in number and offered trade articles that the tribe prized. Discovery of gold led to more garimpeiros, however, which in turn caused conflict. The effect of such conflict on the Yanomamis of Roraima has been the most widely studied case. In 1985, defying FUNAI attempts to keep miners off the Indian lands, garimpeiro leader José Altino Machado led a party into the Yanomami reserves to assert by force the miners' right to exploit tin and gold deposits found there. In the ensuing conflict, the garimpeiros murdered a number of Indians (Yanomami culture prohibits mention of the name of a deceased person, hindering FUNAI's attempts to determine exactly how many had been killed). Contact with the garimpeiros and other outsiders also spread disease. Between 1988 and 1990, perhaps 15 percent of the Yanomami died from diseases that they had no immunity to. The Indians lacked scientific explanations for the epidemics that afflicted them, but they associated the diseases with mining. They believed that the natural environment was inhabited by spirits, one of which, Xawara, was a vapor that harmed them when miners released it from the soil.[40]

The Yanomami conflict epitomized the dilemma that confronted the government as it tried to reconcile mining's economic importance with the need to defend Indian tribes and their environment. This, of course, was similar to the dilemma confronting the sixteenth-century Spanish monarchy, which attempted to protect its indigenous vassals while also filling its treasure fleets with silver. The main difference was that the modern Brazilians did not force the Amazonian Indians to work in the mines. Pressed by international and Brazilian advocates for the Yanomamis, the national government began in the early 1990s to expel garimpeiros from the Yanomami reserves. Police dynamited landing strips in the jungle so that miners could not fly food and other supplies in. The state government, however, supported the miners, who had more political clout and who offered more to the regional economy than the Indians did.

The national government compromised with the mining interests in 1992 when it reduced the size of the Yanomami lands by 70 percent and divided the remainder into nineteen discrete reserves, opening more lands to mining.[41] Even so, it proved difficult to keep garimpeiros from sneaking into the remaining Yanomami territories. In 1993, miners attacked the village of Haximu and murdered nineteen Yanomamis, a massacre that heightened international concern over the conflict between exploiting the economic benefits of mining and protecting indigenous rights. In many ways, the situation was reminiscent of the sixteenth-century Spanish monarchy's attempts to balance its lust for gold and silver with its concern for the welfare of its indigenous subjects.

Andean Culture, the Mines, and Harmony

Mining caused tremendous environmental and social stress, and nowhere was this more clear than in Peru and Bolivia. Yet the culture of their Quechua and Aymara ancestors helped Andean miners withstand the awful effects of laboring in the mines. Ethnic traditions strengthened the miners' resilience and helped them harmonize their work with their Andean world. Their ancestors mined before the Spaniards arrived and had religious explanations of the underworld they encountered while they extracted silver, copper, and mercury ores. As farmers and as miners they appealed for aid to Pachamama, the great Andean earth mother deity. Rituals and sacrifices enticed her to bless their fields and flocks and to protect against the frosts and droughts that brought famine and disease. Pachamama was also intimately involved with mining. Her entrails produced the gold and silver prized by Incas and Spaniards alike. "The mine is definitively a woman, the maternal womb, the feminine reproduction of the species. The mine is fertility."[42] Ores grew like potatoes in the ground. Mountains and hills which contained Pachamama's precious gifts were huacas, worshipped by the Andeans.

Indigenous cosmology prepared workers for the physical and psychological burdens of mine work. Their culture helped them overcome the apparent dissonance between farming and toiling underground, between life in the peasant village and the harsh modernity of the mining camp. In pre-Hispanic times,

> those who went to the mines worshiped the hills where they worked and the mines themselves, which they call *coya*. They asked the mines for their metals, and in order to obtain what they asked for, they stayed up at night drinking and dancing as a sign of reverence to the hills. They also worshiped the metals which they call *mama* and the

rocks called *corpa* which contain these metals. They would kiss these rocks and perform other ceremonies with them.[43]

Mining held great religious meaning.

Ayni, or harmony, was a powerful concept in Andean culture. It implied reciprocity and mutual help, an exchange in which someone gave goods or performed services with the expectation of receiving even more goods or services in return.[44] The Inca ruler demanded tribute and obedience from his subjects but in return provided them sustenance and protection in order to preserve ayni. Entering the tunnels of Potosí to tear out riches from the bowels of Mother Earth, miners offered gifts to Pachamama, who could reward them with mineral bonanzas and personal safety. Mitayos marching off to serve at Potosí saw ayni in the king's gift of lands to farm in return for their labor at the mines. Their descendants remembered that "the 'grandfathers' had earned the land (*jallp'a*), eating earth in the mills" at Potosí.[45]

In many respects, mining was an activity that upset ayni. Spaniards destroyed harmony by refusing to pay travel costs, demanding excess labor, and inflicting other abuses, without reciprocation. The twentieth-century peasant, a descendant of the colonial mitayos, felt an intense loss of harmony as he went off to the mines to suffer as a locatario. He left behind not only his village but its cultural security, from village rituals and fiestas to his family members and farmlands. He was attracted by the money, the freedom, and perhaps even the educational opportunities available for his children, yet repelled by the dangers and depressing conditions of the mines and the mining camps. "How many of them return, young still, with their eyes sunk in deep sockets, the skin pallid and stuck to the bones, the chest shrunken and panting and their breathing broken, to their little indigenous farms to die poor and abandoned in a few months!"[46]

Mining disrupted ayni more and more during the twentieth century, as mechanization transformed the traditional methods of exploiting Bolivia's mineral riches. This was especially true at the great mines of Patiño and the other tin barons that later fell under the control of COMIBOL and the government. A cultural transformation of the workers unfolded. Miners became more proletarianized, working full-time at the mines and depending on their wages for survival. They no longer returned to their villages to help with agriculture and benefit from the harvests. Management provided the workers with pulperías and commissaries, which lessened their direct dependence on the agriculture of the surrounding countryside.[47] This weakened economic and social links between the miners and the peasantry that had existed since the sixteenth century. Of the men arriving at the mines, a labor leader remarked in the late 1970s: "The peasants that come to the mine learn to use toothpaste, they learn what a cinema is, they learn what civilization is."[48] At a great COMIBOL complex such as the Siglo XX mine, a company miner received free housing and electricity plus subsidized food and other goods at the company's store. Many intended to spend only a few weeks or months at the mines and then work elsewhere but eventually found it difficult to leave.

Patiño reasoned that he could not transform workers from the nearby villages into permanent full-time miners. These workers would abandon the mines to work their fields or to participate in fiestas and other local rituals. To ease the cultural transformation, Patiño managers at Catavi brought in workers from distant Cochabamba rather than recruit in the surrounding Aymara-speaking ayllus. Living simply from their flocks and fields, the Aymaras found little attraction in the Underground. They recalled the suffering their ancestors had endured because of the Potosí mita and looked on the mines as "death's waiting room."[49]

That belief had a double meaning. Visiting the Pulacayo mines at Huanchaca, Bolivia, at the end of the nineteenth century, French traveler André Bellessort recalled the silver cross in a chapel at the mine entrance. The miners, he reported, believed the cross protected them from the devil who lived deep in the mine and who killed them, "crushing them under falling rocks. Day and night, these two enemy forces, the Cross and the Devil, duel each other, with the miners' lives at stake."[50] Workers refused to enter the mine when the cross was paraded through the streets at carnival time, believing that with the cross absent, Pulacayo lay under the demon's complete control. An astute observer of conditions at the tin mines, journalist Norman Gall reported: "The miner's life is haunted always by such spirits. There are 500 miles of tunnel within the Siglo Veinte mine. In one of the lower enclosures stands a statue of the Devil called the Tío (Uncle), fashioned in the grotesque Indian style of the altiplano's Lenten carnivals. . . . The Tío is regarded as the promoter of cave-ins, and miners vanishing at the lower levels are believed to have been dragged by it into Hell."[51]

What neither the Frenchman nor Gall fully understood, however, was that for Andeans the mines were, in a religious sense, the realm of the dead, whose spirits inhabited the Underground. To work there, the miner had to commune with the phantoms and shadows whose realms he had entered. Such beliefs helped the miners cope with proletarianization and the

Figure 15. Tío Jorge, one of the *supays*, or devils, worshipped in the Rosario mine in the Cerro Rico. He is a human-sized figure, with horns and miner's boots. Worshippers have covered his lap with coca leaves and inserted a lit cigarette in his lips. Colorful ribbons decorate his horns and shoulders.

technology of modern mining. Miners made offerings to the earth mother, but once inside the mines they also supplicated her male consorts, threatening deities who roamed the ukhupacha and controlled access to the rich ores. Miners referred to them as *pachachata*, supay, and *muqui*, transformed versions of the ancestral phantoms. In the mountains of central Peru, miners generally called them muqui, whereas in Bolivia they were called supay or Tío. The muqui had a diminutive human form, the size of a ten-year-old child, and could make the ore bodies appear or disappear. Muquis moved through subterranean passageways, transporting ore on llama-back. They made it available to miners of "good heart," who lived by the Andean principle of ayni, making reciprocal offerings to the muqui and living in harmony with their fellows. Some miners claimed that the muqui ate human feces and converted this into gold and other metals. The workers consequently defecated near rich ore bodies as an offering to the muqui. This fit with their belief that the living mine replenished itself.

Individual miners as well as the collective labor force entered into reciprocal agreements with the muqui or supay. Miners offered alcohol, coca leaves, cigarettes, and brightly colored ribbons to the muqui or entered into more serious and sinister vows in exchange for a bonanza of ore or their personal safety within the mine. They thus strengthened their relationship with the deities of the mine, reciprocating their revelations of rich ore and protection from danger while working underground. Miners who ignored their dependence on the supay violated his sacred realm and endangered themselves and their fellow workers.[52] According to Bernabé Mamani, a miner in the Candelaria Baja Mineshaft at Potosí: "If you see the Tío, the devil, walking around, you can go crazy or die of fear. The Tío is God here: if he wants accidents, he will have them."[53] Such fear was *haperk'a*, which Andeans treated as a physical illness that could only be cured by reestablishing ayni.[54]

Just as miners displayed a heightened sense of masculinity, the muqui or supay exuded an extraordinary sexuality. "Some miners say that the Muqui possesses a sexual organ so large that he sometimes wraps it around his waist like a belt, but at other times he leaves it loose in the galleries like a snake. . . . The miners must be careful when entering the mine not to step on the god's penis; women must not enter the mines because they might be 'abused' by the Muki."[55] Some miners sought aid from the Tío if they felt their own sexual potency waning.[56]

The Bolivian miners' cosmology combined Christian and Andean gods and beliefs. They prayed to Christ and to the Virgin before entering the tunnels but once inside turned their attention to the Tío, who could show them where to find good ore: "Tíos, help me see the metal," they might pray, whereupon to their minds the devil gathered ore and showed it to them. Miners set aside Tuesdays and Fridays for the *ch'alla*, or offering to Pachamama and the Tío, especially at midnight and at midday. A miner at Oruro reported:

> We begin to *ch'alla* in the working areas within the mine. We bring in banners, confetti and paper streamers, all those things. First we begin with the *Tio*. We put a cigarette in his mouth. After this we scatter the alcohol on the ground for the *Pachamama*. I and my partner do it. We are "politicos," a kind of team. We scatter the alcohol and then give some to the *Tio*. Then we take out our coca and begin to chew, and we smoke. We serve liquor from the bottles each of us brings in. We light the *Tio's* cigarette, and we say, "*Tio*, help us in our work. Don't let any accidents happen." We do not kneel before him as we would before a saint, because that would be sacrilegious. Then everyone begins to get drunk. We begin to talk about our work, about the sacrifice that we make. When this is finished, we wind the streamers around the neck of the *Tio*. We prepare our mesas [tables with offerings of herbs, a llama fetus, cakes depicting monsters or desired goods, which the miners burn before the Tío]. After some time, we say, "Let's go." Some have to carry the others out if they are drunk.[57]

Thus continue age-old rituals, echoes of the pre-Hispanic Andes. Like their ancestors, many Andeans considered mountains and hills to be *achachilas*, ancestors who had given life to the people and demanded their worship.[58] Certain ore-bearing hills and their mines became huacas: "Festivals were held in their honor at which the miners danced and drank chicha all night."[59] A couple of times during the year the miners made a special offering, or *k'araku*, which usually included the sacrifice of a llama. Never completely divorced from his roots as a Bolivian cholo, the great tin baron Patiño continued to make offerings to the Tío as a wealthy and powerful capitalist.[60] Managers at his mines provided llamas for sacrifice. Miners who refused to worship the Tío might suffer accidents or even death, and the devil might hide the ore veins from them.

Yet Bolivian miners did not restrict their worship to the old Andean deities. If Tuesdays and Fridays belonged to the Tío and Pachamama, the miners dedicated Sundays and saints' days and early mornings and vespers to Catholic practices. As one commented: "God is in his glory, Pachamama is in the earth, and the Tío is there below with us in the mines."[61] Even the Virgin assumed pre-Hispanic characteristics. Miners described her as "bad," meaning that she was powerful, sometimes destructively so, but she could also grant them great blessings: "The Virgin is very bad. Each Sunday we take candles to illuminate her niche. The Virgin could eat us."[62] As a result, the cosmology of Bolivian miners was neither wholly Catholic nor completely Andean. It melded or harmonized the two, but the result was neither authentically Andean nor truly Catholic.

The miners' cultural insistence on harmony even strengthened their labor unions. As they ritually exchanged gifts with the gods of the mines, the ch'alla and k'araku brought workers together and increased their sense of solidarity. At times, such as during the government of René Barrientos in the 1960s, management tried to prevent such rituals, fearing that they would heighten revolutionary sentiment.[63] A labor leader remarked that in the ch'alla the miners

> give voice to their social problems, they give voice to their work problems, they give voice to all the problems they have, and there is born a new generation so revolutionary that the workers begin thinking of making structural change. This is their university. The experience they have in the *ch'alla* is the best experience inside the mine.[64]

Such rituals bound the workers together in cosmological and vocational solidarity to strengthen their unions. [65]

Andean cosmology and the miners' emphasis on harmony and reciprocity thus helped them withstand the destructive forces of modern mining. Basilia of Oruro saw such reciprocity as a reason for having children: "The children are going to return to you the ayni."[66] Reciprocity also made miners sensitive to the

> organic and spiritual life of the mine . . . the miners are preoccupied with the life of the mine as a living entity . . . they care for the mine. Their attitude is more than respect: it is reverential, stemming from the interaction on which the miners depend. . . . It is also the sensibility of coparticipation with the ways of the mine itself.[67]

Andeans could not escape the dangers of the mines, the exploitation by the foreign companies, the mismanagement by government bureaucrats, or the environmental depredations. But ayni helped them deal with their trials deep in the bowels of Pachamama. It was nonetheless a life of suffering and foreboding, of physical exhaustion and illness. A Bolivian writer captured the ethos in one of his short stories:

> He again untied his nylon sack, and the other miner sat down. Chewing coca leaves they talked, that the work was too much, a crazy effort, little pay, you quickly got sick, you already were spitting blood, you soon died, you seemed older than you were, you had begun working as a youth, eight years ago, two more to live, you don't want to abandon the mine, you don't want to go to the fields, when you are spitting up blood and you leave the mine you soon die, the mine sustains you, gives life to the sick, he knows of many that have left and have died, they had fewer years of work, he doesn't want to die, he will keep working inside the mine, until I die, do you hear, two more years.[68]

Over the centuries, Latin American mines have killed tens of thousands of workers through cave-ins, mercury poisoning, and massacres perpetrated by company management and government forces. Laboring to produce gold, silver, tin, and copper has cut short the lives of millions more miners, who died from silicosis, pneumonia, and malnutrition.

Mining and the Environment

Besides its high social costs, mining has also proved destructive to Pachamama herself, inflicting widespread environmental devastation. Harm to the environment grew over the centuries. Small-scale preconquest indigenous mining scarred the landscape and disturbed the environment. Its effect was slight, however, compared to the impact of colonial mining, and trivial when contrasted with the depredations of the modern mechanized mining industry. Modern miners continue to seek harmony with nature through their ritual offerings. José Rojas, who worked in Cerro de Pasco's smelter at La Oroya, Peru, complained of stomach pains, physical weakness, and mine dust "despite the libations [to the gods] that I make. . . . Now I can't work."[69] The old rituals no longer seem able to restore the harmony disrupted by modern mining.

Harmony with nature did not preoccupy the Spaniards, Portuguese, and their cultural descendants. Europeans offered nature no ritual libations but saw the earth as something to be controlled and subdued for mankind's benefit. They developed their attitude in part from their Judeo-Christian beliefs. Genesis states: "And God blessed them. And God said to them, 'Be fruitful and multiply and fill the earth and subdue it and have dominion over the fish of the sea and over the birds of the heavens and over every living thing that moves on the earth.'"[70] Psalms echoes the theme of man's mastery over nature: "Thou madest him to have dominion over the works of thy hands: thou hast put all things under his feet."[71] The nature of Europeans was not enlivened by a spirit, such as Pachamama; it was a neutral ground instead of a living entity. For Westerners, even those who saw nature as divinely created, the environment existed for the benefit of those who could control and exploit it. The great seventeenth-century scientist and philosopher Francis Bacon, for example, saw the unfolding scientific revolution as a way that mankind brought into being humanity's divinely mandated dominion over nature.[72] This understanding opened wide the door to scientific and technological manipulation of nature. For mining companies and their investors, the industry was engaged in "creative destruction."[73] By digging in the earth and transforming the landscape, they were taking out metals to build things of value in the service of mankind. Unfortunately, the "destruction" usually occurred in one geographical location while the "creation" took place in and benefited someplace else entirely. Modern mining plundered Mother Earth but in the Andes reciprocated not at all, ignoring the demands of ayni.

At the end of the twentieth century, mechanization had transformed large-scale Andean mining to such an extent that companies were profitably processing forty tons of rock to produce a single ounce of gold. Despite the wonders of mechanization and the wealth that came from the concentration of ownership, many workers in the industry continued to scratch out a meager existence and endured hardships reminiscent of colonial times. This inevitably raised the question of what mining had achieved and at what cost. There were no simple answers.

Over the centuries, Latin American mining had consistently promised wealth to individuals and economic development to colonial administrations and later to national governments. The region's mineral resources, it is true, offered a seemingly perpetual treasure. From Europe's discovery of the "New World," Columbus saw the region as a land that would supply the gold needed to satisfy his view of humanity's greatest need: the wealth to launch the Final Crusade and usher in the end of time with Christ's return. As it turned out, however, the region's promise proved illusory. With its great Rich Hill, Potosí yielded vast amounts of bullion, but the poverty of twentieth-century Bolivia revealed little benefit from the silver that the Cerro Rico produced. It had spilled forth a stream of silver that flowed away, to Lima, Europe, and beyond. Spanish American silver and Brazilian gold had monetized the world economy, facilitating international trade and laying the foundation for Europe's industrialization. Yet the human costs were horrific and the anticipated results ephemeral. The seemingly inexhaustible veins gave out, the silver lodes were spent, and the silver stream slowed to a trickle. Later, northward in Potosí province, the Catavi, Siglo XX, and Uncía mines of the great Llallagua complex promised another treasure trove to a later generation, this time consisting of tin. The mines enriched Simón Patiño and laid the foundation of a great family fortune. The Bolivian government and economy depended on it, but in less than a century tin also faded, again at great human cost. A similar story played out elsewhere in the mining countries of Latin America, albeit on a scale less extreme in its rewards and its failures.

It would be too much, of course, to expect only mining to offer a long-term solution to imperial or national economic problems. Although gold has held its worth relatively well since the sixteenth century, silver, tin, and even diamonds have dropped in value. When silver lost its international position as a monetary standard, its value plummeted. By the late twentieth century, the gold-to-silver ratio stood at approximately 1:75, compared with approximately 1:12 in the colonial period. Only the De Beers monopoly's assiduous control of world diamond supplies prevents the price of that mineral from plummeting. Production of artificial diamonds for some industrial applications has already cut into the demand. Meanwhile, economic development in China, India, Russia, and Brazil has increased demand for industrial metals. Tin lost its economic role with the emergence of plastic and aluminum substitutes for the tin can. Consumption of copper, and thus its value, has held up better than that of tin, but modern industry has also found substitutes for copper, including fiber-optic wires, aluminum, and plastic. Undersea cables used for communication have given way to satellite transmissions, and wireless telephones have proliferated everywhere. Metal recycling has also reduced the need for mining expansion. Labor unrest and political turmoil in countries such as Bolivia and Chile perhaps motivated industrialists and manufacturers to find substitutes for the metals mined in Latin America.

The export of staple goods such as minerals and metals offered no permanent security to Latin American economies, although in and of themselves such exports were not necessarily bad. Exports give a country the opportunity to produce a capital surplus and then reinvest it to reduce its dependency on mining. All too often in Latin America, however, foreign competition and weak links between mining and the rest of the economy heightened rather than reduced the nation's dependence on mining. The mining industry had the features of an enclave that is isolated from other sectors of the economy. It often created little local demand for other domestic industries or products, and compared with agriculture provided relatively little employment.[74] Thus, it was not surprising that a critic of Bolivian mining would write:

> Mining is the hole through which the vitality of the country escapes. In more than three centuries, it left nothing, absolutely nothing. That which was built in its service is already useless or soon will be. Commerce and agriculture suffer its ups and downs. The railroads, without the necessary cargo, travel through zones that are not justified without the ores. Even cities like Potosí and Oruro, at another time beneficiaries of the ephemeral mining prosperity, are being converted into empty shells.[75]

The minerals often proved more profitable to others than those who mined them.

A high percentage of Latin America's ghost towns are related to played-out mines, and by the late twentieth century some of the settlements near Bolivia's great tin mines had become depopulated. After 1986, Siglo XX, near the Catavi mine, was a shadow of its former self. Demand for tin had dropped, and management decided to curtail production. The miners' union protested but gave in when management cut food supplies. "In the end it's the hunger that wears you down," recalled activist Domitila Chungara. "It's the children crying to be fed, and having to get up in the morning and pawn whatever you've got left to buy four rolls for breakfast or a kilo of sugar. In the end, despite our efforts and those of friends, we just had to go."[76]

Eventually, five-sixths of Catavi's workers accepted a meager severance pay and abandoned the site. The remaining five hundred or so stayed to maintain the mine, in case it someday should resume operations. A visitor to late-twentieth-century Catavi or to the Rich Hill of Potosí found conditions in many respects reminiscent of colonial rather than modern mechanized mining. In the final years that COMIBOL operated the mines, and even afterward when miners' cooperatives exploited many of the diggings, jucos and locatarios worked old, played-out pits. Desperate peasants, former miners, and palliris dug through the old dumps in the hope of finding something worth selling.

This does not contradict the fact, of course, that Latin American mines have yielded vast fortunes over centuries of exploitation. The gold, silver, tin, copper, and other minerals were crucial to the world economy. But individuals and even nations that relied on mining for their livelihood were gambling. The great economist Adam Smith noted that,

> [o]f all those expensive and uncertain projects . . . which bring bankruptcy upon the greater part of the people who engage in them, there is none perhaps more perfectly ruinous than the search after new silver and gold mines. It is perhaps the most disadvantageous lottery in the world, or the one in which the gain of those who draw the prizes bears the least proportion to the loss of those who draw the blanks.[77]

Even when nations won the mineral lottery, as Bolivia and other Latin American countries did, the jackpot was not necessarily profitable. In one of Brazil's gold districts, "the most striking feature of the history of Nova Lima [was] the contrast between the poverty of its people and the immense wealth they extract from the Morro Velho mine."[78] All too often, mining failed to deliver the treasure, especially for local populations.

Social costs remained high. The mines, especially the underground diggings, were dangerous. Accidents and the prolonged agony of silicosis claimed many lives:

> Workers of 38 years are already old. For every year of work in deep, hot, poorly ventilated mines they age three. Silicon particles produced by drills perforating the rock adhere to their lungs, hardening them gradually until producing death clearly and gradually. . . . Emaciated, their complexions a deathly pallor, their eyes inflamed, dominated by an enormous fatigue, they return to the tunnel to take their daily dose of annihilation. Where possible they hide the illness for which there is no cure nor drugs, but the burning eyes, the skin stuck like dried leather on the cheeks and the constant fatigue cannot be hidden for long. He and his comrades know what is happening; the women also:

when the first symptoms appear—vomiting blood—they keep silent.
There are no desperate gestures. They understand and are resigned.[79]

That workers entered the mines at all is a testament to both their desperate economic circumstances and the courage and determination of the human spirit.

More so than in the past, miners labored with hope for the future of their
children. Workers pressed for higher wages rather than seeking to escape the
mines. The new opportunities for miners' children were one of the chief social
achievements of mining. Educational possibilities at mines, at least for children
of workers at large corporations and the state-owned mines, gave the miners
hope that the next generation would have it better. That was certainly not true
during colonial times, when ethnic divisions and the emphasis upon preserva-
tion of villages and village culture meant that each generation expected to fill
the role of mitayo.

Conclusion

Latin American mines have produced great wealth, whether it be Brazilian
and Colombian gold, Mexican and Andean silver, Chilean copper, or Brazilian
iron and manganese. The golden dream that inspired Columbus, Cortés, and
countless other conquistadores continues to lure Latin Americans into mining. They take great risks to toil at strikes like Serra Pelada in Brazil. Slavery
and other forms of forced labor have disappeared from the mining fields.
Desperation born of poverty entices many into the adits and pits, sometimes
with disastrous consequences. In 2001, for example, more than forty miners
died in a Colombian gold mine near Filadelfia and Quinchía. Dozens of families were working the abandoned mine when their haphazard use of explosives caused the mine to collapse.[80]

During more than five centuries, mining has played a prominent role on
the Latin American economic stage. For the foreseeable future, mining will
remain a major part of economic life in Latin America and will have profound
social, cultural, and environmental consequences for the region. Economic
development throughout the world stimulates demand for metals and other
mining products. Even when demand declines for a particular metal, such as
tin, it usually grows for another, such as aluminum, that replaces the original in importance. Currently, demand for lithium promises to open mining
opportunities in Latin America. As the automobile industry makes a transition to gasoline-electric hybrids and all-electric vehicles, it is creating a huge

market for batteries, which are lithium-based. In the early twenty-first century, Chile and Argentina have established major lithium-mining operations, and a Mexican firm has announced the discovery of lithium deposits in the states of San Luis Potosí and Zacatecas.[81] In its Uyuni province west of Potosí, Bolivia claims half of the known world reserves of lithium.[82] Will the soft, silver-white metal provide Bolivia with ephemeral riches, as its silver and tin did, or will lithium mining offer the nation a more widespread prosperity? History has shown, of course, the benefits and costs of counting on mining to generate economic and social development. Whether silver or lithium, gold or copper, Latin America's mineral resources are finite. Their exploitation will become more expensive, unless technological innovation discovers less costly means of extracting and processing the ores. Metal recycling will undoubtedly offset some demand for increased mining but will likely have only a marginal effect. Intensified mining and refining will create greater conflict with communities concerned about the environmental and social effects.[83] Large mechanized mines will pay well by local standards. Meanwhile, driven by cultural inclination or by economic desperation, some Latin Americans will continue to exploit small diggings and old high-grade mines and dumps.

For much of its history, Latin American mining has offered the region and the miners themselves a bargain with the devil. The image of the Cerro Rico still looms over Bolivia and, metaphorically speaking, over all of Latin America. It provokes impressions of great wealth and profound poverty, of ecological devastation and creative destruction, of workers both ecstatic over the discovery of a bonanza and drained of their life force by brutal labor and devastating illness. Yet if those impressions are stripped away, behind them the Tío waits to welcome the next shift of workers, promising them wealth and protection and sometimes delivering on those promises. The miners hope that by establishing ayni with him, they can impose order and control over the dangers of the mine.

Two incidents illustrate Latin America miners' bargain with the devil. The first occurred in 1786 at Huancavelica's Santa Barbara mercury mine. Two centuries of exploiting the cinnabar deposits to provide mercury for Andean silver refiners had left the mine depleted of rich ore. To meet demand for mercury, government managers began to mine the natural ore-bearing buttresses that earlier generations of workers had left to support the mine. Masonry walls and arches were constructed to replace the natural buttresses. On September 25, 1786, the top half of the mine collapsed. Administrators tried unsuccessfully to convince viceregal authorities that an earthquake had caused the cave-in. But the scope of the disaster soon became clear: the upper sections of Santa Barbara, which lay near the top of the hill, were inaccessible, although tunnels dug lower on the hillside to intersect the lower pits still made it possible to reach the deeper workings. All that meant little to the local population, however, which mourned the deaths of more than two hundred workers entombed by the collapse.[84] How many survived the initial catastrophe, perhaps by taking refuge in surviving pits or air pockets, could not be determined. The mine operators lacked accurate maps of the mine and had no machinery capable of quickly moving rubble or boring holes to extricate victims. Any trapped survivors were left to die horrifically from injuries and asphyxiation in the total darkness of the mine that became their tomb.

The second incident occurred near in the San José gold and copper mine near Copiapó, Chile, in 2010. On August 5, 2010, part of the mine caved in, trapping thirty-three miners nearly half a mile underground. Operated by the San Esteban mining company, San José had a checkered safety record, but the high price of gold made its continued operation an attractive business for investors and for the miners themselves, for they needed the wages. Initial attempts to rescue the trapped men proved futile when a second cave-in completely blocked access to the lower reaches of the mine. At that point it was not clear how many workers, if any, had survived. The company drilled several exploratory six-inch-wide boreholes in an attempt to reach places at the bottom of San José, where, it was hoped, survivors might have taken refuge. On August 22, seventeen days after the initial cave-in, drillers finally broke through into the area where the miners had retreated. When the drillers retracted their probe, they found attached to it a scrawled message: "We are well in the shelter, the 33 of us." The workers had survived more than two weeks by carefully sharing emergency rations that were intended to last for two days. But the rations had run out.

What the twenty-first-century Chilean workers had, in contrast to the eighteenth-century Peruvians at Huancavelica, was the knowledge that machinery and technology made their rescue possible and the hope that they might be reached in time to save them. Between August 5 and August 22 they united to strengthen one another emotionally to fight despair and deprivation. Comforted by the breakthrough on August 22, they still had to wait anxiously for the drilling of another shaft wide enough to permit a rescue capsule to lift them, one by one, to the surface. Three large drilling rigs had begun perforating separate shafts. Psychologists counseled the workers on how to deal with the terrors they had experienced. Personnel from the U.S. National Aeronautics and Space Administration (NASA) arrived to apply the knowledge NASA had gained from extended space travel to help the miners cope with their prolonged isolation. Meanwhile, the workers communicated with their families and rescue personnel via the boreholes and received food, medicine, and other provisions. They had no guarantee, however, that these efforts would succeed in extricating them. The shaft drilled by one of the rigs broke through into the refuge chamber on October 9, more than two months after the cave-in. All thirty-three men were safely and triumphantly extracted on October 12 and 13 from what had nearly been their tomb, almost half a mile underground. The rescue cost tens of millions of dollars and required the technical cooperation of personnel from around the globe. Its final phase was carried worldwide on live television. Physically, the workers were in generally good condition, but it remains to be seen what types of psychological scars they will bear.

The Huancavelica and San José disasters bring to mind a story ethnographer June Nash heard while interviewing mine workers in Oruro, Bolivia. One worker told her about a miner who made offerings to the Tío and was rewarded with a good vein that he worked. One night the Tío, a tall blond man, appeared in the tunnel and offered to help the Indian in exchange for a jug of alcohol. To pay for the drink, the Tío gave the miner some dirt, which to his amazement turned mysteriously into gold. This he used to purchase the liquor. The Tío then reciprocated by giving him rich ores. First, however, he ordered the miner not to turn around and look to see where the ore was hidden or how it was being extracted. The miner obeyed, took his bonanza to the surface, bought a truck and house, and within a month had spent his treasure. He went back to the mine. Once again the Tío reappeared. He offered to help the miner one last time, again on the condition that he not look back. But the miner's curiosity and greed got the better of him, and he turned. "He saw the devil with his horns shining. The rock closed on him and he stayed inside buried."[85]

Like that mine worker, laborers at both Huancavelica and the San José mine had entered the Tío's world. Capital investment and modern technology made the San José rescue feasible, and public pressure on the company and the Chilean government required that it be attempted. Most mining catastrophes, of course, do not yield such joyous results. At Huancavelica in 1786, rescuers lacked adequate technology for such a rescue and given the racial and ethnic prejudices of the period, it is doubtful the colonial government would have spent tens of millions of pesos in an attempt to save two hundred Indian workers. Nonetheless, both events show that mining is a hard world. It can reward operators, and sometimes even workers, with riches, as Nash's story about the bargain the miner struck with the Tío shows. But it can also leave workers, operators, and nations metaphorically and literally encased in rock. The story of Latin American mining does not reveal whether there is a permanent escape from that rock.

Notes

Chapter 1

1. John H. Parry and Robert G. Keith, eds., *New Iberian World: A Documentary History of the Discovery and Settlement of Latin America to the Early 17th Century* (New York: Times Books, 1984), 2:268.

2. Juan Gil, *Mitos y utopías del descubrimiento* (Madrid: Alianza Editorial, 1989), 1:50–56.

3. See, for example, Kozo Yamamura and Tetsuo Kamiki, "Silver Mines and Sung Coins—A Monetary History of Medieval and Modern Japan in International Perspective," in *Precious Metals in the Later Medieval and Early Modern Worlds*, ed. John F. Richards (Durham, NC: Carolina Academic Press, 1983), 329–62.

4. "La gente della coge el oro con candelas de noche en la playa," in *The Diario of Christopher Columbus's First Voyage to America, 1492–1493*, trans. and ed. Oliver Dunn and James E. Kelley Jr. (Norman: University of Oklahoma Press, 1989), 140–43.

5. "The First Voyage of Columbus," in Parry and Keith, *New Iberian World*, 2:45–46.

6. Carlo Ortwin Sauer, *The Early Spanish Main* (Berkeley: University of California Press, 1966), 27.

7. Ibid., 61–62.

8. Columbus to Ferdinand and Isabella, Jamaica, July 7, 1503, in Parry and Keith, *New Iberian World*, 2:118.

9. William M. Denevan, ed., *The Native Population of the Americas in 1492*, 2nd ed. (Madison: University of Wisconsin Press, 1992), xxiii–xxiv.

10. In substitution, a tributary could produce twenty-five pounds of spun cotton. Samuel Eliot Morison, *Admiral of the Ocean Sea* (Boston, MA: Little, Brown, 1942), 491; Kirkpatrick Sales, *The Conquest of Paradise* (New York: Penguin, 1991), 155.

11. Silvio Zavala, *Estudios indianos* (Mexico: Colegio Nacional, 1948), 145.

12. *Colección de documentos inéditos relativos al descubrimiento, conquista y organización de las antiguas posesiones españolas de ultramar*, vol. 5 (Madrid: Real Academia de la Historia, 1890), 312ff.

13. Bartolomé de las Casas, *History of the Indies*, trans. Andrée Collard (New York: Harper, 1971), 192.

14. The Aztecs had soon grown fond of the pork introduced by the Spaniards. The quote is from Miguel Leon-Portilla, ed., *The Broken Spears: The Aztec Account of the Conquest of Mexico* (Boston, MA: Beacon Press, 1962), 51.

15. Bernal Díaz, *The Conquest of New Spain*, trans. J. M. Cohen (Baltimore, MD: Penguin, 1963), 93.

16. J. Alden Mason, *The Ancient Civilizations of Peru* (New York: Penguin, 1957), 267; and Georg Petersen G., *Minería y metalurgía en el antiguo Perú*, Antropológicas 12 (Lima: Museo Nacional de Antropología y Arqueología, 1970).

17. Robert C. West, "Aboriginal Metallurgy and Metalworking in Spanish America: A Brief Overview," in *In Quest of Mineral Wealth: Aboriginal and Colonial Mining and Metallurgy in Spanish America*, ed. Alan K. Craig and Robert C. West, vol. 33, Geoscience and Man (Baton Rouge: Louisiana State University Press, 1994), 5–20.

18. In addition to West, "Aboriginal Metallurgy," see Izumi Shimada, "Pre-Hispanic Metallurgy and Mining in the Andes: Recent Advances and Future Tasks," in Craig and West, eds. *In Quest*, 47–55.

19. Garman Harbottle and Phil C. Weigand, "Turquoise in Pre-Columbian America," *Scientific American* 266 (February 1992): 78–82.

20. Kendall W. Brown and Alan K. Craig, "Silver Mining at Huantajaya, Viceroyalty of Peru," in Craig and West, eds. *In Quest*, 307, 323.

21. Robert S. Haskett, "'Our Suffering with the Taxco Tribute': Involuntary Mine Labor and Indigenous Society in Central New Spain," *Hispanic American Historical Review* 71, no. 3 (August 1991), 449–451.

22. Biblioteca National (Madrid), "Memorial y relación de las minas de azogue del Perú," 1607, mss. 3041, fols. 1–8.

23. Alonso de Morgado, *Historia de Sevilla* [1587] (Seville: Ariza, 1887), 166, 173.

24. Quoted in Miguel de Cervantes Saavedra, "Discurso preliminar," in *Rinconete y Cortadillo*, ed. Francisco Rodríguez Marín (Seville: Francisco de P. Díaz, 1905), 11.

25. Morgado, *Historia de Sevilla*, 169.

26. Pedro de Medina, *Libro de grandezas y cosas memorables de España* (Madrid: Consejo Superior de Investigaciones Científicas, 1944), 74.

27. Ibid., 75.

28. This is particularly true compared with modern values. Around 2000, for example, a troy ounce of gold was worth $300 to $400, compared to $3 to $5 for a troy ounce of silver.

29. Thus, the European value of gold relative to silver declined in the late Middle Ages. In Florence, for example, the gold mark dropped from 13.62 marks of silver in 1324 to 11.98 in 1345 and 9.36 in 1450. In Portugal, a mark of gold was valued successively in 12 marks of silver in 1350, 11.33 marks in 1383, and 10 marks in 1433. Vitorino Magalhães-Godinho, *L'économie de l'empire portugais aux XVe et XVIe siècles*, vol. 26, École Pratique des Hautes Études, VIe Section, Centre de Recherches

Historiques, Ports—Routes—Trafics (Paris: S.E.V.P.E.N., 1969), 39. See also Manuel Moreyra Paz Soldán, *La moneda colonial en el Perú: capítulos de su historia* (Lima: Banco Central de Reserva del Perú, 1980), 69.

30. The foregoing discussion refers to the trends in the value of gold and silver in the Iberian Peninsula.

31. Dennis O. Flynn and Arturo Giraldez, "China and the Manila Galleons," in *Japanese Industrialization and the Asian Economy*, ed. A. J. H. Latham and H. Kawakatsu, (New York: Routledge, 1994), 75. See also Richard Von Glahn, *Fountain of Fortune: Money and Monetary Policy in China, 1000–1700* (Berkeley: University of California Press, 1996), especially chap. 4.

32. Von Glahn, *Fountain of Fortune*, 131.

33. Fernand Braudel, *Capitalism and Material Life, 1400–1800* (New York: Harper and Row, 1973), 341.

34. Inga Clendinnen, *Ambivalent Conquests: Maya and Spaniard in Yucatan, 1517–1570* (New York: Cambridge University Press, 1987), 13–14.

Chapter 2

1. See, for example, Bartolomé Arzáns de Orsúa y Vela, *Anales de la Villa Imperial de Potosí* (La Paz: Ministerio de Educación y Cultura, 1970), 19.

2. A purported interview with Gualpa is contained in "Relación del Cerro de Potosí y su descubrimiento," in *Relaciones geográficas de Indias—Peru*, ed. Marcos Jiménez de la Espada, vol. 183, Biblioteca de Autores Españoles (Madrid: Ediciones Atlas, 1965), 357–61.

3. John J. TePaske used colonial treasury records to calculate this total.

4. Geoffrey Parker, "The Emergence of Modern Finance in Europe, 1500–1730," in *The Fontana Economic History of Europe*, ed. Carlo M. Cipolla, vol. 2, *The Sixteenth and Seventeenth Centuries* (London: Fontana, 1974), 527.

5. Pedro de Cieza de León, *Obras completas* (Madrid: Consejo de Investigaciones Superiores, 1984), 1:133.

6. Guillermo Lohmann Villena, *Las minas de Huancavelica en los siglo XVI y XVII* (Seville: Escuela de Estudios Hispano-Americanos, 1949), 74, 101, 103.

7. These figures, of course, come from treasury records and do not include any contraband production. Real output was undoubtedly higher. Peter Bakewell, who has closely studied Potosí's record for the sixteenth and seventeenth centuries, believes that around 1635 its true production was 12 percent higher than the tax data indicate. Bakewell, "Registered Silver Production in the Potosí District, 1550–1735," *Jahrbuch für Geschichte von Staat, Wirtschaft und Gesellschaft Lateinamerikas*, band 12 (1975): 84.

8. Kenneth J. Andrien, *Crisis and Decline: The Viceroyalty of Peru in the Seventeenth Century* (Albuquerque: University of New Mexico Press, 1985), 62.

9. Testimonio de la Residencia del Dr. Dn. Luis Ambrosio de Alarcón, 1720, ANP, Juicios de Residencia, legajo 37, cuaderno 111, Archivo Nacional, Lima; and Alarcón to the king, October 25, 1719, AGI, Lima 410, Archivo General de Indias, Seville.

10. Bartolomé Arzáns de Orsúa y Vela, *Tales of Potosí*, ed. R. C. Padden, trans. Frances M. López-Morillas (Providence, RI: Brown University Press, 1975), 172–73.

11. Cieza de León, *Obras completas*, 133.

12. Peter Bakewell, *Silver and Entrepreneurship in Seventeenth-Century Potosí: The Life and Times of Antonio López de Quiroga* (Albuquerque: University of New Mexico Press, 1988), 169.

13. Alan K. Craig, *Spanish Colonial Silver Coins in the Florida Collection* (Gainesville: University of Florida Press, 2000), 13.

14. Bakewell, *Silver and Entrepreneurship*, 36–42.

15. Enrique Tandeter, *Coercion and Market: Silver Mining in Colonial Potosí, 1692–1826* (Albuquerque: University of New Mexico Press, 1993), 234.

16. Decree of the Regency, November 13, 1812, AGI, Lima 1335, Archivo General de Indias, Seville.

17. Lewis Hanke and Celso Rodriguez, eds., *Los virreyes españoles en América durante el gobierno de la Casa de Austria*, vol. 282, Biblioteca de Autores Españoles (Madrid: Ediciones Atlas, 1978), 150.

18. Quoted in Garrett Mattingly, *The Armada* (Boston, MA: Houghton Mifflin, 1959), 388.

19. Peter Pierson, *Philip II of Spain* (London: Thames and Hudson, 1975), 69.

20. Quoted in Robert C. West, "Early Silver Mining in New Spain, 1531–1555," in Craig and West, eds., *In Quest*, 122.

21. Haskett, "'Our Suffering,'" 151.

22. Woodrow W. Borah, *New Spain's Century of Depression* (Berkeley: University of California Press, 1951).

23. Borah and Sherburne F. Cook later proposed an even higher population, 25 million, for central Mexico at the time of contact with the Europeans. See *The Aboriginal Population of Central Mexico on the Eve of the Spanish Conquest* (Berkeley: University of California Press, 1963).

24. Diego Holgado to king, accompanying auto, November 12, 1763, fols. 42–43, AGI, Lima 843, Archivo General de Indias, Seville.

25. D. A. Brading, *Miners and Merchants in Bourbon Mexico, 1763–1810* (Cambridge: Cambridge University Press, 1971), 285.

26. Despite his great success at Potosí, López de Quiroga never managed to obtain a title.

27. Quoted in Brading, *Miners and Merchants*, 199.

28. Ibid., 201.

29. Lohmann Villena, *Las minas*, 295–301; Mervyn F. Lang, *El monopolio estatal del mercurio en el México colonial (1550–1710)* (Mexico City: Fondo de Cultura Económica, 1977), 93–94; Antonio Matilla Tascón, *Historia de las minas de Almadén*, vol. 2, *Desde 1646 a 1799* (Madrid, 1987), 19–20.

30. Robert C. West, *Colonial Placer Mining in Colombia* (Baton Rouge: Louisiana State University Press, 1952), 5.

31. Ibid., 62.

32. On the Brazilian gold rush, see Manoel Cardozo, "The Brazilian Gold Rush," *The Americas* 3, no. 2 (October 1946): 137–60; and C. R. Boxer, *The Golden Age of Brazil, 1695–1750* (Berkeley: University of California Press, 1962).

33. See, for example, Boxer, *Golden Age*, 47–48.

34. André João Antonil, *Cultura e Opulência do Brasil* (São Paulo: Companhia Editora Nacional, 1967), 304.

35. Boxer, *Golden Age*, 205–6.

36. Ibid., 224–25.

37. Dennis O. Flynn, "Comparing the Tokugawa Shogunate with Hapsburg Spain: Two Silver-Based Empires in a Global Setting," in *The Political Economy of Merchant Empires: State Power and World Trade, 1350–1750*, ed. James D. Tracy (Cambridge: Cambridge University Press, 1997), 353.

38. Kenneth Maxwell, *Pombal: Paradox of the Enlightenment* (New York: Cambridge University Press, 1993), 43.

39. Parker, "Emergence," 529–30.

40. Charles P. Kindleberger, *Spenders and Hoarders: The World Distribution of Spanish American Silver, 1550–1750* (Singapore: Institute of Southeast Asian Studies, 1989), 2.

41. Flynn, "Tokugawa Shogunate," 332–335. Some economic historians argue that less American silver arrived in the Far East, largely because they consider the flow across the Pacific to have been lower. See, for example, Ward Barrett, "World Bullion Flows, 1450–1800," in *The Rise of Merchant Empires*, ed. James D. Tracy (Cambridge: Cambridge University Press, 1993), 248–50.

42. See, for example, Carlos Sempat Assadourian's cogent analysis in *El sistema de la economía colonial: el mercado interior, regiones y espacio económico* (Mexico City: Editorial Nueva Imagen, 1983).

43. Von Glahn, *Fountain of Fortune*, 5–6.

44. Quoted in Andrien, *Crisis and Decline*, 18.

45. Kindleberger, *Spenders and Hoarders*, 27.

46. Stuart B. Schwartz, "Free Labor in a Slave Economy: the *Lavradores de Cana* of Colonial Bahia," in *Colonial Roots of Modern Brazil*, ed. Dauril Alden (Berkeley: University of California Press, 1973), 194, 196.

47. Richard L. Garner, *Economic Growth and Change in Bourbon Mexico* (Gainesville: University of Florida Press, 1993), 140.

Chapter 3

1. Flynn and Giraldez, "Manila Galleons," 78.

2. Peter Bakewell, *Miners of the Red Mountain: Indian Labor in Potosí, 1545–1650* (Albuquerque: University of New Mexico Press, 1984), 51; and Jeffrey Cole,

The Potosí Mita, 1573–1700: Compulsory Indian Labor in the Andes (Palo Alto, CA: Stanford University Press, 1985), 3.

3. The transition in labor systems at Potosí is best analyzed by Bakewell, *Miners*, 61–135.

4. Juan de Matienzo, *Gobierno del Perú (1567)* (Paris: Institut Français d'Études Andines, 1967), 135–36.

5. Ricardo Beltrán y Rozpide and Angel de Altolaguirre, eds., *Colección de las memorias ó relaciones que escribieron los virreyes del Perú* (Madrid: Imprenta Mujeres Españolas, 1921), 1:87, 93.

6. Pedro Vicente Cañete y Domínguez, *Guía histórica, geográfica, física, política, civil y legal del Gobierno e Intendencia de la Provincia de Potosí* (Potosí: Editorial Potosí, 1952), 100.

7. An institutional study of indigenous tribute is in Ronald Escobedo, *El tributo indígena en el Perú (siglos XVI–XVII)* (Pamplona: Ediciones Universidad de Navarra, 1979).

8. On the repartos, see Jürgen Golte, *Repartos y rebeliones: Túpac Amaru y las contradicciones de la economía colonial* (Lima: Instituto de Estudios Peruanos, 1980); Javier Tord and Carlos Lazo, *Hacienda, comercio, fiscalidad y luchas sociales (Perú colonial)* (Lima: Biblioteca Peruana de Historia, Economía y Sociedad, 1981), 117–90; and Karen Spalding, *Huarochirí: An Andean Society Under Inca and Spanish Rule* (Palo Alto, CA: Stanford University Press, 1984), 188–204.

9. Although conditions at quicksilver mines were even more dangerous than at Potosí until the eighteenth century, Huancavelica's mita was much smaller, and after 1700 many of the subject provinces commuted service for money payment. See Kendall W. Brown, "Workers' Health and Colonial Mercury Mining at Huancavelica, Peru," *The Americas* 57, no. 4 (April 2001): 467–96. General studies of Huancavelica include Arthur P. Whitaker, *The Huancavelica Mercury Mine; a Contribution to the History of the Bourbon Renaissance in the Spanish Empire* (Cambridge, MA: Harvard University Press, 1941); and Lohmann Villena, *Las minas*.

10. Cole, *Potosí Mita*, 20.

11. Felipe Guaman Poma de Ayala, *The First New Chronicle and Good Government, Abridged*, trans. David Frye (Indianapolis, IN: Hackett Publishing, 2006), 180.

12. Enrique Tandeter, "Trabajo forzado y trabajo libre en el Potosí colonial tardío," *Desarrollo Económico* 3, no. 6 (1981): 514–16; and Bakewell, *Miners*, 181.

13. Luis Capoche, *Relación general de la villa imperial de Potosí*, vol. 122, Biblioteca de Autores Españoles (Madrid: Ediciones Atlas, 1959), 109.

14. The earliest documents referring to the practice as the kajcha date from the early 1700s. Tandeter, *Coercion and Market*, 95.

15. The best description of the early *rescate*, or trade in ore, is Capoche, *Relación general*, 160–67.

16. Tandeter, *Coercion and Market*, 92.

17. Ibid., 102–14.

18. Jiménez de la Espada, "Descripción," 377.

19. On women at Potosí, see particularly Jane E. Mangan, *Trading Roles: Gender, Ethnicity, and the Urban Economy in Colonial Potosí* (Durham, NC: Duke University Press, 2005).

20. Carmen Bancora, "Las remesas de metales preciosos desde El Callao a España en la primera mitad del siglo XVII," *Revista de Indias* 29, no. 75 (January–March 1959): 45.

21. Bakewell, *Silver and Entrepreneurship*, 74–78.

22. Thierry Saignes, "Capoche, Potosí y la coca: el consumo popular de estimulantes en el siglo XVII," *Revista de Indias* 48, no. 182–83 (1988): 207–35.

23. Arzáns de Orsúa y Vela, *Tales of Potosí*, 117–18.

24. Arzáns de Orsúa y Vela reported his own experience with coca leaves: "As soon as I placed two leaves in my mouth, my tongue seemed to grow so thick that there was no room for it in my mouth, and it burned and prickled so much that, unable to bear it, I told the miner that I could not enter the mine owing to the effects of the coca. He laughed at me and gave me a small piece of a doughy substance resembling a black lozenge, saying that it was called 'sugar' and that if I took it along with the coca the bad effects that it had caused would disappear. I took it into my mouth believing that it was what he had said, and I swear that I have never tasted anything so bitter in my life, so much so that I spit out the so-called sugar together with the herb I had in my mouth and would have vomited up my entrails after them had not the symptoms passed." Ibid., 118. The lozenge was llijta.

25. Saignes, "Capoche, Potosí," 214–15.

26. José de Acosta, *The Natural and Moral History of the Indies* (London: Hakluyt Society, 1880), 1:207–8. I have modernized the spelling.

27. Capoche, *Relación general*, 109.

28. A. Arregui, F. León Velarde, and M. Valcárcel, *Salud y minería: el riesgo del mal de montaña crónico entre mineros de Cerro de Pasco* (Lima: Asociación Laboral para el Desarrollo, 1990), 14–41.

29. Acosta, *Natural and Moral History*, 1:207.

30. John Miller, *Memoirs of General Miller in the Service of the Republic of Peru* (New York: AMS, 1979), 1:3–4.

31. Doris Ladd vividly depicts the ravages of silicosis in *The Making of a Strike: Mexican Silver Workers' Struggles in Real del Monte, 1766–1775* (Lincoln: University of Nebraska Press, 1988), 24–25.

32. José Parés y Franqués, *Catástrofe morboso de las minas mercuriales de la villa de Almadén del Azogue* [1778], ed. Alfred Menéndez Navarro (Cuenca, Spain: Universidad de Castilla–La Mancha, 1998), 114.

33. Mervyn Lang, "El derrumbe de Huancavelica en 1786. Fracaso de una reforma borbónica," *Histórica* 10, vol. 2 (December 1986): 213–26.

34. Cañete y Domínguez, *Guía*, 619–21.

35. Capoche, *Relación general*, 158.

36. Jiménez de la Espada, "Descripción," 378.

37. Bakewell, *Miners*, 146.

38. Brading, *Miners and Merchants*, 146.

39. Roberto Moreno, "Régimen de trabajo en la minería del siglo XVIII," in *Labor and Laborers through Mexican History*, ed. Elsa Cecilia Frost, Michael C. Meyer, and Josefina Zoraida Vázquez (Tucscon: University of Arizona Press, 1979), 242.

40. Bakewell, *Miners*, 164–65.

41. Bakewell, *Silver Mining and Society in Colonial Mexico: Zacatecas, 1546–1700* (Cambridge: Cambridge University Press, 1971), 125.

42. Brading, *Miners and Merchants*, 147.

43. Antonil, *Cultura e Opulência*, 263–64.

44. Arlei B. Macedo, "500 Years of Mining in Brazil: Environmental Aspects," *Ciência e Cultura* 51, no. 3/4 (1999): 303.

45. Herbert S. Klein, *The Middle Passage: Comparative Studies in the Atlantic Slave Trade* (Princeton, NJ: Princeton University Press, 1978), 17.

46. Julio Pinto Vallejos, "Slave Control and Slave Resistance in Colonial Minas Gerais, 1700–1750," *Journal of Latin American Studies* 17 (1985): 2–3.

47. A similar situation held sway in the diamond fields discovered at Serro do Frio around 1727, where slaves worked under the overseers' close supervision. When so many diamonds were gathered that their price dropped sharply, the Crown attempted to limit diamond mining. It restricted the number of masters and slave gangs permitted to work at Serro do Frio and proscribed the presence of freedmen or other prospectors. A valuable contribution to the history of the diamond region is Joaquim Felício dos Santos, *Memórias do distrito diamantino* (Belo Horizonte: Editora Itatiaia, 1976).

48. A. J. R. Russell-Wood, *The Black Man in Slavery and Freedom in Colonial Brazil* (New York: St. Martin's Press, 1982), 111.

49. Donald Ramos, "Community, Control and Acculturation: A Case Study of Slavery in Eighteenth Century Brazil," *The Americas* 42, no. 4 (1986): 425–27.

50. See, for example, Donald Ramos, "Marriage and the Family in Colonial Vila Rica," *Hispanic American Historical Review* 55, no. 2 (May 1975): 200–225; and A. J. R. Russell-Wood, "Technology and Society: The Impact of Gold Mining on the Institution of Slavery in Portuguese America," *Journal of Economic History* 31, no. 1 (1977): 71–72.

51. Quoted in Pierre Vilar, *A History of Gold and Money, 1450 to 1920* (New York: Verso, 1976), 126.

Chapter 4

1. On Quispe, see Arzáns de Orsúa y Vela, *Anales*, chapters 6–7.

2. Gerald Taylor, "Supay," *Amérindia* 5 (1980): 58.

3. Fernando A. Iwasaki Cauti, "Simbolismos religiosos en la minería y metalurgía prehispánicas," *Anuario de Estudios Americanos* 41 (1984): 118.

4. Cristóbal de Molina, *Ritos y fábulas de los incas* [1575] (Buenos Aires: Futuro, 1959), 100.

5. Tristan Platt, "Conciencia andina y conciencia proletaria: Qhuyaruna y ayllu en el norte de Potosí," *HISLA* 2 (1983): 49.

6. José R. Deustua, "Transiciones y manifestaciones culturales de la minería americana entre los siglos XVI–XIX: un primer intento de aproximación," *Histórica* 22, no. 2 (1998): 219–22.

7. June C. Nash, *We Eat the Mines and the Mines Eat Us: Dependency and Exploitation in Bolivia Tin Mines* (New York: Columbia University Press, 1979), 140–41.

8. Platt, "Conciencia andina," 56.

9. Scarlett O'Phelan Godoy, *Rebellions and Revolts in Eighteenth Century Peru and Upper Peru* (Cologne: Böhlau, 1985), 48.

10. See, for example, Luis Miguel Glave, *Trajinantes: caminos indígenas en la sociedad colonial, siglos XVI/XVII* (Lima: Instituto de Apoyo Agrario, 1989), 191.

11. Mine and mill owners did not always use the silver paid by the ayllu to hire substitutes. Sometimes they simply pocketed the money if they were not actively mining or refining ore. Some had exhausted mines that were too costly to work but that still had the right to mitayos. This practice, called *faltriquera*, was illegal but relatively common. Spaniards who engaged in the practice obviously had little incentive to force the ayllus to send mitayos in person, preferring instead to receive the money.

12. For a perceptive discussion of these points, see Thierry Saignes, "Notes on the Regional Contribution to the *Mita* in Potosí in the Early Seventeenth Century," *Bulletin of Latin American Research* 4, no. 1 (1985): 65–76.

13. Jiménez de la Espada, "Descripción," 377, 380.

14. Saignes, "Regional Contribution," 66, 74.

15. O'Phelan Godoy, *Rebellions and Revolts*, 14.

16. Tandeter, *Coercion and Market*, 19.

17. Glave, *Trajinantes*, 295n; Tandeter, *Coercion and Market*, 243–44.

18. Cañete y Domínguez, *Guía*, 112.

19. Tandeter, *Coercion and Market*, 41–42.

20. Russell-Wood, *Black Man*, 117–18; and Kátia M. de Queirós Mattoso, *To Be a Slave in Brazil, 1550–1888* (New Brunswick, NJ: Rutgers University Press, 1989), 118–19.

21. Kathleen J. Higgins, "Masters and Slaves in a Mining Society: A Study of Eighteenth-Century Sabará, Minas Gerais," *Slavery and Abolition* 11, no. 1 (May 1990): 59.

22. Quoted in Russell-Wood, "Technology and Society," 74–75.

23. Mattoso, *To Be a Slave*, 94.

24. Boxer, *Golden Age*, 165. In a letter to the king, the governor of the Captaincy of Rio de Janeiro wrote that the Mina slaves were reputed to be superior miners and added, "I believe them to have earned that reputation because they are believed to be sorcerers, who have the devil in them, so that only they are capable of finding gold, and for the same reason no miner can live without at least one Mina woman, saying that only these will give them luck." (Translation of letter transcribed in Pinto Vallejos, "Slave Control," 33.)

25. Antonil, *Cultura e Opulência*, 303–4.

26. Higgins, "Masters and Slaves," 63–64.

27. Sergio Serulnikov, *Reivindicaciones indígenas y legalidad colonial. La rebelión de Chayanta (1777–1781)* (Buenos Aires: 1989); and "Disputed Images of Colonialism: Spanish Rule and Indian Subversion in Northern Potosí, 1777–1780," *Hispanic American Historical Review* 76, no. 2 (May 1996): 189–226.

28. O'Phelan Godoy, *Rebellions and Revolts*, 194.

29. Ibid., 244, 266.

30. Ann Zulawski, *They Eat from Their Labor: Work and Social Change in Colonial Bolivia* (Pittsburgh: University of Pittsburgh Press, 1995), chapter 5.

31. Ibid., 124–36.

32. Pinto Vallejos, "Slave Control," 7–8.

33. Donald Ramos, "Slavery in Brazil: A Case Study of Diamantina, Minas Gerais," *The Americas* 45, no. 1 (1988): 51.

34. Carlos Magno Guimarães, *Uma negação da ordem escravista: quilombos em Minas Gerais no século XVIII* (São Paulo: Icone Editora, 1988), 37.

35. Pinto Vallejos, "Slave Control," 23–25, 30–31.

36. Russell-Wood, "Technology and Society," 69–70.

37. See James H. Sweet, *Recreating Africa: Culture, Kinship, and Religion in the African-Portuguese World, 1441–1770* (Chapel Hill: University of North Carolina Press, 2003).

38. See, for example, Russell-Wood, *Black Man*, 113–15.

39. On garimpeiros, see Aires da Mata Machado Filho, *O negro e o garimpo em Minas Gerais*, vol. 88, Coleção Reconquista do Brasil (Belo Horizonte: Editora Itatiaia Limitada, 1985).

40. Ramos, "Slavery in Brazil," 48.

41. Alan Probert, "The Pachuca Papers: The Real del Monte Partido Riots, 1766," *Journal of the West* 12, no. 1 (January 1973): 85–125; Noblet Barry Danks, "The Labor Revolt of 1766 in the Mining Community of Real del Monte," *The Americas* 44, no. 2 (October 1987): 143–65; and Ladd, *Making of a Strike*. Danks and Ladd differ in their views of the unrest, with the former concluding it was "a spontaneous, leaderless rebellion . . . not analogous to modern-day labor strikers" (163). Ladd perceives more planning and solidarity. For documents related to the labor unrest, see Manuel Arellano Z., ed., *Primera huelga minera en Real del Monte, 1766* (Mexico City: Libros de México, 1976).

42. For a window into Terreros's mentality after the riots, see Edith Boorstein Couturier, *The Silver King: The Remarkable Life of the Count of Regla in Colonial Mexico* (Albuquerque: University of New Mexico Press, 2003), especially chapter 8.

43. Ladd, *Making of a Strike*, 94–97.

44. Zulawski, *They Eat*, 124, 134, 148.

45. Charles Gibson, *The Aztecs under Spanish Rule* (Palo Alto, CA: Stanford University Press, 1964), 220–21.

46. Antonio de la Calancha, *Crónica moralizada*, vol. 5, ed. Ignacio Prado Pastor (Lima: Universidad Nacional de San Marcos, 1974), 1680.

47. Miller, *Memoirs*, 1:5.

48. Bakewell, *Miners*, 181–85.

49. John Fisher, "The Miners of Peru in 1790," in *Wirtschaftskräfte und Wirtschaftswege*, vol. 4, *Übersee und Allgemeine Wirtschaftsgeschichte*, ed. Jürgen Schneider (Stuttgart: Klett-Cotta, 1978), 124–25.

50. Alejandro de Humboldt, *Ensayo político sobre el reino de la Nueva España*, vol. 3 (Mexico City: Editorial Pedro Robredo, 1941), 14.

51. Cole, *Potosí Mita*, 19.

Chapter 5

1. María Eugenia Romero Sotelo, *Minería y guerra: la economía de Nueva España, 1810–1821* (Mexico City: El Colegio de México, 1997), 85.

2. Margaret E. Rankine, "The Mexican Mining Industry in the Nineteenth Century with Special Reference to Guanajuato," *Bulletin of Latin American Research* 11, no. 1 (1992): 29.

3. John Coatsworth, "Economic and Institutional Trajectories in Nineteenth-Century Latin America," in *Latin America and the World Economy Since 1800*, ed. John H. Coatsworth and Alan M. Taylor (Cambridge, MA: Harvard University, David Rockefeller Center for Latin American Studies, 1998), 23–24. See also Stephen Haber, *How Latin America Fell Behind: Essays on the Economic Histories of Brazil and Mexico, 1800–1914* (Palo Alto, CA: Stanford University Press, 1997).

4. J. Fred Rippy, *British Investments in Latin America, 1822–1949; a Case Study of the Operations of Private Enterprise in Retarded Regions* (Minneapolis: University of Minnesota Press, 1959), 17.

5. Edmond Temple, *Travels in Various Parts of Peru, Including a Year's Residence in Potosi* (London: Henry Colburn and Richard Bentley, 1830), 1:283–84.

6. Potosí had 130–140 refining mills in operation in its early-seventeenth-century glory days. Daniel J. Santamaría, "Potosí entre la plata y el estaño," *Revista Geográfica* 79 (1973): 79.

7. For Sanz's activities at Potosí, see Guillermo Claudio Mira Delli-Zotti, "Ilustración y reformismo borbónico en el Alto Perú: el intendente Sanz y la minería de Potosí a fines del período colonial" (PhD dissertation, Universidad Complutense de Madrid, 1990).

8. Temple, *Travels*, 1:309.

9. John Barclay Pentland, *Report on Bolivia, 1827*, in *Camden Miscellany*, 4th ser., vol. 13 (London: Royal Historical Society, 1974), 193.

10. Quoted in Frank Griffith Dawson, *The First Latin American Debt Crisis: The City of London and the 1822–25 Loan Bubble* (New Haven, CT: Yale University Press, 1990), 120.

11. Temple, *Travels*, 2:200.

12. Ibid., 1:333.

13. Santamaría, "Potosí," 107.

14. See Pentland, *Report on Bolivia*, 188–89.

15. Marvin Bernstein, *The Mexican Mining Industry, 1890–1950: A Study of the Interaction of Politics, Economics, and Technology* (Albany: State University of New York, 1965), 12.

16. Enrique Cárdenas, "A Macroeconomic Interpretation of Nineteenth-Century Mexico," in Haber, ed., *How Latin America*, 67–74.

17. Richard J. Salvucci, "Mexican National Income in the Era of Independence, 1800–40," in Haber, ed., *How Latin America*, 231–34.

18. H. G. Ward, *Mexico* (London: Henry Colburn, 1829), 1:413–14.

19. Rankine, "Mexican Mining Industry," 30–32.

20. Ward, *Mexico*, 1:424; Robert W. Randall, *Real del Monte: A British Mining Venture in Mexico* (Austin: University of Texas Press, 1972), 52–60; and Alan Probert, "Mules, Men, and Mining Machinery: Transport on the Veracruz Road," *Journal of the West* 14, no. 2 (1975): 104–13.

21. Only in 1892 did Mexican law permit foreign ownership.

22. Carlos Contreras, "La minería hispanoamericana después de la independencia. Estudios comparativo de Bolivia, Chile, México y Perú," in *Dos décadas de investigación en historia económica comparada en América Latina: Homenage a Carlos Sempat Assadourian*, ed. Margarita Megegus Bornemann (Mexico City: El Colegio de México, Centro de Estudios Históricos, 1999), 266, 268–69.

23. Frances Calderón de la Barca, *Life in Mexico: The Letters of Fanny Calderón de la Barca*, ed. Howard Fisher and Marion Hall Fisher (Garden City, NY: Anchor Books, 1970), 239

24. Ward, *Mexico*, 1:422–23.

25. Ibid., 415.

26. Rankine, "Mexican Mining Industry," 30–36.

27. Heraclio Bonilla, ed., *Gran Bretaña y el Perú: Informes de los cónsules británicos: 1826–1900* (Lima: Instituto de Estudios Peruanos, 1975), 1:5, 9, 13–14. On the steam pumps, see John Fisher, *Minas y mineros en el Perú colonial, 1776–1824* (Lima: Instituto de Estudios Peruanos, 1977), 240–41.

28. José R. Deustua, *The Bewitchment of Silver: The Social Economy of Mining in Nineteenth-Century Peru* (Athens: Ohio University Press, 2000), 25–27.

29. Marshall C. Eakin, *British Enterprise in Brazil: The St. John d'el Rey Mining Company and the Morro Velho Gold Mine, 1830–1960* (Durham, NC: Duke University Press, 1989), 14–15, 31–33.

30. Ibid., 199–201.

31. W. L. von Eschwege, *Pluto Brasiliensis* (São Paulo: Editora da Universidade de São Paulo, 1979), 249.

32. Tandeter, *Coercion and Market*, 222.

33. Miller, *Memoirs*, 2:284.

34. Antonio Mitre, *Los patriarcas de la plata: estructura socioeconómica de la minería boliviana en el siglo XIX* (Lima: Instituto de Estudios Peruanos, 1981), 138–43.

35. An American mining engineer working at Potosí in the mid-twentieth century recalled that while working in one of the galleries "one day we broke into an ancient room that turned out to be the sala de ahorca that we had heard rumors of. Chains hung from eye bolts in the back and there were many skeletons." Sheldon Wimpfen, "Tin Peaks and Silver Streams," http://www.bureauofmines.com/TPSS_04.HTM, accessed April 5, 2006 (site discontinued).

36. Enrique Tandeter, "Crisis in Upper Peru, 1800–1805," *Hispanic American Historical Review* 71, no. 1 (February 1991): 67.

37. Gustavo Rodríguez Ostria, "Industrialización, tiempo y cultura minera," *Estado y sociedad* 3, no. 4 (December 1987): 70; and André Bellessort, *La jeune Amérique: Chili et Bolivie* (Paris: Perrin et Cie, 1897), 287–98.

38. Gustavo Rodríguez Ostria, "*Kajchas*, trapicheros y ladrones de mineral en Bolivia (1824–1900)," *Siglo XIX* 4, no. 8 (July–December 1989): 127.

39. Ibid., 128–29.

40. Indeed, the refiners were building upon a theoretical foundation laid in the seventeenth century Andes by Alvaro Alonso Barba, as shown by Tristan Platt, "The Alchemy of Modernity. Alonso Barba's Copper Cauldrons and the Independence of Bolivian Metallurgy (1790–1890)," *Journal of Latin American Studies* 32 (2000): 14–25. For a description of the Ortiz machinery, see Tristan Platt, "Historias unidas, memorias escindidas: las empresas mineras de los hermanos Ortiz y la construcción de las élites nacionales. Salta y Potosí, 1800–1880," in *Dos décadas de investigación en historia económica comparada en América Latina*, ed. Margarita Menegus Bornemann (Mexico City: Centro de Estudios Históricos, Colegio de México: Centro de Investigaciones y Estudios Superiores en Antropología Social: Instituto Doctor José María Luis Mora: Centro de Estudios sobre la Universidad, UNAM, 1999), 300–335.

41. Brian Loveman, *Chile: The Legacy of Hispanic Capitalism* (New York: Oxford University Press, 1988), 143.

42. William W. Culver and Cornel J. Reinhart, "The Decline of a Mining Region and Mining Policy: Chilean Copper in the Nineteenth Century," in *Miners and Mining in the Americas*, ed. Thomas C. Greaves and William Culver (Dover, NH: Manchester University Press, 1985), 68–81.

43. William W. Culver and Cornel J. Reinhart, "Capitalist Dreams: Chile's Response to Nineteenth-Century World Copper Competition," *Comparative Studies in Society and History* 31, no. 4 (1989): 725, 729–39; and Loveman, *Chile*, 144–45.

44. J. R. Brown, "The Frustration of Chile's Nitrate Imperialism," *Pacific Historical Review* 32, no. 4 (1963): 387–388.

45. Such attempts at self-regulation and price fixing by the companies worked only temporarily, however, because some low-cost producers refused to participate and there was a tendency for others to exceed their assigned quotas. New combinations consequently had to be negotiated. For an analysis of the combinations, see J. R. Brown, "Nitrate Crises, Combinations, and the Chilean Government in the Nitrate Age," *Hispanic American Historical Review* 43, no. 2 (May 1963): 230–46.

46. Mitre, *Los patriarcas*, 46–49.

47. Miller, *Memoirs*, 2:280, 290.

48. Contreras, "La minería hispanoamericana," 261.

49. Mitre, *Los patriarcas*, 116–21.

50. Bernstein, *Mexican Mining Industry*, 32. In Mexico, the first railroad was completed in 1850, but it ran between Mexico City and the great port of Vera Cruz, the traditional conduit through which goods from Europe passed into the country and from which exports departed to the North Atlantic.

51. Ibid., 32–34.

52. William R. Summerhill, "Market Intervention in a Backward Economy: Railway Subsidy in Brazil, 1854–1913," *Economic History Review* 51, no. 3 (1998): 542.

53. Ian Thomson and Dietrich Angerstein, *Historia del ferrocarril en Chile* (Santiago: Dibam, 1997), 42–43.

54. John Coatsworth, *Growth against Development: The Economic Impact of Railroads in Porfirian Mexico* (DeKalb: Northern Illinois Press, 1981), 35–36.

55. Bernstein, *Mexican Mining Industry*, 32–34.

56. Ibid., 32; Robert W. Randall, "Mexico's Pre-Revolutionary Reckoning with Railroads," *The Americas* 42, no. 1 (July 1985): 25; and Coatsworth, *Growth against Development*, 35.

57. More promoter and entrepreneur than skilled engineer, Meiggs "made a fortune, much of it from bribes, swindles, and kickbacks, which he spent lavishly on high living and charitable donations. He died poor and heavily in debt in 1877. . . . His legacy, however, was one of the most spectacular railroad systems in the world, having sent locomotives higher than they had ever been before." Peter F. Klaren, *Peru: Society and Nationhood in the Andes* (New York: Oxford University Press, 2000), 176–77.

The Central Line had to climb rapidly out of Lima to a height of more than fifteen thousand feet above sea level. This achievement eventually opened the possibility of sending railroads to mining sites such as Cerro de Pasco and Huancavelica. By the time Meiggs died, he had completed about 700 of the 990 miles of track he had contracted to build. Peruvian guano financed the Meiggs projects, but Peru's defeat in the War of the Pacific and declining guano profits provoked a severe financial crisis. The government signed the so-called Grace Contract of 1886 to continue building the railroad, but in so doing surrendered control of the railways to a British company, the Peruvian Corporation, for sixty-six years. It completed the Southern in 1908 and extended the Central Railroad to Huancayo the following year. See also Sir Robert Marrett, *Peru* (New York: Praeger, 1969), 102; and Watt Stewart, *Henry Meiggs: Yankee Pizarro* (Durham, NC: Duke University Press, 1946). On the challenges and risks inherent in building the Peruvian railroads, see the comments of British consul Spenser St. John in 1878 in Bonilla, *Informes*, 1:196–99.

58. Klaren, *Peru*, 197, 206–7.

59. Milton Vargas, "Origem e Desenvolvimento da Geotecnologia no Brasil," *Quipu* 2, no. 2 (May–August 1985): 267–68; and Steven Topik, *The Political Economy of the Brazilian State, 1889–1930* (Austin: University of Texas Press, 1987), 121. See also Eakin, *British Enterprise*, 51.

60. Richard Graham, *Britain and the Onset of Modernization in Brazil, 1850–1914* (Cambridge: Cambridge University Press, 1972), 70–71.

61. Bernstein, *Mexican Mining Industry*, 41–44, 159–60.

62. Ibid., 44; and Alan Lougheed, "The Cyanide Process and Gold Extraction in Australia and New Zealand, 1888–1913," *Australian Economic History Review* 27, no. 1 (1987): 47–48.

63. Rankine, "Mexican Mining Industry," 45.

64. Bernstein, *Mexican Mining Industry*, 44–48.

65. Silver sulfide ores, known as negrillos, were also very difficult for colonial refiners to process through amalgamation. They had to add special ingredients such as pyrites and antimony to free the silver from the other compounds so that it could freely combine with the mercury. The exact additions depended on the type of complex silver ores, and refiners discovered them more through art than chemical analysis.

66. Jeremy Mouat, "The Development of the Flotation Process: Technological Change and the Genesis of Modern Mining, 1898–1911," *Australian Economic History Review* 36, no. 1 (1996): 6.

67. Bernstein, *Mexican Mining Industry*, 137–42.

68. More significant, however, was the discovery and exploitation of nitrate deposits near Mejillones. The nitrate fields attracted Chilean capital and the development of port and railroad facilities. Eventually Chile and Bolivia fought over the Atacama, with the Chileans triumphing in the War of the Pacific (1879–1884). Their seizure of the Atacama left Bolivia landlocked.

69. Mitre, *Los patriarcas*, 59–64.

70. In addition to Bolivians resident in Paris, the Huanchaca Company's initial backers included Chileans and Europeans. In 1899, however, the U.S.-based Guggenheims acquired a 50 percent interest in it. Mitre, *Los patriarcas*, 98–103, 122–23.

71. Bonilla, *Informes*, 1:247, 283, 302–3.

72. See Bellessort, *La jeune Amérique*, 317–18.

73. See, for example, Gustavo Rodríguez Ostria, "Las compañeras del mineral," *Nueva Sociedad* 93 (January–February 1988): 177–79.

74. Rodríguez Ostria, "Industrialización," 73–74.

75. Julio Pinto Vallejos and Luis Ortega Martínez, *Expansión minera y desarrollo industrial: un caso de crecimiento asociado (Chile, 1850–1914)* (Santiago: Departmento de History, Universidad de Santiago de Chile, 1991), 55.

76. For a perceptive discussion of the barreteros' entrepreneurship, see David E. Hojman, "On Miners, Mining Firms and Technology: From the *Barretero* to Anaconda and Kennecott," *Bulletin of Latin American Research* 2, no. 2 (May 1983): 123–26. Barreteros were not always individual workers, however, and sometimes headed

teams of facemen, timbermen, and ore carriers, with each receiving a negotiated portion of the partido.

77. Nineteenth-century labor actions at Real del Monte and Pachuca are discussed in Robert W. Randall, "Militant Mineworkers in Pre-Revolutionary Mexico," *Duquesne Review* 28, no. 2 (Fall 1973): 35–55. The quote is on page 44.

78. Quoted in ibid., 48.

79. Cuauhtémoc Velasco Avila, "Labour relations in mining: Real del Monte and Pachuca, 1824–1874," in Greaves and Culver, *Miners and Mining*, 47–67. At Real del Monte in Mexico, detailed financial and administrative records running from the late eighteenth to the end of the nineteenth centuries provide a unique opportunity to analyze the various forms of labor and how workers in each category were compensated. British administrators and technical personnel, backed by British capital, controlled Real del Monte from 1824 to 1849, whereupon a Mexican mining company took over operations.

80. Quoted in Julio Pinto Vallejos, "La transición laboral en el norte salitrero: la provincia de Tarapacá y los orígenes del proletariado en Chile 1870–1890," *Historia* 25 (1990): 211.

81. Loveman, *Chile*, 173–74, 181–90. For the political context of the strike and war, see Michael Monteón, *Chile in the Nitrate Era: The Evolution of Economic Dependence, 1880–1930* (Madison: University of Wisconsin Press, 1982), 37–41.

Chapter 6

1. Quoted in Manuel Carrasco, *Simón I. Patiño, un procer industrial*, 2nd ed. (Cochabamba, Bolivia: Editorial Canelas, 1964), 61.

2. Charles F. Geddes, *Patino: The Tin King* (London: Robert Hale, 1972), 63.

3. Ibid., 43.

4. John T. Thoburn, *Tin in the World Economy* (Edinburgh: Edinburgh University Press, 1994), 4.

5. For an analysis of tin mining in Bolivia during the nineteenth century, see John Hillman, "The Emergence of the Tin Industry in Bolivia," *Journal of Latin American Studies* 16, no. 2 (November 1984): 403–37.

6. Herbert S. Klein, "The Creation of the Patino Tin Empire," *Inter-American Economic Affairs* 19, no. 2 (1965): 6–7.

7. Klein, "Patino Tin Empire," 16.

8. Gregorio Iriarte, *Galerías de la muerte: vida de los mineros bolivianos* (Montevideo, Uruguay: Tierra Nueva, 1972), 65.

9. John Hillman, "Bolivia and the International Tin Cartel, 1931–1941," *Journal of Latin American Studies* 20 (May 1988): 108.

10. Iriarte, *Galerías de la muerte*, 65.

11. In addition to Patiño, Avelino Aramayo relocated to Switzerland, and Moritz ("Mauricio") Hochschild represented Chilean interests. Meanwhile, several U.S.

corporations set up mining operations in Bolivia, including the Guggenheims, Easley and Inslee, Golden Center Mines, and W. R. Grace. See Steven S. Volk, "Class, Union, Party: The Development of a Revolutionary Union Movement in Bolivia (1905–1952): Part 1: Historical Background," *Science and Society* 39, no. 1 (1975): 31.

12. Timothy J. LeCain, *Mass Destruction: The Men and Giant Mines that Wired America and Scarred the Planet* (New Brunswick, NJ: Rutgers University Press, 2009), chap. 1, discusses Jackling's innovation in the copper industry and his method's environmental legacy.

13. Loveman, *Chile*, 187–88.

14. Such is a central argument of Peter de Shazo in *Urban Workers and the Labor Unions in Chile, 1902–1927* (Madison: University of Wisconsin Press, 1983).

15. For a labor leader's account of the massacre, see José Santos Morales, "Relato de un proscrito. Mi escapada," in *Santa María de Iquique, 1907: documentos para su historia*, ed. Pedro Bravo Elizondo (Santiago: Ediciones del Litoral, 1993), 181–87. See also Eduardo Devés, *Los que van a morir te saludan. Historia de una masacre. Escuela Santa María, Iquique, 1907* (Santiago: Ediciones Documentas, América Latina Libros, Nuestra América, 1988).

16. See, for example, Bravo Elizondo, *Santa María de Iquique*, 205–6.

17. Loveman, *Chile*, 214.

18. Lessie Jo Frazier, *Salt in the Sand: Memory, Violence, and the Nation-State in Chile, 1890 to the Present* (Durham, NC: Duke University Press, 2007), 99–106.

19. Raymond F. Mikesell, *The World Copper Industry: Structure and Economic Analysis* (Baltimore, MD: Johns Hopkins University Press for Resources for the Future, 1979), 7–8.

20. Loveman, *Chile*, 213–14.

21. J. Douglas Porteous, "Social Class in Atacama Company Towns," *Annals of the Association of American Geographers* 64, no. 3 (September 1974): 409–17.

22. Sheldon Wimpfen, "Tin Peaks and Silver Streams," http://www.bureauofmines. com/TPSS_08.HTM, accessed May 12, 2005 (site discontinued).

23. These comments about Chilean miners come from the perceptive analysis of Thomas Miller Klubock, "Working-Class Masculinity, Middle-Class Morality and Labor Politics in the Chilean Copper Mines," *Journal of Social History* 30, no. 2 (Winter 1996): 435–63; and Klubock, *Contested Communities: Class, Gender, and Politics in Chile's El Teniente Copper Mine, 1904–1951* (Durham, NC: Duke University Press, 1998), 60–62.

24. Klubock, *Contested Communities*, 189–202.

25. Alan Knight, *The Mexican Revolution* (Lincoln: University of Nebraska Press, 1986), 1:440.

26. Ramón Eduardo Ruíz, *The Great Rebellion: Mexico, 1905–1924* (New York: Norton, 1980), 70.

27. Knight, *Mexican Revolution*, 1:143.

28. Michael J. Gonzales, "United States Copper Companies, the State, and Labour Conflict in Mexico, 1900–1910," *Journal of Latin American Studies*, 26, no. 3 (October 1994): 659.

29. Knight, *Mexican Revolution*, 1:177–78, 437–48.

30. Michael J. Gonzales, "U.S. Copper Companies, the Mine Workers' Movement, and the Mexican Revolution, 1910–1920," *Hispanic American Historical Review* 76, no. 3 (August 1996): 504.

31. Knight, *Mexican Revolution*, 1:144–45.

32. Bernstein, *Mexican Mining Industry*, 143.

33. Juan Luis Sariego and Raúl Santana Paucar, "Transición tecnológica y resistencia obrera en la minería mexicana," *Cuadernos políticos* 31 (January–March 1982): 19.

34. The foregoing analysis is based on ibid., 17–20.

35. Bernstein, *Mexican Mining Industry*, 228–29.

36. Juan Luis Sariego, "La reconversión industrial en la minería cananaense," *Nueva Antropología* 9, no. 32 (November 1987): 20–21.

37. Sariego and Santana Paucar, "Transición tecnológica," 25.

38. The best analysis of the company's first three decades in Peru is Alberto Flores Galindo, "Los mineros de Cerro de Pasco, 1900–1930," in *Obras completas* (Lima: Fundación Andina, Sur, Casa de Estudios del Socialismo, 1993), 1:11–179. It serves as the basis for much of the following several paragraphs.

39. Elizabeth Dore, "Social Relations and the Barriers to Economic Growth: The Case of the Peruvian Mining Industry," *Nova Americana* 1 (1978): 251.

40. Quoted in Flores Galindo, "Los mineros," 40.

41. Paul Rizo-Patrón Boylan, "La minería entre 1900 y 1950," in *Historia de la minería en el Perú*, ed. José Antonio del Busto Duthurburu and Susana Aldana (Lima: Milpo, 1999), 330.

42. Carlos Contreras, "Mineros, arrieros y ferrocarril en Cerro de Pasco, 1870–1904," *HISLA* 4, no. 2 (1984): 3–20.

43. Adrian Dewind, "From Peasants to Miners: The Background to Strikes in the Mines of Peru," *Science & Society* 39, no. 1 (Spring 1975): 57–59.

44. Florencia Mallon, *The Defense of Community in Peru's Central Highlands: Peasant Struggle and Capitalist Transition, 1860–1940* (Princeton, NJ: Princeton University Press, 1983), 229–30.

45. Flores Galindo, "Los mineros," 15.

46. Mallon, *Defense of Community*, 243.

47. Dore, "Social Relations," 264–65.

48. The quote is from Dewind, "Peasants to Miners," 63.

49. The quote and accompanying information in this paragraph are from Dewind, "Peasants to Miners," 64–67.

50. Antonio Mitre, *Bajo un cielo de estaño; fulgor y ocaso del metal en Bolivia* (La Paz: Asociación Nacional de Mineros Medianos, ILDIS, 1993), 220.

51. Ibid., 228–29.

52. Manuel E. Contreras, "La mano de obra en la minería estañífera de principios de siglo, 1900–1925," *Historia y Cultura* 8 (1985): 107.

53. Wimpfen, "Tin Peaks and Silver Streams," http://www.bureauofmines.com/TPSS_08.HTM, accessed March 21, 2006 (site discontinued).

54. June C. Nash, "Conflicto industrial en los Andes: Los mineros bolivianos del estaño," *Estudios Andinos* 4, no. 2 (1964–1976): 226.

55. Quoted in Contreras, "La mano de obra," 102.

56. June C. Nash, "Mi vida en las minas: la autobiografía de una mujer boliviana," *Estudios Andinos* 5 (1976), 141; Norman Gall, Norman Gall Publications, "'Bolivia: The Price of Tin,' Part 1, Patiño Mines and Enterprises," http://www.normangall.com/bolivia_art2.htm, accessed February 18, 2011. For the testimony of a Bolivian palliri and political activist, see Domitila Barrios de Chungara and Moema Viezzer, *Let Me Speak! Testimony of Domitila, a Woman of the Bolivian Mines* (New York: Monthly Review Press, 1978), which portrays the challenges that the miners and their families faced following the 1952 revolution and especially in the years of the Barriento dictatorship.

57. Nash, "Mi vida," 141.

58. Francisco Zapata, "Los mineros como actores sociales y políticos en Bolivia, Chile y Perú durante el siglo XX" (paper presented at the VIII Reunión Internacional de Historiadores de la Minería Latinoamericana, Guanajuato, Mexico, March 24, 2004).

59. See Volk, "Class, Union, Party, 1," 43.

60. E. P. Thompson, *Making of the English Working Class* (New York: Pantheon, 1964), 9–10.

61. Francisco Zapata, "Mineros y militares en la conyuntura actual de Bolivia, Chile y Perú (1976–1978)," *Revista Mexicana de Sociología* 42, no. 4 (October–December 1980): 1451–452.

62. Zapata, "Los mineros como actores."

63. Nash, "Mi vida," 145.

64. Steven S. Volk, "Class, Union, Party: The Development of a Revolutionary Movement in Bolivia (1905–1952): Part 2: From the Chaco War to 1952," *Science and Society* 39, no. 2 (1975): 187–97.

Chapter 7

1. On the Bolivian Revolution, see Robert J. Alexander, *The Bolivian National Revolution* (New Brunswick, NJ: Rutgers University Press, 1958); James M. Malloy, *Bolivia: The Uncompleted Revolution* (Pittsburgh, PA: University of Pittsburgh Press, 1970); Jonathan Kelley and Herbert S. Klein, *Revolution and the Rebirth of Inequality: A Theory Applied to the National Revolution in Bolivia* (Berkeley: University of California Press, 1981); and Herbert S. Klein, *Bolivia: The Evolution of a Multi-Ethnic Society* (New York: Oxford University Press, 1982).

2. The quote is from Hugo Roberts Barragán, *La revolución del 9 de abril* (La Paz, 1971), 190.

3. Malloy, *Uncompleted Revolution*, 175; and Klein, *Bolivia*, 232–34, 240.

4. Bernstein, *Mexican Mining Industry*, 58–59, 154–56, 192–99, 265–67.

5. "Discurso pronunciado por el Comandante Fidel Castro Ruz, primer secretario del comité central del Partido Comunista de Cuba y primer ministro del Gobierno Revolucionario, a los mineros de Chuquicamata, Chile, el 14 de noviembre de 1971," accessed August 6, 2008, http://www.cuba.cu/gobierno/discursos/1971/esp/f141171e.html.

6. Norman Gall, "Chile: The Struggle in the Copper Mines," *Dissent* (Winter 1973): 101–2. For a study of labor in the copper industry during the Allende and early Pinochet periods, see Manuel Barrera, "El conflicto obrero en el enclave cuprífero chileno," *Revista Mexicana de Sociología*, 40, no. 2 (1978): 609–82.

7. Iriarte, *Galerías de la muerte*, 73.

8. In the great Siglo XX mine, expropriated from the Patiño holdings, for example, the average tin content of the ores declined from 9 percent in 1924 to 2.45 percent in 1938 to 1.11 percent in 1952 to 0.50 percent in 1970. Norman Gall, "'Bolivia: the Price of Tin,' Part 2, The Crisis of Nationalization," accessed February 18, 2011, http://www.normangall.com/bolivia_art3.htm.

9. Kelley and Klein, *Revolution and Rebirth*, 128–29.

10. Norman Gall, "Slow Death in Bolivia," *The New Leader* (June 6, 1966), accessed February 18, 2011, http://www.normangall.com/bolivia_art1.htm.

11. Ricardo A. Godoy, "Technical and Economic Efficiency of Peasant Miners in Bolivia," *Economic Development and Cultural Change* 34, no. 1 (October 1985): 106–9; Olivia Harris and Xavier Albó, *Monteras y guardatojos: campesinos y mineros en el norte de Potosí*, (La Paz: CIPCA, 1986), 24–29; and Barrios de Chungara and Viezzer, *Let Me Speak!*, 22–23.

12. Segundino Pelaez R. and Marina Vargas S., *Estaño, sangre y sudor (tragedia del minero locatario)* (Oruro, Bolivia: Editorial Universitaria, 1980), 8.

13. Pelaez R. and Vargas S., *Estaño, sangre y sudor*, 33.

14. Gall, "Slow Death."

15. Rodríguez Ostria, "Las compañeras," 178.

16. Guillermo Lora, *El movimiento obrero de Bolivia* (Cochabamba, Bolivia: Los Amigos del Libro, 1969–1971), 1:27.

17. René Poppe, *Interior mina (testimonio)* (La Paz: Biblioteca Popular Boliviana de "Ultima Hora," 1986), 49.

18. Guillermo Delgado P., "Industrial Stagnation and Women's Strategies for Survival at the Siglo XX and Uncía Mines," in Greaves and Culver, *Miners and Mining*, 162–68.

19. Harris and Albó, *Monteras y guardatojos*, 24–29.

20. Poppe, *Interior mina*, 47.

21. Thomas C. Greaves, Xavier Albó, and Godofredo S. Sandoval, "Becoming a Tin Miner," in Greaves and Culver, *Miners and Mining*, 176–80.

22. Harris and Albó, *Monteras y guardatojos*, 49.

23. Sophia Tickell, "Domitila—the Forgotten Activist," *New Internationalist* 200 (October 1989), http://www.newint.org/issue200/domitila.htm.

24. Greaves, Albó, and Sandoval, "Becoming a Tin Miner," 187.

25. Sergio Paz Almaraz, *Bolivia: Réquiem para una República* (Montevideo, Uruguay: Biblioteca de Marcha, 1970), 78–79.

26. Harris and Albó, *Monteras y guardatojos*, 22.

27. Nash, "Mi vida," 146.

28. Kelley and Klein, *Revolution and Rebirth*, 129.

29. Gall, "Slow Death."

30. Ibid.

31. Jack Brown, Rafael Valdieviese, and Marcelo Sangines Uriarte, *Informe Cornell: el minero boliviano de Colquiri* (La Paz: Universidad Mayor de San Andrés, 1968), 64–65.

32. Iriarte, *Galerías de la muerte*, 24–26.

33. Norman Gall, "The Price of Tin, Part 2," accessed February 18, 2011, http://www.normangall.com/bolivia_art2.htm.

34. Barrios de Chungara and Viezzer, *Let Me Speak!*, 24–25.

35. Ricardo A. Godoy, *Mining and Agriculture in Highland Bolivia: Ecology, History, and Commerce among the Jukumanis* (Tucson: University of Arizona Press, 1990), 103–7.

36. Ibid., 103.

37. Claudio Scliar, *Geopolítica das Minas do Brasil: a Importância da Mineracão para a Sociedade* (Rio de Janeiro: Editora Revan, 1996), 80, 86–87.

38. Ibid., 76.

39. Edward J. Rogers, "Brazilian Success Story: Volta Redonda Iron and Steel Project," *Journal of Inter-American Studies* 10, no. 4 (October 1968): 648.

40. Scliar, *Geopolítica*, 120.

41. CVRD was privatized in 1997.

42. Business News Americas website, Mining page, "CVRD Hires 896 New Workers," published January 19, 1998, accessed February 3, 2011, http://www.bnamericas.com/news/mining/CVRD_Hires_896_New_Workers.

43. *Os Carvoeiros*, directed by Nibel Noble (Les Zazen Produções, 1999).

44. Bloomberg website, News page, "CVRD Won't Sell Iron Ore to Producers That Allow Slave Labor," accessed November 25, 2008, http://www.bloomberg.com/apps/news?pid=newsarchive&sid=arPjegyeQ7ik.

45. The quote is from Antônio da Justa Feijão and José Armindo Pinto, "Amazônia e a saga aurífera do século XX," in *Garimpo, Meio Ambiente e Sociedades Indígenas*, ed. Lívia Barbosa, Ana Lucia Lobato, and José Augusto Drummond (Niterói, Brazil: Universidade Federal Fluminense, 1992), 20.

46. Ivan F. Machado, *Recursos minerais: Política e sociedade* (São Paulo: Editora E. Blucher, 1989), 200–201.

47. Ibid., 186.

48. Ricardo Kotscho, *Serra Pelada: Uma Ferida Aberta na Selva* (São Paulo: Brasiliense, 1984), 68.

49. In the language of the *fofoca*, in fact, an established garimpeiro, who recognized the interdependence, was a *manso* or "tamed" one. David Cleary, *Anatomy of the Amazon Gold Rush* (Iowa City: University of Iowa Press, 1990), 134.

50. Ibid., 164.

51. Ibid., 174.

52. Their supposed liberalism was of an odd sort, because Curió was implicated in a number of human rights abuses during the dictatorship.

53. Kotscho, *Serra Pelada*, 43.

54. Feijão and Pinto, "Amazônia," 33.

55. A third of the homes had a living room, 40 percent a dining room, and 40 percent had only one bedroom. Two-thirds of the houses had a separate kitchen, and three-quarters of the homes had a bathroom.

56. David J. Fox, "Bolivian Mining, a Crisis in the Making," in Greaves and Culver, *Miners and Mining*, 108.

Chapter 8

1. Miguel Agia, *Servidumbres personales de indios* (Seville: Escuela de Estudios Hispano-Americanos, 1946), 62; and Report of Damián de Jeria, January 10, 1604, AGI, Lima 34, Archivo General de Indias, Seville.

2. Brown, "Worker's Health," 491.

3. "Emergency Preparedness and Response: APELL for Mining," *Industry and Environment* 23 (2000): 70.

4. Antônio Carlos Diegues, "Os impactos da mineração sobre as áreas úmidas da Amazônia e suas populações humanas," in Barbosa, Lobato, and Drummond, *Garimpo*, 14.

5. Macedo, "500 Years of Mining," 303.

6. See, for example, Gordon Macmillan, *At the End of the Rainbow? Gold, Land, and People in the Brazilian Amazon* (London: Earthscan Publications, 1995), 159; and Marcello M. Veiga, "Mercury in Artisanal Gold Mining in Latin America: Facts, Fantasies and Solutions" (UNIDO Expert Group Meeting, Vienna, July 1–3, 1997), accessed March 16, 2006, http://www.facome.uqam.ca/pdf/veiga_02.pdf.

7. World Health Organization, Task Group on Environmental Health Criteria for Methylmercury, *Methylmercury* (Geneva: World Health Organization, 1990), 69.

8. Organization of Teratology Information Specialists Fact Sheet, "Methylmercury and Pregnancy," (October 2004), accessed May 27, 2011, http://www.otispregnancy.org/files/methylmercury.pdf.

9. On the Madeira River, some garimpeiros had mercury levels in their hair measuring as high as 26.7 ppm, and Indians on the Tapajós River, another site of garimpagem, tested as high as 29 ppm. Diegues, "Os impactos," 15. See also B. S. Leady and J. G. Gottgens, "Mercury Accumulation in Sediment Cores and Along Food Chains in Two Regions of the Brazilian Pantanal," *Wetlands Ecology*

and Management 9, no. 4 (2001): 349–61, which traces elevated levels of mercury to garimpeiro activity.

10. Dan Biller, "Informal Gold Mining and Mercury Pollution in Brazil" (Washington, D.C.: World Bank, Policy Research Dept., Public Economics Division, 1994), 6.

11. World Health Organization, *Methylmercury*, 26.

12. Feijão and Pinto, "Amazônia," 19.

13. Almaraz Paz, *Bolivia*, 78–79.

14. Ricardo Zelaya, *Minería o medio ambiente: el gran dilema* (La Paz: CEDOIN, 1998), 35.

15. Zelaya, *Minería*, 76; and Hans Möeller Schroeter, *Dinamitas y contaminantes: cooperativas mineras y su incidencia en la problemática ambiental* (La Paz: PIEB, 2002), 113–15.

16. Jiménez de la Espada, "Descripción," 373.

17. Dick Kamp, "Mexico's Mines: Source of Wealth or Woe?," *Business Mexico* 3, no. 1 (1993).

18. On the ecological consequences of the La Oroya smelter, see Carlos Alarcón Aliaga, *Catástrofe ecológica en la sierra central del Perú: Incidencia de la actividad minero-metalúrgica en el medio ambiente* (Lima: IPEMIN, 1994).

19. "La Oroya se encuentra entre las ciudades más contaminadas del mundo," *El Comercio* (Lima), accessed October 19, 2006, http://www.elcomercioperu.com. pe/EdicionOnline/Html/2006-10-19.htm, (site discontinued).

20. Doria Balvín Díaz, Juan Tejedo Huamán, and Humberto Lozada Castro, *Agua, minería y contaminación: el caso de Southern Peru* (Ilo, Peru: Ediciones Laboral, 1995), 90–122.

21. Located about thirty miles southwest of the Cerro Rico, Porco was the site of Incan silver mines that passed into the hands of the Pizarro brothers immediately after the conquest. The first silver rush to Potosí flowed from Porco.

22. Hugh Jones, "Designer Waste," *Industry and Environment* 23 (2000): 76; and "Water Pollution in Latin America," *The Global Change Game*, accessed March 24, 2006, http://www.mts.net/~gcg/resources/latam/index06.html, (site discontinued).

23. Rob Edwards, "Toxic Sludge Flows Through the Andes," *New Scientist* 152 (November 23, 1996): 4.

24. Gary McMahon, José Luis Evia, Alberto Pascó-Font, and José Miguel Sánchez, *An Environmental Study of Artisanal, Small, and Medium Mining in Bolivia, Chile, and Peru* (Washington, D.C.: World Bank, 1999), 1–2. For purposes of the study, a medium-size operation handled one thousand to five thousand tons of rock per day and had annual sales of $10 to $100 million; the small category extracted less than one thousand tons daily and sold less than $10 million per year. Artisanal mining operations were characterized by their lack of mechanization.

25. Ibid., 11.

26. Ibid., 21.

27. Boxer, *Golden Age*, 37.

28. Macedo, "500 Years of Mining," 304.

29. MacMillan, *End of the Rainbow?*, 157

30. Anthony L. Hall, *Developing Amazonia: Deforestation and Social Conflict in Brazil's Carajás Programme* (New York: Manchester University Press, 1991), 169–70.

31. David Treece, *Bound in Misery and Iron: The Impact of the Grande Carajás Programme on the Indians of Brazil* (London: Survival International, 1987), 79.

32. William F. Laurance, Ana K. M. Albernaz, and Carlos da Costa, "Is Deforestation Accelerating in the Brazilian Amazon," *Environmental Conservation* 28, no. 4 (2001): 305–11.

33. Feijão and Pinto, "Amazônia," 18.

34. Brian J. Godfrey, "Migration to the Gold-Mining Frontier in Brazilian Amazônia," *Geographical Review* 82, no. 4 (October 1992): 461.

35. Orlando Valverde, *Grande Carajás: Planejamento da Destruição* (Rio de Janeiro: Forense Universitária, 1989), 120.

36. Feijão and Pinto, "Amazônia," 19.

37. Valverde, *Grande Carajás*, 126–29.

38. Lúcio Flávio Pinto, *Carajás: o ataque ao coração da Amazônia*, 2nd ed. (Rio de Janeiro: Editora Marco Zero, 1982), 93.

39. Patrice M. Franko, *The Puzzle of Latin American Economic Development* (Lanham, MD: Rowman and Littlefield, 1999), 422.

40. MacMillan, *End of the Rainbow?*, 47–51.

41. Robert Borofsky, *Yanomami: The Fierce Controversy and What We Can Learn from It* (Berkeley: University of California Press, 2005), 8.

42. Deustua, "Transiciones y manifestaciones," 223.

43. Bernabé Cobo, *Inca Religion and Customs*, trans. and ed. Roland Hamilton (Austin: University of Texas Press, 1990), 45.

44. Nash, *We Eat the Mines*, 140–41.

45. Platt, "Conciencia andina," 50.

46. Iriarte, *Galerías de la muerte*, 8–9.

47. In the 1970s COMIBOL provided only subsidized bread, rice, sugar, and meat. Iriarte, *Galerías de la muerte*, 30.

48. Quoted in Platt, "Conciencia andina," 48.

49. Harris and Albó, *Monteras y guardatojos*, 37–38.

50. Bellessort, *La jeune Amérique*, 290.

51. Gall, "Slow Death."

52. Carmen Salazar-Soler, "La Divinidad de las Tinieblas," *Bulletin de l'Institut Francais d'Études Andines*, Numéro Special, Biblioteca Digital Andina, 1997, http://www.comunidadandina.org/bda/docs/IF-CA-0001.pdf.

53. Stephen Ferry, *I Am Rich Potosí: The Mountain That Eats Men* (New York: Monacelli Press, 1999), 21.

54. Nash, *We Eat the Mines*, 202.

55. Carmen Salazar-Soler, "La Divinidad de las Tinieblas," *Bulletin de l'Institut Francais d'Études Andines*, Numéro Special, Biblioteca Digital Andina, 1997, http://www.comunidadandina.org/bda/docs/IF-CA-0001.pdf, 6.

56. Nash, *We Eat the Mines*, 203.

57. June Nash, "The Devil in Bolivia's Nationalized Tin Mines," *Science and Society* 36, no. 2 (1972): 226. Interpolation from original.

58. Manuel Rigoberto Paredes, *Mitos, supersticiones y supervivencias populares de Bolivia*, 4th ed. (La Paz: Ediciones "Burgos," 1973), 45.

59. John Howland Rowe, "Inca Culture at the Time of the Spanish Conquest," in *Handbook of South American Indians*, ed. Julian H. Steward, vol. 2, *The Andean Civilizations* (Washington, D.C.: Government Printing Office), 246.

60. Ibid., 227.

61. Nash, "Mi vida," 148–49.

62. Ibid., 149.

63. June Nash, "Religión, rebelión y conciencia de clase en las comunidades mineras del estaño de Bolivia," *Revista del Instituto Pastoral Andina* 26 (1985): 124.

64. Nash, "The Devil," 232.

65. Philippe Zevaco, "Indian Mythology and Mining Conditions in Bolivia," *Cultures* 1, no. 2 (1973): 93–94. Bolivian miners' sacrifices and supplications to the Tío differed slightly from the cosmological beliefs that held sway in Chilean mines. In both Bolivia and Chile, miners saw the earth as a female deity, but in Chile the spirit controlling the mine underground was also female. Some associated her with the Virgin Mary, others as a vicious or tempestuous woman. They placated her for their own safety and to find the treasures she had hidden in the bowels of the earth. Klubock, "Working Class Masculinity," 443.

66. Nash, "Mi vida," 144.

67. Michael T. Taussig, *The Devil and Commodity Fetishism in South America* (Chapel Hill: University of North Carolina Press, 1980), 145–46.

68. René Poppe, *Cuentos mineros* (La Paz: Ediciones ISLA, 1985), 95.

69. Quoted in Alarcón Aliaga, *Catástrofe ecológica*, 27.

70. Gen. 1:28 (King James Version).

71. Ps. 8:6 (King James Version).

72. Richard Bauckham, "Modern Domination of Nature—Historical Origins and Biblical Critique," in *Environmental Stewardship: Critical Perspectives, Past and Present*, ed. R. J. Berry (New York: T and T Clark, 2006), 37.

73. McMahon, Evia, Pascó-Font, and Sánchez, *Environmental Study*, 1.

74. Franko, *Puzzle*, 41.

75. Almaraz Paz, *Bolivia*, 83–84.

76. Tickell, "Domitila."

77. Adam Smith, *An Enquiry Into the Nature and Causes of the Wealth of Nations* (New York: Modern Library, 1940), 529–30.

78. Eakin, *British Enterprise in Brazil*, 194.

79. Almaraz Paz, *Bolivia*, 79–80.

80. "Al menos 40 muertos en Colombia tras el derrumbe de una mina de oro abandonada," *El Mundo* (Spain), November 23, 2001.

81. BloggingStocks website, "Mexican Mining Firm Finds a Huge Lithium Deposit," blog entry by Connie Madon, October 11, 2009, accessed November 16, 2010, http://www.bloggingstocks.com/2009/10/11/mexican-mining-firm-finds-a-huge-lithium-deposit/.

82. The *New York Times* website, "Bolivia Has Lithium, and President Intends to Make World Pay for It," by Simon Romero, February 2, 2009, accessed November 15, 2010, http://www.nytimes.com/2009/02/02/world/americas/02iht-lithium.4.19877751.html.

83. Northcutt Ely, "The Earth's Natural Resources Budget," in *Earth Resources*, ed. Charles F. Park Jr. (Washington, D.C.: Voice of America Forum Series, 1980), 289–97.

84. Mervyn F. Lang, "El derrumbe de Huancavelica," 213–26.

85. Nash, *We Eat the Mines*, 191–92.

Glossary

acullicar. To chew or suck on coca leaves.

alcalde mayor de minas. Mining magistrate.

altiplano. Andean high plateau, about twelve thousand feet above sea level.

amaru. Serpent.

apiri. Andean ore carrier.

arastre. Ore-crushing mill.

arroba. Twenty-five pounds.

ayllu. Andean clan or ethnic group.

ayni. Harmony, reciprocity.

azogue. Mercury (quicksilver).

azoguero. Amalgamator, silver refiner.

bamburrado. In Brazil, someone who strikes a bonanza.

bandeirante. A Brazilian frontiersman, prospector, explorer, and Indian slaver, usually from the region of São Paulo.

barranco. In Brazil, a mining claim.

barrenador. Drillman (see barretero and coheteador).

barretero. Miner, drillman, one who works on the rock face (see barrenador and coheteador).

bateia. Wooden or metal pan used to pan for gold.

blefado. Someone who loses the fortune he made through mining.

bossale. Brazilian slave born in Africa.

bota. Bag for carrying ore (see tenate).

braça. Linear measurement of approximately six feet.

brazos caídos. Labor strike.

brujo. Andean shaman.

buho. Owl; sometimes used as a synonym for juku because jukus often go into the mines at night to steal ore (see juku).

buscón. Prospector (see faiscador and garimpeiro).

cajón. Flagstone box in which ore, magistral, salt, and mercury were mixed during amalgamation at Potosí during colonial times.

carretero. Mine worker who pushes ore carts.

Casa de la Moneda. The mint at Potosí.

Cerro Rico. The "Rich Hill" at Potosí.

chacaneador. Teamster who uses llamas to haul ore from a mine to the mill.

ch'alla. Ritual conducted by workers inside a mine to placate Pachamama and the Tío.

charrismo. Condition in which labor leaders sell out the mine workers' interests to the company or the government.

ch'askiri. Worker who loads and dumps ore carts.

chicha. Maize beer.

cholo. Mestizo or hispanicized Andean Indian.

coartação. Conditional manumission of a slave in which eventual full liberty depended on the slave's complying with specified conditions.

coartado. Slave who lived in coartação.

coatéquitl. Pre-Hispanic labor draft in Mexico. It was used by the Spaniards, particularly in the sixteenth century, to provide mine workers in densely populated central Mexico.

COB. Central Obrera Boliviana (Bolivian Workers Central).

cocales. Coca plantations.

coheteador. Drillman (see barrenador and barretero).

colorado. Silver chloride ore.

COMIBOL. Corporación Minera Boliviana (Bolivian Mining Corporation).

condenados. The damned.

copajira. Mineralized acidic liquid in a mine.

corpa. Ore-bearing rock; in Bolivia, a mine worker's share of the ore.

corregidor. Provincial governor.

correspondencia. Ratio between the quantity of mercury used in the amalgamation process and the amount of silver the process produces.

cortes. Medieval feudal assembly; Iberian equivalent of French Estates-General.

coya. Pre-Hispanic Andean word for "mine"; principal wife of an Incan ruler.

cuadrilla. Labor gang.

destajo. Work that is compensated at a per-piece rate.

diezmo. Tithe, or tenth; in colonial times, a ten-percent tax on mining production.

efectivo. A mitayo who appeared in person to work in a mine.

emboaba. Derogatory term used by paulistas to describe Portuguese and other outsiders in the goldfields of Minas Gerais.

encomendero. Person who holds an encomienda.

encomienda. Grant of indigenous tribute, either in money or kind.

enganchador. Labor contractor.

enganche. Labor recruitment, often by unscrupulous methods.

estado. A length equivalent to a man's height.

faiscador. Prospector (see buscón and garimpeiro).

faltriquera. Accepting a money payment to hire mitayos without doing so.

ficha. Chit or card a mine worker can redeem for merchandise at the company store.

forastero. Outsider; an Andean who abandons his or her ayllu.

formiga. "Ant"; in Brazil, an ore carrier.

FSTMB. Federación Sindical de Trabajadores Mineros de Bolivia (Bolivia Mine Workers Syndical Federation).

FUNAI. Fundação Nacional do Índio (Indian Affairs Foundation, Brazil).

garimpagem. Extralegal prospecting and mining.

garimpeiro. Prospector or miner who engages in illegal mining activity (see buscón and faiscador).

grimpa. Body of running water, stream.

guayra. Andean ceramic smelting furnace (also spelled wayra).

hacendado. Landowner.

hacienda de minas. In Mexico, a refining mill.

haperk'a. Terror produced by the Tío or "devil" of a mine.

hatunruna. Andean peasant.

horno busconil. Oven for distilling mercury, invented by Lope de Saavedra Barba at Huancavelica.

huaca. An Andean sacred place, shrine, or deity.

huachaca. In Peru, a mine worker's share of the ore.

indio de plata. "Silver Indian," a worker hired by the azoguero with funds provided by an ayllu to replace a missing mitayo.

ingenio. Mill; refining complex where ore is ground and amalgamated.

jagua. Black sand that contains gold flakes and iron oxide.

jallp'a. Land for cultivation.

janajpacha. In Andean cosmology, the overworld.

jaqi. Authentic person, one who has earned respect.

juku. Modern equivalent of the colonial kajcha (see buho).

kaipiri. Person who carries ore.

kajcha. One who works the kajcheo.

kajcheo. Weekend mining at Potosí by mitayos and mingados; the ore thus produced belonged to the workers rather than the mine owner and was an important supplement to a miner's wages.

kanchiri. In colonial times, a worker who illuminated the mine.

k'araku. Mining ritual that includes the sacrifice of a llama to Pachamama and the Tío.

kaypacha. In Andean cosmology, the world in which humans live.

kuraka. Andean ethnic lord; chieftain.

lamero. Person who reworks tailings and slimes.

lavra. A workplace where a slave gang used sluices and other equipment to process gold-bearing alluvium and earth.

layrani. Aymara term for someone "with eyes," who knows how to read and write and is dissatisfied with indigenous culture.

lazador. Labor recruiter who often uses unscrupulous methods.

leguaje. Travel expenses paid by azogueros to Potosí mitayos; it was based on the number of leagues the mitayo had to travel to reach the mines.

llijta. Alkaline lozenge miners place in their mouth with coca leaves to release the leaves' ecognine.

locatario. Pieceworker who typically reworks old mines and ore dumps.

magistral. Copper sulfates, iron pyrites, and other minerals used during amalgamation to initiate a chemical reaction when added to silver ore, mercury, and salt.

malacate. Horse-operated whim.

mama. Metal; also woman, lady.

mancomunal. Chilean workers' cultural society and proto-union.

mingado. In colonial times, free laborer at Potosí whose wages were generally three or four times that received by a mitayo.

mita. Colonial Andean system of forced labor.

mitayo. Worker serving in the mita labor draft.

MNR. Movimiento Nacionalista Revolucionario (National Revolutionary Movement, Bolivia).

muqui. Deity of the mine.

negrillo. Silver sulfide ore.

Pachamama. Andean earth mother goddess.

paco. Silver chloride ore.

palla. Work quota.

pallayta. Work done by the palliri.

palliri. High-grader, often a woman, who searches through discarded earth and stone from the mine for rich bits of ore that can be retrieved and sold. This work is generally done in dumps outside the mine.

partido. Share of ore received by a miner (see pepena).

paulista. Person from São Paulo, Brazil.

pepena. Share of ore received by a miner (see partido).

piña. "Pineapple"; porous, spongelike silver left after a silver amalgam has been heated to drive off the mercury.

platino. "Silverlike"; platinum.

PRI. Partido Revolutionario Institucional (Institutional Revolutionary Party, Mexico).

pulpería. Grocer's shop at a mine, sometimes operated by the mining company or the government.

puna. Plateau, especially in the mountains.

q'ara. Andean who has partially abandoned indigenous culture and perhaps even become lighter-complexioned.

quilombo. Community of runaway slaves in the Brazilian interior.

quinto real. "Royal fifth," in colonial times, a twenty-percent tax on mineral production.

quitapepena. Overseer who verifies that miners have not taken an excess share of the ore they produce.

real de minas. Mining district.

recogedor. Labor recruiter.

repartimiento. Distribution; in colonial Mexico, term used for forced labor draft similar to the Andean mita.

reparto de mercancías. Forced distribution of merchandise among Andeans by the corregidor.

St. Monday. Worker absenteeism on Monday.

sistema de cama-caliente. Rotating use of a bed and house by workers unrelated to the house's owners; used during housing shortage at a mine.

socavón. Nearly horizontal passage that gives access to a mine.

soroche. Altitude sickness.

supay. In Andean cosmology, a dead ancestor living in the underground; deity of the underground, particularly in a mine; Tío.

supaymarca. In Andean cosmology, the land of the shadows.

tenate. In Mexico, bag for carrying ore (see bota).

tenatero. In Mexico, ore carrier.

tienda de raya. Company store.

tlatoque. In Mexico, indigenous community ruler.

tío. uncle, guy; (cap.) in Bolivia, deity of a mine (see supay).

tracción a sangre. Worker who not only has to mine ore but also has to haul it out himself.

trapiche. Small indigenous mill and smelting operation.

ukhupacha. In Andean cosmology, the underworld.

veedor. Mine inspector.

venerista. Pieceworker, usually part of a cooperative.

yanacona. In colonial Andes, someone who lacked ayllu affiliation and had a
    dependent relationship with a Spaniard.

Bibliography

~✦~

Archival Sources

Archivo General de Indias. Seville.

Archivo Nacional. Lima.

Biblioteca Nacional. Madrid.

Books, Articles, and Internet Sources

Acosta, José de. *The Natural and Moral History of the Indies.* 2 vols. London: Hakluyt Society, 1880.

Agia, Miguel. *Servidumbres personales de indios.* Seville: Escuela de Estudios Hispano-Americanos, 1946.

Alarcón Aliaga, Carlos. *Catástrofe ecológica en la sierra central del Perú: Incidencia de la actividad minero-metalúrgica en el medio ambiente.* Lima: IPEMIN, 1994.

Alexander, Robert J. *The Bolivian National Revolution.* New Brunswick, NJ: Rutgers University Press, 1958.

Almaraz Paz, Sergio. *Bolivia: Réquiem para una República.* Montevideo, Bolivia: Biblioteca de Marcha, 1970.

Andrien, Kenneth J. *Crisis and Decline: The Viceroyalty of Peru in the Seventeenth Century.* Albuquerque: University of New Mexico Press, 1985.

Antología de poemas de la revolución. La Paz: Publicaciones SPIC, 1954.

Antonil, André João. *Cultura e Opulência do Brasil.* São Paulo: Companhia Editora Nacional, 1967.

Arellano Z., Manuel, ed. *Primera huelga minera en Real del Monte, 1766.* Mexico City: Libros de México, 1976.

Arregui, A., F. León Velarde, and M. Valcárcel. *Salud y minería: el riesgo del mal de montaña crónico entre mineros de Cerro de Pasco.* Lima: Asociación Laboral para el Desarrollo, 1990.

Arzáns de Orsúa y Vela, Bartolomé. *Anales de la Villa Imperial de Potosí*. La Paz: Ministerio de Educación y Cultura, 1970.

———. *Tales of Potosí*. Edited by R. C. Padden. Translated by Frances M. López-Morillas. Providence, RI: Brown University Press, 1975.

Bakewell, Peter. *Miners of the Red Mountain: Indian Labor in Potosí, 1545–1650*. Albuquerque: University of New Mexico Press, 1984.

———. "Registered Silver Production in the Potosí District, 1550–1735." *Jahrbuch für Geschichte von Staat, Wirtschaft und Gesellschaft Lateinamerikas*, band 12 (1975): 67–103.

———. *Silver and Entrepreneurship in Seventeenth-Century Potosí: The Life and Times of Antonio López de Quiroga*. Albuquerque: University of New Mexico Press, 1988.

———. *Silver Mining and Society in Colonial Mexico: Zacatecas, 1546–1700*. Cambridge: Cambridge University Press, 1971.

Balvín Díaz, Doris, Juan Tejedo Huamán, and Humberto Lozada Castro. *Agua, minería y contaminación: el caso de Southern Peru*. Ilo, Peru: Ediciones Laboral, 1995.

Bancora, Carmen. "Las remesas de metales preciosos desde El Callao a España en la primera mitad del siglo XVII." *Revista de Indias* 29, no. 75 (January–March 1959): 35–88.

Barbosa, Livia, Ana Lucia Lobato, and José Augusto Drummond, eds. *Garimpo, Meio Ambiente e Sociedades Indígenas*. Niterói, Brazil: Universidade Federal Fluminense, 1992.

Barrera, Manuel. "El conflicto obrero en el enclave cuprífero chileno." *Revista Mexicana de Sociología* 40, no. 2 (1978): 609–82.

Barrett, Ward. "World Bullion Flows, 1450–1800." In *The Rise of Merchant Empires: Long-Distance Trade in the Early Modern World, 1350-1750*, edited by James D. Tracy, 224–254. Cambridge: Cambridge University Press, 1993.

Barrios de Chungara, Domitila, and Moema Viezzer. *Let Me Speak! Testimony of Domitila, a Woman of the Bolivian Mines*. New York: Monthly Review Press, 1978.

Bauckham, Richard. "Modern Domination of Nature—Historical Origins and Biblical Critique." In *Environmental Stewardship: Critical Perspectives, Past and Present*, edited by R. J. Berry, 37–53. New York: T and T Clark, 2006.

Bellessort, André. *La jeune Amérique: Chili et Bolivie*. Paris: Perrin et Cie, 1897.

Beltrán y Rozpide, Ricardo, and Angel de Altolaguirre, eds. *Colección de las memorias ó relaciones que escribieron los virreyes del Perú*. 2 vols. Madrid: Imprenta Mujeres Españolas, 1921–1930.

Bernstein, Marvin. *The Mexican Mining Industry, 1890–1950: A Study of the Interaction of Politics, Economics, and Technology*. Albany: State University of New York, 1965.

Biller, Dan. *Informal Gold Mining and Mercury Pollution in Brazil*. Washington, D.C.: World Bank, Policy Research Dept., Public Economics Division, 1994.

Bonilla, Heraclio, ed. *Gran Bretaña y el Perú: Informes de los cónsules británicos: 1826–1900*. 5 vols. Lima: Instituto de Estudios Peruanos, 1975–1976.

Borah, Woodrow W. *New Spain's Century of Depression*. Berkeley: University of California Press, 1951.

Borah, Woodrow W., and Sherburne F. Cook. *The Aboriginal Population of Central Mexico on the Eve of the Spanish Conquest.* Berkeley: University of California Press, 1963.

Borofsky, Robert. *Yanomami: The Fierce Controversy and What We Can Learn from It.* Berkeley: University of California Press, 2005.

Boxer, C. R. *The Golden Age of Brazil, 1695–1750.* Berkeley: University of California Press, 1962.

Brading, D. A. *Miners and Merchants in Bourbon Mexico, 1763–1810.* Cambridge: Cambridge University Press, 1971.

Braudel, Fernand. *Capitalism and Material Life, 1400–1800.* New York: Harper and Row, 1973.

Bravo Elizondo, Pedro, ed. *Santa María de Iquique, 1907: documentos para su historia.* Santiago: Ediciones del Litoral, 1993.

Brown, J. R. "The Frustration of Chile's Nitrate Imperialism." *Pacific Historical Review* 32, no. 4 (1963): 383–96.

———. "Nitrate Crises, Combinations, and the Chilean Government in the Nitrate Age." *Hispanic American Historical Review* 43, no. 2 (May 1963): 230–46.

Brown, Jack, Rafael Valdieviese, and Marcelo Sangines Uriarte. *Informe Cornell: el minero boliviano de Colquiri.* La Paz: Universidad Mayor de San Andrés, 1968.

Brown, Kendall W. "Workers' Health and Colonial Mercury Mining at Huancavelica, Peru." *The Americas* 57, no. 4 (April 2001): 467–96.

Brown, Kendall W., and Alan K. Craig. "Silver Mining at Huantajaya, Viceroyalty of Peru." In *In Quest of Mineral Wealth: Aboriginal and Colonial Mining and Metallurgy in Spanish America*, edited by Alan K. Craig and Robert C. West, 303–28. Baton Rouge: Louisiana State University Press, 1994.

Calancha, Antonio de la. *Crónica moralizada.* Edited by Ignacio Prado Pastor. 6 vols. Lima: Universidad Nacional de San Marcos, 1974–1981.

Calderón de la Barca, Frances. *Life in Mexico: The Letters of Fanny Calderón de la Barca.* Edited by Howard Fisher and Marion Hall Fisher. Garden City, NY: Anchor Books, 1970.

Cañete y Domínguez, Pedro Vicente. *Guía histórica, geográfica, física, política, civil y legal del Gobierno e Intendencia de la Provincia de Potosí.* Potosí, Bolivia: Editorial Potosí, 1952.

Capoche, Luis. *Relación general de la villa imperial de Potosí.* Biblioteca de Autores Españoles, vol. 122. Madrid: Ediciones Atlas, 1959.

Cárdenas, Enrique. "A Macroeconomic Interpretation of Nineteenth-Century Mexico." In *How Latin America Fell Behind: Essays on the Economic Histories of Brazil and Mexico, 1800–1914*, edited by Stephen Haber, 65–92. Palo Alto, CA: Stanford University Press, 1997.

Cardozo, Manoel. "The Brazilian Gold Rush." *The Americas* 3, no. 2 (October 1946): 137–60.

Carrasco, Manuel. *Simón I. Patiño, un procer industrial.* 2nd ed. Cochabamba, Bolivia: Editorial Canelas, 1964.

Casas, Bartolomé de las. *History of the Indies.* Translated by Andrée Collard. New York: Harper, 1971.

Cervantes Saavedra, Miguel de. *Rinconete y Cortadillo.* Edited by Francisco Rodríguez Marín. Seville: Francisco de P. Díaz, 1905.

Cieza de León, Pedro de. *Obras completas.* Madrid: Consejo de Investigaciones Superiores, 1984.

Cleary, David. *Anatomy of the Amazon Gold Rush.* Iowa City: University of Iowa Press, 1990.

Clendinnen, Inga. *Ambivalent Conquests: Maya and Spaniard in Yucatan, 1517–1570.* New York: Cambridge University Press, 1987.

Coatsworth, John. "Economic and Institutional Trajectories in Nineteenth-Century Latin America." In *Latin America and the World Economy Since 1800*, edited by John H. Coatsworth and Alan M. Taylor, 23–54. Cambridge, MA: Harvard University, David Rockefeller Center for Latin American Studies, 1998.

———. *Growth against Development: The Economic Impact of Railroads in Porfirian Mexico.* DeKalb: Northern Illinois Press, 1981.

Cobo, Bernabé. *Inca Religion and Customs.* Translated and edited by Roland Hamilton. Austin: University of Texas Press, 1990.

Colección de documentos inéditos relativos al descubrimiento, conquista y organización de las antiguas posesiones españolas de ultramar. 42 vols. Madrid: Real Academia de la Historia, 1885–1932.

Cole, Jeffrey. *The Potosí Mita, 1573–1700: Compulsory Indian Labor in the Andes.* Palo Alto, CA: Stanford University Press, 1985.

Contreras, Carlos. "La minería hispanoamericana después de la independencia. Estudios comparativo de Bolivia, Chile, México y Perú." In *Dos décadas de investigación en historia económica comparada en América Latina: Homenage a Carlos Sempat Assadourian*, edited by Margarita Megegus Bornemann, 255–83. Mexico: El Colegio de México, Centro de Estudios Históricos, 1999.

———. "Mineros, arrieros y ferrocarril en Cerro de Pasco, 1870–1904," *HISLA* 4, no. 2 (1984): 3–20.

Contreras, Manuel E. "La mano de obra en la minería estañífera de principios de siglo, 1900–1925." *Historia y Cultura* 8 (1985): 97–134.

Couturier, Edith Boorstein. *The Silver King: The Remarkable Life of the Count of Regla in Colonial Mexico.* Albuquerque: University of New Mexico Press, 2003.

Craig, Alan K. *Spanish Colonial Silver Coins in the Florida Collection.* Gainesville: University of Florida Press, 2000.

Craig, Alan K., and Robert C. West, eds. *In Quest of Mineral Wealth: Aboriginal and Colonial Mining and Metallurgy in Spanish America.* Geoscience and Man, vol. 33. Baton Rouge: Louisiana State University Press, 1994.

Culver, William W., and Cornel J. Reinhart. "Capitalist Dreams: Chile's Response to Nineteenth-Century World Copper Competition." *Comparative Studies in Society and History* 31, no. 4 (1989): 722–44.

——. "The Decline of a Mining Region and Mining Policy: Chilean Copper in the Nineteenth Century." In *Miners and Mining in the Americas*, edited by Thomas C. Greaves and William Culver, 68–81. Dover, NH: Manchester University Press, 1985.

Danks, Noblet Barry. "The Labor Revolt of 1766 in the Mining Community of Real del Monte." *The Americas* 44, no. 2 (October 1987): 143–65.

Dawson, Frank Griffith. *The First Latin American Debt Crisis: The City of London and the 1822–25 Loan Bubble*. New Haven, CT: Yale University Press, 1990.

Delgado P., Guillermo. "Industrial Stagnation and Women's Strategies for Survival at the Siglo XX and Uncía Mines." In *Miners and Mining in the Americas*, edited by Thomas C. Greaves and William Culver, 162–70. Dover, NH: Manchester University Press, 1985.

Denevan, William M., ed. *The Native Population of the Americas in 1492*. 2nd ed. Madison: University of Wisconsin Press, 1992.

Deustua, José R. *The Bewitchment of Silver: The Social Economy of Mining in Nineteenth-Century Peru*. Athens: Ohio University Press, 2000.

——. "Transiciones y manifestaciones culturales de la minería americana entre los siglos XVI–XIX: un primer intento de aproximación." *Histórica* 22, no. 2 (1998): 209–26.

Devés, Eduardo. *Los que van a morir te saludan. Historia de una masacre. Escuela Santa María, Iquique, 1907.* Santiago: Ediciones Documentas, América Latina Libros, Nuestra América, 1988.

Dewind, Adrian. "From Peasants to Miners: The Background to Strikes in the Mines of Peru." *Science & Society* 39, no. 1 (Spring 1975): 44–72.

Diaz, Bernal. *The Conquest of New Spain*. Translated by J. M. Cohen. Baltimore, MD: Penguin, 1963.

Diegues, Antônio Carlos. "Os impactos da mineração sobre as areas úmidas da Amazônia e suas populações humanas." In *Garimpo, Meio Ambiente e Sociedades Indigenas*, edited by Livia Barbosa, Ana Lucia Lobato, and José Augusto Drummond, 7–17. Niterói, Brazil: Universidade Federal Fluminense, 1992.

Dore, Elizabeth. "Social Relations and the Barriers to Economic Growth: The Case of the Peruvian Mining Industry." *Nova Americana* 1 (1978): 245–87.

——. "Una interpretación socio-ecológica de la historia minera latinoamericana." *Ecología política* 7 (1994): 49–68.

Dunn, Oliver, and James E. Kelley Jr., eds. and trans. *The Diario of Christopher Columbus's First Voyage to America 1492–1493*. Norman: University of Oklahoma Press, 1989.

Eakin, Marshall C. *British Enterprise in Brazil: The St. John d'el Rey Mining Company and the Morro Velho Gold Mine, 1830–1960*. Durham, NC: Duke University Press, 1989.

Edwards, Rob. "Toxic Sludge Flows Through the Andes." *New Scientist* 152 (November 23, 1996): 4.

Ely, Northcutt. "The Earth's Natural Resources Budget." In *Earth Resources*, edited by Charles F. Park Jr., 289–97. Washington, D.C.: Voice of America Forum Series, 1980.

"Emergency Preparedness and Response: APELL for Mining." *Industry and Environment* 23 (2000): 70.

Eschwege, W. L. von. *Pluto Brasiliensis.* São Paulo: Editora da Universidade de São Paulo, 1979.

Escobedo, Ronald. *El tributo indígena en el Perú (siglos XVI–XVII).* Pamplona: Ediciones Universidad de Navarra, 1979.

Feijão, Antônio da Justa, and José Armindo Pinto. "Amazônia e a saga aurífera do século XX." In *Garimpo, Meio Ambiente e Sociedades Indigenas,* edited by Livia Barbosa, Ana Lucia Lobato, and José Augusto Drummond, 18–36. Niterói, Brazil: Universidade Federal Fluminense, 1992.

Ferry, Stephen. *I Am Rich Potosí: The Mountain That Eats Men.* New York: Monacelli Press, 1999.

Fisher, John. *Minas y mineros en el Perú colonial, 1776–1824.* Lima: Instituto de Estudios Peruanos, 1977.

———. "The Miners of Peru in 1790." In *Wirtschaftskräfte und Wirtschaftswege: IV Übersee und Allgemeine Wirtschaftsgeschichte,* edited by Jürgen Schneider, 117–27. Stuttgart: Klett-Cotta, 1978.

Flores Galindo, Alberto. "Los mineros de Cerro de Pasco, 1900–1930." In *Obras completas.* 5 vols. Lima: Fundación Andina, Sur, Casa de Estudios del Socialismo, 1993.

Flynn, Dennis O. "Comparing the Tokugawa Shogunate with Hapsburg Spain: Two Silver-Based Empires in a Global Setting." In *The Political Economy of Merchant Empires: State Power and World Trade, 1350–1750,* edited by James D. Tracy, 332–59. Cambridge: Cambridge University Press, 1997.

Flynn, Dennis O., and Arturo Giraldez. "China and the Manila Galleons." In *Japanese Industrialization and the Asian Economy,* edited by A. J. H. Latham and H. Kawakatsu, 71–90. New York: Routledge, 1994.

Fox, David J. "Bolivian Mining, a Crisis in the Making." In *Miners and Mining in the Americas,* edited by Thomas C. Greaves and William Culver, 108–33. Dover, NH: Manchester University Press, 1985.

Franko, Patrice M. *The Puzzle of Latin American Economic Development.* Lanham, MD.: Rowman and Littlefield, 1999.

Frazier, Lessie Jo. *Salt in the Sand: Memory, Violence, and the Nation-State in Chile, 1890 to the Present.* Durham, NC: Duke University Press, 2007.

Gall, Norman. "Chile: The Struggle in the Copper Mines." *Dissent* (Winter 1973).

———. "Slow Death in Bolivia." *The New Leader* (June 6 1966). http://www.normangall.com/bolivia.art1.htm.

Garner, Richard L. *Economic Growth and Change in Bourbon Mexico.* Gainesville: University of Florida Press, 1993.

———. "Long-Term Silver Mining Trends in Spanish America: A Comparative Analysis of Peru and Mexico." *American Historical Review* 93, no. 4 (October 1988): 898–935.

Geddes, Charles F. *Patiño: The Tin King.* London: Robert Hale, 1972.

Gibson, Charles. *The Aztecs under Spanish Rule.* Palo Alto, CA: Stanford University Press, 1964.

Gil, Juan. *Mitos y utopías del descubrimiento.* 3 vols. Madrid: Alianza Editorial, 1989.

Glave, Luis Miguel. *Trajinantes: caminos indígenas en la sociedad colonial, siglos XVI/XVII.* Lima: Instituto de Apoyo Agrario, 1989.

Godfrey, Brian J. "Migration to the Gold-Mining Frontier in Brazilian Amazônia." *Geographical Review* 82, no. 4 (October 1992): 458–69.

Godoy, Ricardo A. *Mining and Agriculture in Highland Bolivia: Ecology, History, and Commerce among the Jukumanis.* Tucson: University of Arizona Press, 1990.

———. "Technical and Economic Efficiency of Peasant Miners in Bolivia." *Economic Development and Cultural Change* 34, no. 1 (October 1985): 103–20.

Golte, Jürgen. *Repartos y rebeliones: Túpac Amaru y las contradicciones de la economía colonial.* Lima: Instituto de Estudios Peruanos, 1980.

Gonzales, Michael J. "United States Copper Companies, the State, and Labour Conflict in Mexico, 1900–1910." *Journal of Latin American Studies* 26, no. 3 (October 1994): 651–81.

———. "U.S. Copper Companies, the Mine Workers' Movement, and the Mexican Revolution, 1910–1920." *Hispanic American Historical Review* 76, no. 3 (August 1996): 503–34.

Graham, Richard. *Britain and the Onset of Modernization in Brazil, 1850–1914.* Cambridge: Cambridge University Press, 1972.

Greaves, Thomas C., and William Culver, eds. *Miners and Mining in the Americas.* Dover, NH: Manchester University Press, 1985.

Greaves, Thomas C., Xavier Albó, and Godofredo S. Sandoval. "Becoming a Tin Miner." In *Miners and Mining in the Americas,* edited by Thomas C. Greaves and William Culver, 171–91. Dover, NH: Manchester University Press, 1985.

Guaman Poma de Ayala, Felipe. *The First New Chronicle and Good Government, abridged.* Translated by David Frye. Indianapolis, IN: Hackett Publishing, 2006.

Guimarães, Carlos Magno. *Uma negação da ordem escravista: quilombos em Minas Gerais no século XVIII.* São Paulo: Icone Editora, 1988.

Haber, Stephen, ed. *How Latin America Fell Behind: Essays on the Economic Histories of Brazil and Mexico, 1800–1914.* Palo Alto, CA: Stanford University Press, 1997.

Hall, Anthony L. *Developing Amazonia: Deforestation and Social Conflict in Brazil's Carajás Programme.* New York: Manchester University Press, 1991.

Hanke, Lewis and Celso Rodriguez, eds. *Los virreyes españoles en América durante el gobierno de la Casa de Austria.* Biblioteca de Autores Españoles, vol. 282. Madrid: Ediciones Atlas, 1978.

Harbottle, Garman, and Phil C. Weigand. "Turquoise in Pre-Columbian America." *Scientific American* 266 (February 1992): 78–84.

Harris, Olivia, and Xavier Albó. *Monteras y guardatojos: campesinos y mineros en el norte de Potosí.* La Paz: CIPCA, 1986.

Haskett, Robert S. "'Our Suffering with the Taxco Tribute': Involuntary Mine Labor and Indigenous Society in Central New Spain." *Hispanic American Historical Review* 71, no. 3 (August 1991): 447–75.

Higgins, Kathleen J. "Masters and Slaves in a Mining Society: A Study of Eighteenth-Century Sabará, Minas Gerais." *Slavery and Abolition* 11, no. 1 (May 1990): 58–73.

Hillman, John. "Bolivia and the International Tin Cartel, 1931–1941." *Journal of Latin American Studies* 20 (May 1988).

———. "The Emergence of the Tin Industry in Bolivia." *Journal of Latin American Studies* 16, no. 2 (November 1984): 403–37.

Hojman, David E. "On Miners, Mining Firms and Technology: From the *Barretero* to Anaconda and Kennecott." *Bulletin of Latin American Research* 2, no. 2 (May 1983): 123–26.

Humboldt, Alejandro de. *Ensayo político sobre el reino de la Nueva España*. 5 vols. Mexico: Editorial Pedro Robredo, 1941.

Iriarte, Gregorio. *Galerías de la muerte: vida de los mineros bolivianos*. Montevideo, Uruguay: Tierra Nueva, 1972.

Iwasaki Cauti, Fernando A. "Simbolismos religiosos en la minería y metalurgía prehispánicas." *Anuario de Estudios Americanos* 41 (1984): 93–141.

Jiménez de la Espada, Marcos, ed. "Descripción de la villa y minas de Potosí." In *Relaciones geográficas de Indias—Perú*. Biblioteca de Autores Españoles, vol. 183. Madrid: Ediciones Atlas, 1965.

Jones, Hugh. "Designer Waste." *Industry and Environment* 23 (2000): 76–78.

Kamp, Dick. "Mexico's Mines: Source of Wealth or Woe?" *Business Mexico* 3, no. 1 (1993).

Kelley, Jonathan, and Herbert S Klein. *Revolution and the Rebirth of Inequality: A Theory Applied to the National Revolution in Bolivia*. Berkeley: University of California Press, 1981.

Kindleberger, Charles P. *Spenders and Hoarders: The World Distribution of Spanish American Silver, 1550–1750*. Singapore: Institute of Southeast Asian Studies, 1989.

Klaren, Peter F. *Peru: Society and Nationhood in the Andes*. New York: Oxford University Press, 2000.

Klein, Herbert S. *Bolivia: The Evolution of a Multi-Ethnic Society*. New York: Oxford University Press, 1982.

———. "The Creation of the Patino Tin Empire." *Inter-American Economic Affairs* 19, no. 2 (1965): 3–23.

———. *The Middle Passage: Comparative Studies in the Atlantic Slave Trade*. Princeton, NJ: Princeton University Press, 1978.

Klubock, Thomas Miller. *Contested Communities: Class, Gender, and Politics in Chile's El Teniente Copper Mine, 1904–1951*. Durham, NC: Duke University Press, 1998.

———. "Working-Class Masculinity, Middle-Class Morality and Labor Politics in the Chilean Copper Mines." *Journal of Social History* 30, no. 2 (Winter 1996): 435–63.

Knight, Alan. *The Mexican Revolution*. 2 vols. Lincoln: University of Nebraska Press, 1986.

Kotscho, Ricardo. *Serra Pelada: Uma Ferida Aberta na Selva*. São Paulo: Brasiliense, 1984.

Ladd, Doris. *The Making of a Strike: Mexican Silver Workers' Struggles in Real del Monte, 1766–1775*. Lincoln: University of Nebraska Press, 1988.

Lang, Mervyn. F. "El derrumbe de Huancavelica en 1786. Fracaso de una reforma borbónica." *Histórica* 10, no. 2 (December 1986): 213–26.

———. *El monopolio estatal del mercurio en el México colonial (1550–1710)*. Mexico City: Fondo de Cultura Económica, 1977.

Laurance, William F., Ana K. M. Albernaz, and Carlos da Costa. "Is Deforestation Accelerating in the Brazilian Amazon." *Environmental Conservation* 28, no. 4 (2001): 305–11.

Leady, B. S., and J. G. Gottgens. "Mercury Accumulation in Sediment Cores and Along Food Chains in Two Regions of the Brazilian Pantanal." *Wetlands Ecology and Management* 9, no. 4 (August 2001): 349–61.

LeCain, Timothy J. *Mass Destruction: The Men and Giant Mines that Wired America and Scarred the Planet*. New Brunswick, NJ: Rutgers University Press, 2009.

Leon-Portilla, Miguel, ed. *The Broken Spears: The Aztec Account of the Conquest of Mexico*. Boston: Beacon Press, 1962.

Lohmann Villena, Guillermo. *Las minas de Huancavelica en los siglos XVI y XVII*. Seville: Escuela de Estudios Hispano-Americanos, 1949.

Lora, Guillermo. *El movimiento obrero de Bolivia*. 3 vols. Cochabamba, Bolivia: Los Amigos del Libro, 1969–1971.

Lougheed, Alan. "The Cyanide Process and Gold Extraction in Australia and New Zealand, 1888–1913." *Australian Economic History Review* 27, no. 1 (1987): 44–60.

Loveman, Brian. *Chile: The Legacy of Hispanic Capitalism*. New York: Oxford University Press, 1988.

Macedo, Arlei B. "500 Years of Mining in Brazil: Environmental Aspects." *Ciência e Cultura* 51, no. 3/4 (1999): 302–10.

Machado, Ivan F. *Recursos minerais: Política e sociedade*. São Paulo: Editora E. Blucher, 1989.

Machado Filho, Aires da Mata. *O negro e o garimpo em Minas Gerais*. Coleção Reconquista do Brasil, vol. 88. Belo Horizonte: Editora Itatiaia Limitada, 1985.

MacMillan, Gordon. *At the End of the Rainbow? Gold, Land, and People in the Brazilian Amazon*. London: Earthscan Publications, 1995.

Magalhães-Godinho, Vitorino. *L'économie de l'empire portugais aux XVe et XVIe siècles*. École Pratique des Hautes Études, VIe Section, Centre de Recherces Historiques, Ports—Routes—Trafics, vol. 26. Paris: S.E.V.P.E.N., 1969.

Mallon, Florencia. *The Defense of Community in Peru's Central Highlands: Peasant Struggle and Capitalist Transition, 1860–1940*. Princeton, NJ: Princeton University Press, 1983.

Malloy, James M. *Bolivia: The Uncompleted Revolution*. Pittsburgh, PA: University of Pittsburgh Press, 1970.

Mangan, Jane E. *Trading Roles: Gender, Ethnicity, and the Urban Economy in Colonial Potosí*. Durham, NC: Duke University Press, 2005.

Marrett, Robert. *Peru*. New York: Praeger, 1969.

Mason, J. Alden. *The Ancient Civilizations of Peru*. New York: Penguin, 1957.

Matienzo, Juan de. *Gobierno del Perú (1567)*. Paris: Institut Français d'Études Andines, 1967.

Matilla Tascón, Antonio. *Historia de las minas de Almadén*. Vol. 2, *Desde 1646 a 1799*. Madrid, 1987.

Mattingly, Garrett. *The Armada*. Boston, MA: Houghton Mifflin, 1959.

Mattoso, Kátia M. de Queirós. *To Be a Slave in Brazil, 1550–1888*. New Brunswick, NJ: Rutgers University Press, 1989.

Maxwell, Kenneth. *Pombal: Paradox of the Enlightenment*. New York: Cambridge University Press, 1993.

McMahon, Gary, José Luis Evia, Alberto Pascó-Font, and José Miguel Sánchez. *An Environmental Study of Artisanal, Small, and Medium Mining in Bolivia, Chile, and Peru*. Washington, D.C.: World Bank, 1999.

Medina, Pedro de. *Libro de grandezas y cosas memorables de España*. Madrid: Consejo Superior de Investigaciones Científicas, 1944.

Mikesell, Raymond F. *The World Copper Industry: Structure and Economic Analysis*. Baltimore, MD: Johns Hopkins University Press for Resources for the Future, 1979.

Miller, John. *Memoirs of General Miller in the Service of the Republic of Peru*. 2 vols. New York: AMS, 1979.

Mira Delli-Zotti, Guillermo Claudio. "Ilustración y reformismo borbónico en el Alto Perú: el intendente Sanz y la minería de Potosí a fines del período colonial." PhD diss., Universidad Complutense de Madrid, 1990.

Mitre, Antonio. *Bajo un cielo de estaño; fulgor y ocaso del metal en Bolivia*. La Paz: Asociación Nacional de Mineros Medianos, ILDIS, 1993.

———. *Los patriarcas de la plata: estructura socioeconómica de la minería boliviana en el siglo XIX*. Lima: Instituto de Estudios Peruanos, 1981.

Möeller Schroeter, Hans. *Dinamitas y contaminantes: cooperativas mineras y su incidencia en la problemática ambiental*. La Paz: PIEB, 2002.

Molina, Cristóbal de. *Ritos y fábulas de los incas*. 1575. Buenos Aires: Futuro, 1959.

Monteón, Michael. *Chile in the Nitrate Era: The Evolution of Economic Dependence, 1880–1930*. Madison: University of Wisconsin Press, 1982.

Moreno, Roberto. "Régimen de trabajo en la minería del siglo XVIII." In *Labor and Laborers through Mexican History*, edited by Elsa Cecilia Frost, Michael C. Meyer, and Josefina Zoraida Vázquez, 242–67. Tucson: University of Arizona Press, 1979.

Moreyra Paz Soldán, Manuel. *La moneda colonial en el Perú: capítulos de su historia*. Lima: Banco Central de Reserva del Perú, 1980.

Morgado, Alonso de. *Historia de Sevilla*. 1587. Seville: Ariza, 1887.

Morison, Samuel Eliot. *Admiral of the Ocean Sea*. Boston, MA: Little, Brown and Company, 1942.

Mouat, Jeremy. "The Development of the Flotation Process: Technological Change and the Genesis of Modern Mining, 1898–1911." *Australian Economic History Review* 36, no. 1 (1996): 3–28.

Nash, June C. "Conflicto industrial en los Andes: Los mineros bolivianos del estaño." *Estudios Andinos* 4, no. 2 (1964–1976): 219–57.

———. "The Devil in Bolivia's Nationalized Tin Mines." *Science and Society* 36, no. 2 (1972): 221–33.

———. "Mi vida en las minas: la autobiografía de una mujer boliviana." *Estudios Andinos* 5 (1976): 139–50.

———. "Religión, rebelión y conciencia de clase en las comunidades mineras del estaño de Bolivia." *Revista del Instituto Pastoral Andina* 26 (1985): 113–35.

———. *We Eat the Mines and the Mines Eat Us: Dependency and Exploitation in Bolivia Tin Mines.* New York: Columbia University Press, 1979.

O'Phelan Godoy, Scarlett. *Rebellions and Revolts in Eighteenth Century Peru and Upper Peru.* Cologne: Böhlau, 1985.

Paredes, Manuel Rigoberto. *Mitos, supersticiones y supervivencias populares de Bolivia.* 4th ed. La Paz: Ediciones "Burgos," 1973.

Parés y Franqués, José. *Catástrofe morboso de las minas mercuriales de la villa de Almadén del Azogue.* 1778. Edited by Alfred Menéndez Navarro. Cuenca, Spain: Universidad de Castilla-La Mancha, 1998.

Parker, Geoffrey. "The Emergence of Modern Finance in Europe, 1500–1730." In vol. 2 of *The Fontana Economic History of Europe*, edited by Carlo M. Cipolla, 527–94. London: Fontana, 1974.

Parry, John H., and Robert G. Keith, eds. *New Iberian World: A Documentary History of the Discovery and Settlement of Latin America to the Early 17th Century.* 5 vols. New York: Times Books, 1984.

Pelaez R., Segundino and Marina Vargas S. *Estaño, sangre y sudor (tragedia del minero locatario).* Oruro, Bolivia: Editorial Universitaria, 1980.

Pentland, John Barclay. *Report on Bolivia, 1827.* Edited by J. Valerie Fifer. Vol. 13, *Camden Miscellany*, 4th ser. London: Royal Historical Society, 1974.

Petersen G., Georg. *Minería y metalurgía en el antiguo Perú.* Antropológicas 12. Lima: Museo Nacional de Antropología y Arqueología, 1970.

Pierson, Peter. *Philip II of Spain.* London: Thames and Hudson, 1975.

Pinto, Lúcio Flávio. *Carajás: o ataque ao coração da Amazônia.* 2nd ed. Rio de Janeiro: Editora Marco Zero, 1982.

Pinto Vallejos, Julio. "La transición laboral en el norte salitrero: la provincia de Tarapacá y los orígenes del proletariado en Chile 1870–1890." *Historia* 25 (1990): 207–28.

———. "Slave Control and Slave Resistance in Colonial Minas Gerais, 1700–1750." *Journal of Latin American Studies* 17 (1985): 1–34.

Pinto Vallejos, Julio, and Luis Ortega Martínez. *Expansión minera y desarrollo industrial: un caso de crecimiento asociado (Chile, 1850–1914).* Santiago: Departamento de History, Universidad de Santiago de Chile, 1991.

Platt, Tristan. "The Alchemy of Modernity. Alonso Barba's Copper Cauldrons and the Independence of Bolivian Metallurgy (1790–1890)." *Journal of Latin American Studies* 32 (2000): 1–54.

———. "Conciencia andina y conciencia proletaria: Qhuyaruna y ayllu en el norte de Potosí." *HISLA* 2 (1983): 47–73.

———. "Historias unidas, memorias escindidas: las empresas mineras de los hermanos Ortiz y la construcción de las élites nacionales. Salta y Potosí, 1800–1880." In *Dos décadas de investigación en historia económica comparada en América Latina*, edited by Margarita Menegus Bornemann, 285–362. Mexico City: Centro de Estudios Históricos, Colegio de México: Centro de Investigaciones y Estudios Superiores en Antropología Social: Instituto Doctor José María Luis Mora: Centro de Estudios sobre la Universidad, UNAM, 1999.

Poppe, René. *Cuentos mineros*. La Paz: Ediciones ISLA, 1985.

———. *Interior mina (testimonio)*. La Paz: Biblioteca Popular Boliviana de "Ultima Hora," 1986.

Porteous, J. Douglas. "Social Class in Atacama Company Towns." *Annals of the Association of American Geographers* 64, no. 3 (September 1974): 409–17.

Probert, Alan. "Mules, Men, and Mining Machinery: Transport on the Veracruz Road." *Journal of the West* 14, no. 2 (1975): 104–13.

———. "The Pachuca Papers: The Real del Monte Partido Riots, 1766." *Journal of the West*, 12, no. 1 (January 1973): 85–125.

Ramos, Donald. "Community, Control and Acculturation: A Case Study of Slavery in Eighteenth Century Brazil." *The Americas* 42, no. 4 (1986): 419–51.

———. "Marriage and the Family in Colonial Vila Rica." *Hispanic American Historical Review*, 55, no. 2 (May 1975): 200–225.

———. "Slavery in Brazil: A Case Study of Diamantina, Minas Gerais." *The Americas* 45, no. 1 (1988): 47–59.

Randall, Robert W. "Mexico's Pre-Revolutionary Reckoning with Railroads." *The Americas* 42, no. 1 (July 1985): 1–28.

———. "Militant Mineworkers in Pre-Revolutionary Mexico." *Duquesne Review* 28, no. 2 (Fall 1973): 35–55.

———. *Real del Monte: A British Mining Venture in Mexico*. Austin: University of Texas Press, 1972.

Rankine, Margaret E. "The Mexican Mining Industry in the Nineteenth Century with Special Reference to Guanajuato." *Bulletin of Latin American Research* 11, no. 1 (1992): 29–48.

Rickard, T. A. *Journeys of Observation*. San Francisco: Dewey Publishing, 1907.

Rippy, J. Fred. *British Investments in Latin America, 1822–1949; a Case Study of the Operations of Private Enterprise in Retarded Regions*. Minneapolis: University of Minnesota Press, 1959.

Rizo-Patrón Boylan, Paul. "La minería entre 1900 y 1950." In *Historia de la minería en el Perú*, edited by José Antonio del Busto Duthurburu and Susana Aldana, 315–47. Lima: Milpo, 1999.

Roberts Barragán, Hugo. *La revolución del 9 de abril*. La Paz, 1971.

Rodriguez Ostria, Gustavo. "Industrialización, tiempo y cultura minera." *Estado y sociedad* 3, no. 4 (December 1987): 65–84.

———. "*Kajchas*, trapicheros y ladrones de mineral en Bolivia (1824–1900)." *Siglo XIX* 4, no. 8 (July–December 1989): 125–39.

———. "Las compañeras del mineral." *Nueva Sociedad* 93 (January–February 1988): 177–86.

Rogers, Edward J. "Brazilian Success Story: Volta Redonda Iron and Steel Project." *Journal of Inter-American Studies* 10, no. 4 (October 1968): 637–52.

Romero Sotelo, María Eugenia. *Minería y guerra: la economía de Nueva España, 1810–1821.* Mexico City: El Colegio de México, 1997.

Rowe, John Howland. "Inca Culture at the Time of the Spanish Conquest." In *Handbook of South American Indians*, edited by Julian H. Steward, 198–330. Vol. 2, *The Andean Civilizations* (Washington, D.C.: Government Printing Office), 1946.

Ruíz, Ramón Eduardo. *The Great Rebellion: Mexico, 1905–1924.* New York: Norton, 1980.

Russell-Wood, A. J. R. *The Black Man in Slavery and Freedom in Colonial Brazil.* New York: St. Martin's Press, 1982.

———. "Technology and Society: The Impact of Gold Mining on the Institution of Slavery in Portuguese America." *Journal of Economic History* 31, no. 1 (1977): 59–83.

Saignes, Thierry. "Capoche, Potosí y la coca: el consumo popular de estimulantes en el siglo XVII." *Revista de India*, 48, no. 182–183 (1988): 207–35.

———. "Notes on the Regional Contribution to the *Mita* in Potosí in the Early Seventeenth Century." *Bulletin of Latin American Research* 4, no. 1 (1985): 65–76.

Sales, Kirkpatrick. *The Conquest of Paradise.* New York: Penguin, 1991.

Salvucci, Richard J. "Mexican National Income in the Era of Independence, 1800–40." In *How Latin America Fell Behind: Essays on the Economic Histories of Brazil and Mexico, 1800–1914*, edited by Stephen Haber, 216–42. Palo Alto, CA: Stanford University Press, 1997.

Sanjines C., Javier. "Entre campesinos y mineros: Desestructuración colonial y memoria colectiva en los andes bolivianos." *Estado y sociedad* 7, no. 8 (1991): 61–67.

Santamaría, Daniel J. "Potosí entre la plata y el estaño." *Revista Geográfica* 79 (1973): 71–115.

Santos, Joaquim Felício dos. *Memórias do distrito diamantino.* Belo Horizonte: Editora Itatiaia, 1976.

Santos Morales, José. "Relato de un proscrito. Mi escapada." In *Santa María de Iquique, 1907: documentos para su historia*, edited by Pedro Bravo Elizondo, 181–87. Santiago: Ediciones del Litoral, 1993.

Sariego, Juan Luis. "La reconversión industrial en la minería cananaense." *Nueva Antropología* 9, no. 32 (November 1987): 9–23.

Sariego, Juan Luis and Raúl Santana Paucar. "Transición tecnológica y resistencia obrera en la minería mexicana." *Cuadernos políticos* 31 (January–March 1982): 17–27.

Sauer, Carl Ortwin. *The Early Spanish Main.* Berkeley: University of California Press, 1966.

Schwartz, Stuart B. "Free Labor in a Slave Economy: the *Lavradores de Cana* of Colonial Bahia." In *Colonial Roots of Modern Brazil*, edited by Dauril Alden, 147–98. Berkeley: University of California Press, 1973.

Scliar, Claudio. *Geopolítica das Minas do Brasil: a Importância da Mineração para a Sociedade.* Rio de Janeiro: Editora Revan, 1996.

Sempat Assadourian, Carlos. *El sistema de la economía colonial: el mercado interior, regiones y espacio económico.* Mexico City: Editorial Nueva Imagen, 1983.

Serulnikov, Sergio. "Disputed Images of Colonialism: Spanish Rule and Indian Subversion in Northern Potosí, 1777–1780." *Hispanic American Historical Review* 76, no. 2 (May 1996): 189–226.

———. *Reivindicaciones indígenas y legalidad colonial. La rebelión de Chayanta (1777–1781).* Buenos Aires, 1989.

Shazo, Peter de. *Urban Workers and the Labor Unions in Chile, 1902–1927.* Madison: University of Wisconsin Press, 1983.

Shimada, Izumi. "Pre-Hispanic Metallurgy and Mining in the Andes: Recent Advances and Future Tasks." In *In Quest for Mineral Wealth: Aboriginal and Colonial Mining and Metallurgy in Spanish America*, edited by Alan K. Craig and Robert C. West, 37–74. Baton Rouge: Louisiana State University Press, 1994.

Smith, Adam. *An Enquiry into the Nature and Causes of the Wealth of Nations.* New York: Modern Library, 1940.

Spalding, Karen. *Huarochirí: An Andean Society Under Inca and Spanish Rule.* Palo Alto, CA: Stanford University Press, 1984.

Stegner, Wallace. *Angle of Repose.* New York: Penguin, 1992.

Stewart, Watt. *Henry Meiggs: Yankee Pizarro.* Durham, NC: Duke University Press, 1946.

Summerhill, William R. "Market Intervention in a Backward Economy: Railway Subsidy in Brazil, 1854–1913." *Economic History Review* 51, no. 3 (1998): 542–68.

Sweet, James H. *Recreating Africa: Culture, Kinship, and Religion in the African-Portuguese World, 1441–1770.* Chapel Hill: University of North Carolina Press, 2003.

Tandeter, Enrique. *Coercion and Market: Silver Mining in Colonial Potosí, 1692–1826.* Albuquerque: University of New Mexico Press, 1993.

———. "Crisis in Upper Peru, 1800–1805." *Hispanic American Historical Review* 71, no. 1 (February 1991): 35–71.

———. "Trabajo forzado y trabajo libre en el Potosí colonial tardío." *Desarrollo Económico* 3, no. 6 (1981): 511–48.

Taussig, Michael T. *The Devil and Commodity Fetishism in South America.* Chapel Hill: University of North Carolina Press, 1980.

Taylor, Gerald. "Supay." *Amérindia* 5 (1980): 47–65.

Temple, Edmond. *Travels in Various Parts of Peru, Including a Year's Residence in Potosi.* 2 vols. London: Henry Colburn and Richard Bentley, 1830.

TePaske, John J. *A New World of Gold and Silver.* Edited by Kendall W. Brown. Leiden: Brill, 2010.

Thoburn, John T. *Tin in the World Economy.* Edinburgh: Edinburgh University Press, 1994.

Thompson, E. P. *Making of the English Working Class.* New York: Pantheon, 1964.

Thomson, Ian, and Dietrich Angerstein. *Historia del ferrocarril en Chile.* Santiago: Dibam, 1997.

Tickell, Sophia. "Domitila—the Forgotten Activist." *New Internationalist* 200 (October 1989). http://www.newint.org/issue200/domitila.htm.

Topik, Steven. *The Political Economy of the Brazilian State, 1889–1930.* Austin: University of Texas Press, 1987.

Tord, Javier, and Carlos Lazo. *Hacienda, comercio, fiscalidad y luchas sociales (Perú colonial).* Lima: Biblioteca Peruana de Historia, Economía y Sociedad, 1981.

Treece, David. *Bound in Misery and Iron: The Impact of the Grande Carajás Programme on the Indians of Brazil.* London: Survival International, 1987.

Valverde, Orlando. *Grande Carajás: Planejamento da Destruição.* Rio de Janeiro: Forense Universitária, 1989.

Vargas, Milton. "Origem e Desenvolvimento da Geotecnologia no Brasil." *Quipu* 2, no. 2 (May–August 1985): 263–79.

Velasco Avila, Cuauhtémoc. "Labour relations in mining: Real del Monte and Pachuca, 1824–1874." In *Miners and Mining in the Americas,* edited by Thomas C. Greaves and William Culver, 47–67. Dover, NH: Manchester University Press, 1985.

Vilar, Pierre. *A History of Gold and Money, 1450 to 1920.* New York: Verso, 1976.

Volk, Steven S. "Class, Union, Party: The Development of a Revolutionary Union Movement in Bolivia (1905–1952). Part 1: Historical Background." *Science and Society* 39, no. 1 (1975): 26–49.

———. "Class, Union, Party: The Development of a Revolutionary Movement in Bolivia (1905–1952). Part 2: From the Chaco War to 1952." *Science and Society* 39, no. 2 (1975), 187–97.

Von Glahn, Richard. *Fountain of Fortune: Money and Monetary Policy in China, 1000–1700.* Berkeley: University of California Press, 1996.

Ward, H. G. *Mexico.* 2 vols. London: Henry Colburn, 1829.

West, Robert C. "Aboriginal Metallurgy and Metalworking in Spanish America: A Brief Overview." In *In Quest for Mineral Wealth: Aboriginal and Colonial Mining and Metallurgy in Spanish America,* edited by Alan K. Craig and Robert C. West, 5–20. Baton Rouge: Louisiana State University Press, 1994.

———. *Colonial Placer Mining in Colombia.* Baton Rouge: Louisiana State University, 1952.

———. "Early Silver Mining in New Spain, 1531–1555." In *In Quest for Mineral Wealth: Aboriginal and Colonial Mining and Metallurgy in Spanish America,* edited by Alan K. Craig and Robert C. West, 119–36. Baton Rouge: Louisiana State University Press, 1994.

World Health Organization. Task Group on Environmental Health Criteria for Methylmercury. *Methylmercury.* Geneva: World Health Organization, 1990.

Yamamura, Kozo, and Tetsuo Kamiki. "Silver Mines and Sung Coins—A Monetary History of Medieval and Modern Japan in International Perspective." In *Precious Metals in the Later Medieval and Early Modern Worlds,* edited by John F. Richards, 329–62. Durham, NC: Carolina Academic Press, 1983.

Zapata, Francisco. "Los mineros como actores sociales y políticos en Bolivia, Chile y Perú durante el siglo XX." Paper presented at the VIII Reunión Internacional de Historiadores de la Minería Latinoamericana, Guanajuato, Mexico, March 24, 2004.

———. "Mineros y militares en la conyuntura actual de Bolivia, Chile y Perú (1976–1978)." *Revista Mexicana de Sociología* 42, no. 4 (October–December 1980): 1443–64.

Zavala, Silvio. *Estudios indianos.* Mexico City: Colegio Nacional, 1948.

Zelaya, Ricardo. *Minería o medio ambiente: el gran dilema.* La Paz: CEDOIN, 1998.

Zevaco, Philippe. "Indian Mythology and Mining Conditions in Bolivia." *Cultures* 1, no. 2 (1973): 87–99.

Zola, Emile. *Germinal.* Translated by Leonard Tancock. New York: Alfred A. Knopf, 1991.

Zulawski, Ann. *They Eat from Their Labor: Work and Social Change in Colonial Bolivia.* Pittsburgh, PA: University of Pittsburgh Press, 1995.

Index

— *continued on next page* —

— continued on next page —

The War for Mexico's West: Indians and Spaniards in New Galicia, 1524–1550
—Ida Altman

Damned Notions of Liberty:
Slavery, Culture, and Power in Colonial Mexico, 1640–1769
—Frank Proctor

Irresistible Forces: Latin American Migration to the United States
and its Effects on the South
—Gregory B. Weeks and John R. Weeks

Cuauhtémoc's Bones: Forging National Identity in Modern Mexico
—Paul Gillingham

SERIES ADVISORY EDITOR:
Lyman L. Johnson,
University of North Carolina at Charlotte